'Burgess presents a much-needed path to engage both the wealthy and everyone else. It isn't punitive, it is inclusive. It isn't billionaire bashing, it's bridge building. The principle of 'Income for me/wealth for we' is not just practical, it is executable. This book outlines an agenda to build balance again with greater opportunity, a healthy middle class and a productive environment for the continued creation of wealth for the benefit of all, not just the few.'

> Chuck Collins, author of *Born on Third Base: A One Percenter Makes the Case for Tackling Inequality, Bringing Wealth Home, and Committing to the Common Good*, Senior Scholar, Institute for Policy Studies, Washington DC, and co-editor of Inequality.org. Co-founder of Wealth for the Common Good and Patriotic Millionaires

'Governments across the world are grappling with the increasingly toxic issue of social and economic inequalities. This book by Tom Burgess contributes some bold and imaginative ideas to the ongoing debate with a view to coming up with a package of practical solutions designed to bring about a reduction in financial hardship currently experienced by so many people worldwide.'

> Professor David Wilson, Emeritus Professor and Pro-Chancellor, De Montfort University

'A sound, commonsense approach to engaging business for the greater good where we all can profit. It is not enough for business to have a social conscience. It is the performance that counts. Tom Burgess offers a practical agenda to engage the philosophy of a corporate social conscience through initiatives such as tax reform, profit allocation and self-financing infrastructure investment. A defining statement which should be read by all entrepreneurs who seek a clear alternative perspective to progress their business.'

> David A Kerfoot MBE DL

'Long before Piketty quantified it, some thinkers realized that a chasm of inequality had been opening up over the past twenty-five years between the have-nots and the have-alls (leaving aside the increasingly squeezed middle). Burgess was one of these early thinkers, and his thesis that zero-sum economics is socially and financially destructive is the product of a generation's-worth of hard thinking on the matter. The analysis and solutions Burgess puts forward are radical and urgently in need of implementation.'

Prof. Chris Green, formerly Associate Professor in the Faculty of Humanities, Hong Kong Polytechnic University

'A century ago, civic-minded business people who understood how concentrated wealth undermines our democracy helped launch the struggle that toppled America's original plutocracy. In Income for me/ wealth for we, Burgess reignites that civic-minded spirit.'

Sam Pizzigati, Associate Fellow, Institute for Policy Studies, Washington DC and author of The Rich Don't Always Win

From Here to Prosperity

From Here to Prosperity

An Agenda for Progressive Prosperity
based on an inequality-busting strategy of

Income for me / *wealth for we*

THOMAS J. BURGESS

SHEPHEARD-WALWYN (PUBLISHERS) LTD

First published in 2016 by
Shepheard-Walwyn (Publishers) Ltd
107 Parkway House, Sheen Lane,
London SW14 8LS
www.shepheard-walwyn.co.uk

British Library Cataloguing in Publication Data
A catalogue record of this book
is available from the British Library

ISBN: 978-0-85683-510-0

Typeset by Alacrity, Chesterfield, Sandford, Somerset
Printed and bound in the United Kingdom
by Short Run Press, Exeter

Contents

Acknowledgements

I WOULD particularly like to thank my publisher Anthony Werner, my editors Francis Pearce and Derek Aldous, Tobi Brown and Mary Seivert for the cover design, Lev Janisvilli for providing early feedback and Dena Schneider for helping the initial focus. Also the members of the Economic Study Association who meet regularly to discuss and analyze my father's economic writings. This book would not have been possible without the tireless work of my late parents, my mum Rosemary for getting me through to being a grown-up and my dad, Ronald for introducing me to economics and politics. Also thanks to my friends in the USA and UK for listening to my ideas. Most of all, thanks to a special person Debra Raine for inspiration, support and constant encouragement without whom this book would not have happened.

Linguistic note: Though this book was mainly written while I am in California, it is published in London for distribution in the UK, USA and beyond, I have used the British spellings unless it refers to a specific American instance.

To Carla, Greg and Eve

May you enjoy the freedom of prosperity

Preface

*'Recognition of the inherent dignity and of the equal and inalienable
rights of all members of the human family is the foundation of
freedom, justice and peace in the world...'*

Preamble to the Universal Declaration of Human Rights
adopted in 1948 by the General Assembly
of the United Nations

To me that says it all, it is the basis of how we should live our lives and outlines the tasks for the governments we elect to act on behalf of us all, not just the few.

Though today, nearly seventy years later, the global economic system is creating extreme inequality, causing unnecessary hardship for millions of people. So many have so little, while so few have so much. Where is the progress?

I am frustrated by the lack of action to solve inequality, persistent poverty and slow economic growth. I did not want to write another analysis of the problem, about how bad it is and how it is getting worse. I wanted practical answers, and I was pretty sure there were simple answers, I like simplicity.

I am inspired by my late father, Dr Ronald Burgess, an economist, who had written several economic papers, as well as a 1993 book: *Public Revenue without Taxation*. I always thought this seemed like a great idea and it was indeed simple. However my Dad wrote an academic, learned book. I wanted to propose practical answers written in a more every day language so that you need not be an economist to understand. I did study economics at school and university so I should know the basics!

Just twenty years later, inequality has worsened, poverty is still endemic and the economy of the world is still fragile. It should be strong, given globalisation, technology and advances in healthcare and communication. There should not have been the Great Recession, but there was, we should have recovered much faster. But we are in danger of making the same mistakes again. While I believe we could raise public revenue without taxation (you will need to read his book to find out how!), we now need some urgent action to bring some strong structural changes to correct our economy and make progress for our society in the 21st century.

I have always been fascinated by politics, I was a Student Union President and active in the National Union of Students, later I was a founder member of the Social Democratic Party and twice stood for city council, and also founded and edited a political newspaper. I really wanted to stand for Member of Parliament but there was no party that ideally matched my views. As my headmaster once said in my school report: 'Tom is an individualist' which apparently means one that pursues a markedly independent course in thought or action. I also got busy with my own business and sharing in the joys of bringing up a family, which became my priority. Now that my children are grown up, left home and off the payroll, and now that I have left the business world behind I can now devote my energy to making a difference.

This book is just the start.

Another factor is that I have been fortunate enough to live in both the UK and USA. One of the consequences about being out of your home country is that you can take a more objective view of your home nation, and a much better understanding of the culture, media and politics of the nation you now call home. So I hope I can bring an impartial view.

The longer you live your life and the more you travel, you see the contrasts, in culture, living standards, the variations in income, wealth, opportunity, housing and outlook on life. The businesses I founded have worked for over 500 clients in nearly 100 countries. I have seen and experienced all sides now from the mansions and yachts of the super rich, the smart hotels, impressive boardrooms and excesses of senior corporate executives, to the unemployment, insecurity and frustration of so many people as well as the determination and courage of ordinary working people, trying to make ends meet and lead a fulfilled and purposeful life. Having experienced so much I hope this puts me in a good position to comment and propose some answers to the dilemmas of today. I hope this book will inspire you to realise that if we collaborate, we can bring change and elect a government that truly does work for us, the majority, not just the few.

In *From Here to Prosperity*, I hope to persuade you that together we can build a fairer society that truly provides the opportunity of prosperity for everyone and encourages greater democratic engagement. And I propose to show you how. I want to bring you practical and simple answers. The mechanisms of change that I will describe include measures that will appeal across the whole political spectrum, bar its extremes, and will benefit the vast majority at little expense to the very wealthy few.

I propose an **Agenda for Progressive Prosperity** that aims to minimise extreme inequality and create greater opportunity for all by bringing significant financial relief to the poor and squeezed middle class. It is based on the inequality-busting strategy of *'income for me/wealth for we'*. We each keep the income we earn from the personal effort of our work and we share more equitably the wealth we create jointly. The tax system could be reformed to shift the base from income to wealth and to encourage greater social responsibility. A key tactic to achieve this would be by abolishing income and payroll taxes for the majority of the population. This would be more than covered by a greater contribution, based on a small percentage from the value of personal assets above a threshold from those who have accumulated significant wealth. Everyone will be better off. With more funds brought into circulation, consumer demand will be boosted and more jobs created, leading to greater opportunity for all. This agenda is inclusive and non-partisan; it causes no hardship and could transform our society bringing sustainable growth and greater social justice.

Inequality is not someone else's problem. It is a tragic consequence of a broken system that affects us all and we need to fix it fast. With such high levels of poverty, low wages and weak consumer demand even the wealth of the rich is at risk. If we do not change, change will be thrust upon us by social unrest and revolution. The rapid concentration of wealth into the hands of a tiny minority has drifted us into a plutocracy, government by the rich for the rich. As a believer both in democracy and capitalism, I find this deeply troubling and not just from a moral perspective, though that is critical, but also because my sense of history tells me that it is dangerous. To my mind, it is better to encourage peaceful but profound change whilst we still have the chance.

The Agenda for Progressive Prosperity is built on a five-step process that will bring increased financial security, greater freedom and more choices leading to a more fulfilled and purposeful life for many. The eminent economist Joseph Stiglitz said reform could be achieved through the tax system. I agree. All these five interlinked policies that I propose, con-tribute to reducing inequality by increasing disposable income for lower earners and sharing more equitably the wealth we jointly help create.

- **A living wage to be the minimum wage**: Low wages cause hardship. Five million people in the UK earn less than a living wage (as defined by the Living Wage Foundation) and the British government spends £30 billion topping up low wages. In the USA, where 51 million jobs pay under $15 per hour, the federal government spends $227 billion subsidising low pay. Research shows that paying a living wage would have a minimal effect on company profits, yet most companies still choose not to do it even though higher wages have been proven to bring benefits such as less absenteeism, reduced recruitment costs and better quality of work. This policy is effortless to implement, it just requires raising the minimum wage to an agreed level i.e. a wage based on agreed acceptable living standards. UK Chancellor of the Exchequer George Osborne proposed a 'National Living Wage' of £9 an hour by 2020, in his 2015 budget. This is the minimum wage in new clothing, and not to be confused with the real thing. While small companies may have transitional challenges to living wage, big companies making substantial profits have no excuse, business models may need to be amended but we must do the right thing. The big benefit to us all is greater consumer demand, as Henry Ford found when he increased his employees' wages so they could afford to buy the cars they made.

- **Income tax to be abolished**: Income and payroll taxes significantly reduce the disposable income of the low and middle earners bringing financial pressure and undermining their quality of life. The 80% of UK taxpayers earning below £32,000 and 70% of Americans earning below $50,000 could be freed from income-related taxes, giving each a significant pay rise and stimulating the economy whilst reducing pressure on the welfare budget. The impact on government revenue is small and could be made up in a more equitable manner from the wealth we generate collectively. The impact on disposable income would gradually be improved as, currently, low-income groups, whose pay packets are reduced by taxation, are compensated by tax credits and welfare, requiring a costly bureaucracy taking away with one hand and giving back with another. Overall, it is reasonable to conclude that income taxes, in relation to the lower paid, are expensive to collect for the community as a whole, and self-defeating, as reducing these taxes would almost certainly lead to a degree of economic expansion, and higher tax revenues overall. Progressive taxes on income would still be retained for higher earners, but deliberately rebranded as insurance payments as they would go towards funding health and welfare for all.

- **A tax based on personal assets to be introduced**: As we all participate in wealth creation, the fruits should be shared more equitably, reducing extreme inequality. This does not happen today: on the contrary, the economy performs in such a way that wealth flows from the poor towards the rich. In the USA, the top 1% own more than 40% of the nation's wealth, in the UK, the country's five richest families now own more wealth, than the poorest 20% of the population. Some of this excessive wealth could be returned to those that helped create it through a low percentage tax on all assets over a certain threshold. This percentage would still be less than the expected increase in asset value so the rich would still get richer, but by not quite so much, and more funds would be put into circulation for the benefit of all.

- **Infrastructure investment to be funded through reformed property tax**: Changing the way the out of date property taxes are levied so there is more equitable means of collecting payment for all public services. This could be based on the market or locational value of the land only, and could make infrastructure projects self-financing. As improved infrastructure raises adjoining land values, a Land Value Tax (LVT) based on the market value of each site, would enable government expenditure to be recouped automatically from rising land values, as well as providing more funds for public services. As the rich occupy the most valuable sites, with the most locational advantages provided by society as a whole, they would contribute more to public revenue through what I prefer to describe as a Land Usage Charge but in return for valuable benefits. Firms occupying the best sites and enjoying the greatest advantages would pay more for the privilege. Current property taxes penalise improvements, whereas land use charges encourage best use. Land hoarding and speculation would become unprofitable, and the scope for moving profits off-shore would be reduced. Some transitional relief might be required initially for property owners with a valuable property but low income.

- **The wealth created to be shared through encouraging greater corporate responsibility**: Enterprises, which bring together capital and labour, create wealth, which should be shared more equitably with all the stakeholders, not just the shareholders. By changing the way we raise public revenue from business, we can ensure that the wealth created benefits all. So instead of all the gains going to the shareholders, more of this will go to stakeholders by means of 'social offsetting' as socially responsible companies will contribute less from their profits/wealth to public revenue. This encourages social responsibility while still respecting the profit motive. It could put an end to low wages, excessively high salaries, and the distorting influence of lobbying and vast political contributions, as well as eradicating tax avoidance and many more 'anti-social' corporate activities that have made so many both metaphorically and literally sick. This would encourage business to act in the interests of the wider community not just the shareholders.

All these measures would put more money in the hands of those now in poverty and those of the 'squeezed middle', bringing great relief without causing anyone else further hardship. Increasing the contribution made from those that already have a comfortable lifestyle can offset the reduction in taxes on income. This would mean more cash taken out of 'storage' and put into circulation, therefore increasing economic growth, providing jobs and creating greater opportunity. There would be no need for further austerity measures; the economy would be turbocharged as the funds would be available from the wealth we all create.

I am not content to just lay out the agenda in a book – having spent a career in business, marketing and media relations, I want to make this long overdue agenda a reality. One thing is very clear: voting is not enough. Real social change only happens when there is a mass movement of people who clearly demonstrate their feelings. A constructive practical and fair agenda needs to be offered. Not a rambling collection of patches but a clear vision and a concise strategy. More engagement can be encouraged by the wise application of social media. But we, the majority, have to be confident and to convince ourselves that we can do it. The wealthy need persuading that it is their interests, too. And our politicians need convincing that this is the will of the people. As John F. Kennedy said: *'If a free society cannot help the many who are poor, they cannot save the few who are rich.'*

Practical common sense answers are required. There are many good academic, learned works on economics and inequality, packed with charts, graphs and data, including those by Thomas Piketty, Anthony Atkinson and Joseph Stiglitz (all of whom I have heard talk at the London School of Economics), Emmanuel Saez of University of California, Berkeley whose seminar I attended at the Institute of Fiscal Studies in London, Robert Reich, whose many lectures I joined for a semester at University of California, Berkeley and Professor Sir John Hills and Gabriel Zucman of the LSE who kindly took time to give me some valuable input. I have benefitted from many others too. There is a lot to learn from these studies and the solutions they propose, but now is the time for action so let's keep it simple and effective. If an idea makes sense and is fair, a way can be found to make it happen. The issues of implementation and transition can be overcome by clear creative thinking. While many may not like change, it must happen if we are to survive and prosper, as we have been going the wrong way for some time.

I do not want to give another analysis of the problems and the dire situation that is now upon us; there has been enough talking. Instead I want to build on this with a common sense approach to a political problem that is undermining our society by means of a book that can be understood and acted on by all. It is about putting the wealth we jointly create to work for everyone.

This is not a battle, this is not a fight, but a means to build non-partisan consensus for change. The answers I propose do not involve an attack on any group and are not motivated by a wish to punish anyone. The Agenda for Progressive Prosperity provides a way to bring a better life to those who have been denied the opportunity by a system that is overdue for reform. We need a positive attitude, great determination and a practical, bold agenda.

I hope this book will at least stimulate constructive discussion around a bold vision, a simple, fair approach that will truly give the opportunity of a better life for all and move us all From Here To Prosperity.

PART I

The Challenge
for Change

*'I have a dream that one day this nation will rise up, live out the true
meaning of its creed: We hold these truths to be self evident,
that all men are created equal'*

Martin Luther King 1963

THE TIME has come, to join together, realise that many more people
could lead fulfilled and purposeful lives if we took a different
approach to our society, our economy and our government.

- We let many in the world be hungry when there is plenty.
- We live in democracies but power is in the hands of a few.
- We are still consuming finite resources when there are sustainable options.
- We are killing our planet but we have nowhere else to go.
- We are imposing taxes on people so they cannot build a fulfilled life.
- We allow the rich to get richer and the poor to get poorer.
- We agree with human rights but do not respect the rights of many humans.
- We are still fighting wars in the name of peace.

We can do better.

It is time to put aside the divisions of the past, to move away from right or left wing rhetoric that can alienate and no longer unites. There are many good people with good ideas and intentions, we need to be open, listen, learn and work it out. We have a huge task ahead. Let's work together and make that choice.

Government itself is not the problem: in fact, it is the answer. This does not mean bigger governments but better and bolder governments, with a purpose and vision. This is an Agenda for peaceful but determined action to make the world a better place for many more people.

It is not difficult, it is not simple, but it can be done.

A pivotal point has been reached and unless we act, things could get out of control. What is happening now is not new, it has happened before; we need to learn from our mistakes. We live in an even more highly connected world with rapid communication and instant access to information; we should be wiser and more informed.

Let's seize the opportunity, take up the challenge for change so that real progress can be made.

CHAPTER 1

Where Are We Now?

WE ARE NOT where we could be on the path of human progress. Despite all the advances that have been made in technology, health-care and communications, we still live in a world riddled with inequality, conflict and suffering. Even in the rich nations, we need change and I believe that if we can make it here, to paraphrase the song, we can make it anywhere. At base, almost all our problems stem from inequality of some sort: of wealth, of opportunity, of resources or freedoms. There is no excuse for poverty in the economically advanced countries, no reason why it should persist; there is enough income generated and wealth created to go round in a more equitable manner.

I want to give you some real facts that bring clarity about where we are today and facts that are indisputable. Then to move on to common sense policy ideas that, given the political will, could make a real difference. But that is not enough, the greatest ideas are no good unless implemented, so I want to outline how the environment for change can be created, once we have that, how the policy ideas can be implemented in a realistic time frame. Before the answers, let's review the problems to determine where we are now. I have identified three major issues; while I have taken most of my illustrations from the UK and USA, these problems are applicable to most western democracies and 'advanced' economies.

- Extreme inequality and persistent poverty
- Slow economic progress
- Damaged democracy, a government that isn't working, for us

1.1 Extreme inequality and persistent poverty

The world is getting richer and yet most of its inhabitants are poor or getting poorer. How can this be? Surely, everyone should be getting richer, perhaps not at the same rate and certainly not from the same base, but getting richer, regardless? Well, no. It doesn't work like that, unfortunately, because our economic and political systems drive wealth towards the rich, concentrating more and more of it into a very few hands, and with it, political power. The Equality Trust, which works to improve the quality of life in the UK, says:

> the grotesque concentration of wealth in the hands of a tiny minority is fracturing our society, weakening our economy and giving disproportionate power to the richest. Unless policymakers adopt a clear goal of reducing the gap between the richest and the rest, they will have to govern an increasingly dysfunctional nation.

Some people are very rich, so rich, in fact, that 80 super-rich individuals are as wealthy as all the poorest 3.5 billion combined: half the population of the world. Wealth is so concentrated among the super-rich and so thinly spread among the very poor that when you reverse the equation to see how many people at the top have, say, half the world's wealth it is still only 1%, according to the charity Oxfam. Nor do the 99% share the other half of the world's wealth equally. The gradient is so steep that with wealth amounting to $110 trillion, that richest 1% owns 65 times the total wealth of the bottom half of the world's population. And this tiny group's wealth is not just growing but accelerating. The richest 1% increased their share of income in 24 out of 26 countries for which data is available between 1980 and 2012.

According to the Global Wealth Report by Credit Suisse (published in October 2014), global wealth surged by $20.1 trillion over the previous year to $263 trillion, 20% above the pre-crisis peak in 2007. The countries with the biggest economies benefitted most. Their exact position on the podium varies according to who is doing the measuring – the CIA Handbook, the International Monetary Fund, The United Nations or the World Bank – but the European Union, the USA and China are first, second and third in terms of Gross Domestic Product. In the USA, household wealth rose by $8.9 trillion in the 12 months ending mid-2014. Despite the crisis in the Euro Zone, the European Union enjoyed the second-largest rise of $8.1 trillion. China, with 21.4% of the adult population of the world, added 8.1% of global wealth or $715 billion. The drop-off at that point is sharp.

The World Wealth Report published by Capgemini estimates that in 2014 there were 12 million millionaires (High Net Worth Individuals, HNWI) in the world, each having a net worth of at least $1 million in all assets except their primary residence. Their assets are expected to rise to $55.8 trillion by 2015. The number of multi-millionaires worldwide has grown by 7.1% over the past decade, while millionaire numbers have increased by 58%.

In the USA, the Congressional Budget Office found that the gap in income between the top 1% of the population and the rest tripled between 1979 and 2007, the onset of the Great Recession. After federal taxes and transfer payments, the income of the top 1% increased by 275%, while it increased less than 40% for the middle three quintiles of the population and only 18% for the bottom quintile. In April 2013, Pew Research Center in USA reported that from 2009 to 2011, the mean net worth of households in the upper 7% of wealth distribution rose by an estimated 28%, while the mean net worth of households in the lower 93% dropped by 4%. While a few got much richer, almost all Americans were worse off.

The wealth gap has continued to widen in the recovery; an estimated 15% – that's more than 45 million people – live in poverty in the USA. According to the US Census Bureau, median family and median household incomes have been falling, adjusted for inflation; while according to the data gathered by Emmanuel Saez, at the University of California, Berkley, the income of the wealthiest 1% has risen by 3.1%. Saez has calculated that 95% of all economic gains since the recovery started have gone to the 1%.

Is this because the rich work harder or perhaps because they work just as hard as everyone else but are lucky enough to get paid more for what they do? The answer is neither. In the USA, the top 1% own more than 40% of the nation's approximately $54 trillion wealth; they earn about 19% of the country's income. The difference between what they earn and what they own is explained not by the sweat of their brows but by their accumulation of wealth of stocks, bonds, real estate and so on that continue to increase in value.

With 1% owning so much, it leaves the bottom 80% with just 7% of the wealth, or, to look at it another way, the wealthiest 400 Americans have the same combined wealth as more than 150 million people: the poorest half of the nation's population. About three million people, the 1%, have nearly half the pie while 315 million scrambles for the other half.

Inequality among working-age people has risen faster in Britain than in any other rich nation since the mid-1970s, according to a report by the OECD in 2011. In 2014, according to the Office for National Statistics (ONS), Britain's top 20% of earners saw their annual disposable income rise by £940, while the bottom fifth lost £381 and all other groups lost around £250. By contrast, the share of the top 1% of income earners increased from 7.1% in 1970 to 14.3% in 2005. Astonishingly, the country's five richest families now own more wealth, £28.1 billion, than the poorest 20% of the population who have just £2,230 each on average. Just prior to the global recession, the OECD said the very wealthiest Brits – the 0.1% of highest earners – accounted for a remarkable 5% of total pre-tax income, a level of hoarding not seen since the Second World War.

'There are two ideas of government,' according to soon-to-be US presidential candidate William Jennings Bryan in 1896.

> There are those who believe that if you just legislate to make the well-to-do prosperous, that their prosperity will leak through on those below. The Democratic idea has been that if you legislate to make the masses prosperous their prosperity will find its way up and through every class that rests upon it.

In Bryan's time what we now call trickle down was known as the horse and sparrow theory: If you feed the horse enough oats, some will pass through to the road for the sparrows. However many times it is discredited it keeps coming back. One reason that it does not work is that when the rich grab on to wealth, they cling on to it. ONS says Britain's richest 1% (roughly 600,000 people) have accumulated as much wealth as all the poorest 55% of the population. As one billionaire said, *'I sock my extra money away in savings, where it doesn't do the country much good.'*

In 2012 the Tax Justice Network, a research group that maps and analyses tax avoidance and tax havens, reported that the super-rich hoard at least £13 trillion ($21 trillion) in secret offshore accounts – the equivalent of the combined GDP of the USA and Japan. The study carried out by James Henry, former chief economist at the consultancy McKinsey, showed that the top 10 banks, including Goldman Sachs, UBS and Credit Suisse in Switzerland, managed more than £4 trillion [$6.2 trillion] in 2010, a sharp rise from £1.5 trillion five years earlier. He calculated that if that dead money were to earn just 3% interest and to be taxed at 30%

it would raise $188 billion dollars: more than the rich countries spend on international aid every year. *'The problem here is that the assets of these countries are held by a small number of wealthy individuals while the debts are shouldered by the ordinary people of these countries through their governments,'* the report said.

Britain has more than 25 million working people (about 80% of work-force) earning £32,000 or less. A report published by the Centre for London in September 2014 highlighted the situation in London of a group dubbed 'Endies' (Employed but No Disposable Income or Savings). These are individuals and single parents living on between £20,000 and £33,000 or couples with dependent children having a household income of between £25,000 and £40,000, an estimated 650,000 households in London. Their earnings are kept flat by a fiercely competitive labour market, while living costs, particularly housing, transport and childcare have risen sharply. Endies live quiet and modest lives largely hidden from view for a simple reason: most cannot afford to go out. Life is an endless treadmill of work, commuting and recovering at home, often with the Internet for company and little other respite.

At the end of 2014, the living wage was calculated at £7.85 an hour outside London (about £19,000 a year) and £9.15 an hour in the capital by the Living Wage Foundation, while the National Minimum Wage for adults was set at £6.50, 20% below the living wage. The number of UK workers earning below the living wage has risen to 4.8 million according to 2013 research from Resolution Foundation think tank. This is equivalent to 20% of employees and is up from 3.4 million in 2009. Rachel Reeves, Labour Shadow Treasury minister said in September 2013 that research by the House of Commons library suggested 60% of new jobs created since May 2010 had been in low-pay sectors, where median hourly pay was less than a quarter of the national hourly median. Two-thirds of restaurant and hotel workers earned less than the living wage.

You might argue that some economic inequality is essential to drive growth and progress, rewarding those with talent, skills, and the drive to innovate or take entrepreneurial risks. But the extremes of income and subsequent wealth concentration that we see today threaten to exclude hundreds of millions of people from the rewards of their talents and hard work. Rather than creating an incentive to contribute to society, it removes the point. The harder most of us work, the better off a tiny minority becomes at our expense. Where is the sense in that? Once you are rich, you can't help getting richer. The World Economic Forum has identified increasing economic inequality as a major risk to human progress. In November 2013, it released its 'Outlook on the Global Agenda 2014', in which it ranked widening income disparities as the second greatest worldwide risk in the forthcoming 12 to 18 months. Based on those surveyed, it stated: *'inequality is impacting social stability within countries and threatening security on a global scale.'*

Extreme economic inequality is damaging and worrying for many reasons. Although it has been fuelled by growth, it can also impede it. In August 2014, Standard & Poor's said current inequality levels are hindering US economic growth, and the firm reduced its 10-year US growth forecast to a 2.5% rate, having expected 2.8% five years earlier. While earnings for the top 1% rose 15.1% from 2009 to 2010; for the bottom 90%, income rose slower or fell. This increased reliance on debt, leading to the Great Recession. In the end it will also have affected the educational opportunities open to many Americans and their future earnings potential, dampening social mobility: the loss of the American Dream. A less-educated workforce cannot compete in a changing global economy, resulting in a negative impact on potential long-term growth. Extreme economic inequality can multiply social problems. It can compound other inequalities, such as those between women and men. In many countries, extreme economic inequality is of even greater concern because of the destructive impact that wealth concentrations can have on equitable political representation. The massive concentration of economic resources in the hands of fewer people presents a significant threat to our political and economic systems. Instead of moving forward together, people are increasingly divided by economic and political power, inevitably heightening social tensions and increasing the risk of breakdown in society. Ultimately, the levels of wealth inequality that we are experiencing are bad for business and bad for democracy.

Nobel Prize winning economist, Joseph E. Stiglitz explains why this is bad news:

> Some people look at income inequality and shrug their shoulders. So what if this person gains and that person loses? What matters, they argue, is not how the pie is divided but the size of the pie. That argument is fundamentally wrong. An economy in which most citizens are doing worse year after year – an economy like America's is not likely to do well over the long haul.

The Organisation for Economic Co-operation and Development (OECD) warned of sweeping consequences for rich societies in a report in 2011, pointing to the rash of occupations and protests that year, especially by young people, around the world. It said:

> Youths who see no future for themselves feel increasingly disenfranchised. They have now been joined by protesters who believe they are bearing the brunt of a crisis for which they have no responsibility, while people on higher incomes appeared to be spared.

Thomas Piketty in his well-researched book, *Capitalism in the 21st Century*, noted that:

> when the rate of return on capital exceeds the rate of growth of output and income, as it did in the 19th century and seems quite likely to again in the 21st century, capitalism automatically generates arbitrary and unsustainable inequalities that radically undermine the meritocratic values on which democratic societies are based.

He does, however, give us hope that:

> there are nevertheless ways democracy can regain control over capitalism and ensure that the general interest takes precedence over private interests, while preserving economic openness and avoiding protectionist and nationalist actions.

Persistent Poverty

What is considered the poverty line or threshold varies from country to country depending on the social context. For instance in the USA, the government's definition of poverty is based on total income received; in 2014 it was set at $23,850 (total yearly income) for a family of four. It is estimated that most Americans will spend at least one year below the poverty line at some point between ages 25 and 75.

In November 2012, the US Census Bureau said more than 16% of the population lived in poverty, including almost 20% of American children, up from 14.3% (approximately 43.6 million) in 2009 and to its highest level since 1993. Starting in the 1980s, relative poverty rates have consistently exceeded those of other wealthy nations. Even in California, the so-called Golden State (from where I have been writing most of this book), after declining to a 20-year low of 12% in 2006, the official poverty rate in California spiked upward in the wake of the Great Recession: as of 2011, it was 16.9%. This amounts to more than six million Californians living in households with incomes below the federal poverty level (about

$23,000 for a family of four). The Census 'Supplemental Poverty Measure', which incorporates California's high cost of living and the effect of safety net programs such as food stamps, suggests that California's poverty rate was even higher at 23.5% during 2009-2011. One third of America's welfare recipients live in the state, which only comprises 12% (39m) of the USA population (319m): a reality completely out of line with perception.

In the UK, the most common measure of poverty as used in the UK Child Poverty Act 2010, is *'household income below 60% of median income'*. The median income is where half the households earn above the median and half the households earn below the median income level. Though in 2015 the government announced that it would change the definition, which critics say this would show less in poverty whereas many felt that there were in fact more.

In fact governments are pushing working people below the poverty line by taking away hard earned cash through income related taxes, significantly reducing disposable income, then replacing it with tax credits and other welfare benefits, a bizarre merry go round. Employment doesn't guarantee a life above the poverty line; according to census data, more than one in 10 Americans who work full-time are still poor. In 2013, for the first time, there are more working households living in poverty in the UK than non-working ones, according to the Joseph Rowntree Foundation, the social policy research and development charity. It adds that low pay and part-time work had prompted an unprecedented fall in living standards. This means just over half of the 13 million people in poverty, surviving on less than 60% of the national median (middle) income, were from working families. The Poverty and Social Exclusion project in the UK (PSE), funded by Economic and Social Research Council (ESRC) found that, over the last 30 years, the percentage of households living below society's minimum standard of living has increased from 14% to 33% – despite the fact that the UK economy has doubled in size over the same period.

We need to solve the causes of economic inequality and poverty; this is not just about getting rid of poverty because unless we reduce economic inequality, poverty will always be there. Nor is it just about redistributing the pot. If wealth were to be used more effectively and not hoarded by the few, this would significantly increase economic growth and it would improve the financial status of a huge number of people. The redistribution of wealth and narrowing of income disparity through the old tax system is not the answer. The solution is more fundamental, a system is needed that does not allow these inequalities to get so vast in the first place; structural and radical changes are required to the capitalist system.

1.2 Slow economic progress

On 25th July 2014, George Osborne, the UK Chancellor of the Exchequer was excited: *'Thanks to the hard work of the British people, today we reach a major milestone in our long-term economic plan.'* That milestone was that the UK economy had returned to pre-crisis levels by expanding 0.8% in the second quarter of 2014. On an annual basis Gross Domestic Product (GDP) had expanded by 3.1%. The figures showed the economy was then worth 0.2% more than it was at its peak in 2008. (source: Office for National Statistics). This was hollow optimism; it has been very slow progress, with dire consequences for millions of people hit by persistent and ill-conceived austerity measures. So six years of 'hard work' many were worse off with stagnant wages and higher prices when in fact a more proactive progressive approach could have meant faster progress and less hardship.

A rise in GDP may be good for a country as a whole but it is only good for its people if they actually benefit, and not just the few. Then after all this time, the UK economy was forecast to be the fastest growing among the G7 developed nations, according to the International Monetary Fund (IMF), predicting that the UK would expand by 3.2% in 2014, up from a previous forecast of 2.8%. But would this mean the people would be better off?

Unemployment had fallen. But there were still not enough jobs or, more importantly, there are not enough jobs that pay a decent, living wage. Meanwhile, the USA reported adding 288,000 jobs in June 2014, making the unemployment rate 6.1%, the lowest since September 2008; not as bad as the most recent high point of 10% in October 2009, but nowhere near the 4.4% rate in May 2007 which was preceded by three years of only ever reaching a maximum of 5.6%. However, these slightly improving figures do not give the whole story, as there was a big shift to part time jobs, which accounted for two thirds of all new jobs in June. More companies are shifting to part-time work as it allows them to avoid paying overtime or health insurance and gives them more flexible options to meet demand.

Even when a person has a job with a decent wage, disposable income is decreasing as living costs rise. In addition, in the UK, the average citizen pays over 50% of his or her income in tax (income and consumption related). So this leaves very little disposable income for most people. The average young family in London in April 2015 only had £347 left a year after essential spending and mortgage payments, according to estate agent Hamptons' Ability to Buy study, a points-based index which measures house prices, incomes, interest rates and the cost of living. It suggest this was due to a 17% increase in house prices combined with a 9% rise in childcare costs and a 1.6% fall in average incomes.

A large number of people are under constant pressure to make ends meet; there is no spare cash to save and little prospect of financial security. It need not be like this. The reduction in disposable income for many is a direct result of government action. Budget cutbacks are creating a new group of people, the 'new insecure'. Weaker life-chances, lack of opportunity and increasing insecurity are no longer afflicting only the most excluded groups. Declining real wages and incomes means more people are suffering from uncertainty. The new insecure have to cope with global economic forces and the spread of technology. They struggle to adapt to the social realities of falling living standards, feel the growing pressures of 'earning' and 'caring' in family life, and fear that life for their children will not be as good as for them in the face of pressures on pensions, access to decent health services, the costs of going to university and house price inflation.

The dominant trend in the last two decades has been towards the creation of a '5-75-20' society in the developed western economies: Roughly 5% are enjoying 'runaway' rewards at the top, as asset prices and returns to wealth soar. This group is largely composed of professionals working in finance and property, the corporate elite and successful entrepreneurs, as well as those who inherit significant wealth.

Some 75% in the middle are either in work or have a retirement income, but are relatively insecure and often anxious about the future. Large parts of this group consists not only of 'blue-collar' industrial workers threatened by outsourcing to Asia, but also groups of middle-class professionals who fear their jobs will be next as the emerging 'MINT' economies (Mexico, Indonesia, Nigeria, and Turkey) move up the economic value chain. Once secure professionals, such as academics, mechanical engineers and scientists, who are relatively worse off than their counterparts a generation ago and may be struggling to sustain their standard of living, may also fall into this group.

The 20% at the 'bottom' of society struggle in a vicious cycle of low-wage, irregular work, unemployment and limited access to welfare.

Arguably, they are 'outsiders' in the labour market and victims of entrenched social immobility. It does not take much for many families to go from a relatively well-off, comfortable existence with a bright future, to poverty. There was a moving story told by Darlena Cunha in the *Washington Post* in July 2014 about her experience back in 2008 as a young college educated couple who were bringing in a combined income of $120,000. They bought a house for $240,000; three weeks later it was worth $150,000. She became pregnant with twins which meant leaving her job as a TV news producer. Then, her husband lost his job. Within just two months they had gone to making just $25,000 a year, of which a large amount was going to pay the mortgage they could no longer afford. Their savings dwindled, then disappeared, and she was on welfare, Medicaid and collecting food stamps. '*The reality of poverty can spring up quickly while the psychological effects take longer to surface,*' she said.

> When you lose a job, your first thought isn't, 'Oh my God, I'm poor. I'd better sell all my nice stuff.' It's 'I need another job.' We didn't deserve to be poor, any more than we deserved to be rich. Poverty is a circumstance, not a value judgment.

Six years later, they have now sold that house, her husband found a job that pays well, and they have enough left over for her to go to grad school. As she says, '*President Obama's programs – from the extended unemployment benefits to the tax-free allowance for short-selling a home we couldn't afford – allowed us to crawl our way out of the hole.*' It may be a story with a happy ending but it arose from financial mismanagement – not on her part but on the banks' – and it took much longer to reach a conclusion than it should have because of the way the recovery was handled, again not by her but by government and financial institutions.

A plane that flies too slowly will stall. An economy with slow growth will increase the concentration of wealth and make capital more dominant, according to Thomas Piketty. He adds that other things being equal, faster economic growth will diminish the importance of wealth in a society. There are, however, no 'natural forces' pushing against the steady concentration of wealth; only a burst of rapid growth (from technological progress or rising population) or government intervention can be counted on to keep our economies from drifting into patrimonial capitalism, an economy driven entirely from the top. Piketty recommends that governments step in now, by adopting a global tax on wealth, to prevent soaring inequality contributing to economic or political instability further down the road. In the 18th and 19th centuries western European society was highly unequal. Private wealth dwarfed national income and was concentrated in the hands of the rich families who sat atop a relatively rigid class structure. This system persisted even as industrialisation slowly contributed to rising wages for workers. Although the Great Depression and two world wars that bracketed it disrupted this pattern, a combination of taxes and the creation of the welfare state ushered in a period in which both income and wealth were distributed in relatively egalitarian fashion. On many measures, however, Piketty reckons that the wealth gap is returning to levels last seen before the First World War.

Not only is economic growth dismally slow and well behind our true capability, our infrastructure is crumbling. In the USA, total public spending on transport and water infrastructure has fallen steadily since the 1960s and now stands at 2.4% of GDP. Europe, by contrast, invests 5% of GDP in its infrastructure, while China is racing into the future at 9%. America's spending as a share of GDP has not come close to European levels for over 50 years. Although it still builds roads with enthusiasm, according to the OECD's International Transport Forum, the USA spends considerably less than Europe on maintaining its roads. In 2006 America spent more than twice as much per person as Britain on new construction; but Britain spent 23% more per person maintaining its roads. From personal experience, the UK may have potholes and cracks thanks to its changeable weather, but the roads in California seem no better.

There is little relief either for the weary traveller on America's rail system. The absence of true high-speed rail is a continuing embarrassment to the nation's rail advocates. America's fastest and most reliable line, the north-eastern corridor's Acela, averages a sluggish 70 miles per hour for the 454 miles between Washington and Boston so it is not technically a high speed train by European standards. The French TGV from Paris to Lyons runs at an average speed of 140mph. America's trains are not just slow; they are late. Where European passenger service is punctual around 90% of the time, American short-haul service achieves just a 77% punctuality rating. Long-distance trains are even less reliable. But while the Federal Government seems to understand the necessity of the rail network as it allocated $8 billion for high-speed rail projects as part of the 2009 stimulus, at least three states (Florida, Ohio and Wisconsin) sent the funds back, claiming it was wasteful spending.

This is born out by recent personal experience, travelling on the regular regional Amtrak service from New York to Boston. The train was two hours late leaving New York so in the end it took over seven hours instead of four and half (which would be an average speed of 60 mph) to cover the 265 miles. The week before I was on a train from London to Preston, 225 miles, it took 2 hours 10 minutes, and arrived on time, averaging over 100 mpg). Now, I am lot letting the rail system in the UK off the hook because it leaves a lot to be desired. The system is crowded, and also suffers from delays, and it has just 68 miles of high speed line, one of the lowest in Europe.

Although the accepted version of history is that the railways were a product of gritty, maverick free enterprise, in reality the US and state governments played a huge role from the very beginning by enabling the rail barons to sequester land from native Americans and by using the army and the law to enforce 'progress'. The term 'railroading' for bullying through a plan did not come about by accident. However, towns and cities grew alongside the railways and they were essential to commerce, and it could be argued that the railways gave a point to some territories seeking statehood and admission to the USA, whose growth in turn created a world power.

At roughly the same time, in the UK, despite the scale of the British Empire, poverty and starvation at home were rife. Agricultural pro- ductivity was high, money was pouring into Victorian cities such as Manchester, Bristol and London. But parish and town records show that within miles of major towns, bodies were frequently found whose stomachs, on post-mortem examination, contained little more than grass. One reason was poor communications. Food grown in one county simply couldn't get to people in the next. Then came the railways, or more accurately, the railway mania of the 1830s and 1840s. An astonishing 272 Acts of Parliament were passed permitting the construction of 9,500 miles (15,300 km) of new railways. The government's role was to permit almost every plan (many Members of Parliament were investors themselves) and leave the railways to sort themselves out: 'laissez-faire', let them do what they wanted. It allowed riches for some and ruin for many investors. It was a free for all, a bubble that burst, leaving a third of the proposed railways un-built, often because companies were taken over by rivals and construction was choked off. Nevertheless all those Acts of Parliament created rights of way over land, changing its use and its value, leading eventually to the building of suburbs and, much later, enabling the expansion of the telecoms network that is integral to today's economy.

Despite apparently being 'hands off', the mid-19th-century government of capitalism's golden era played a massive role both literally and metaphorically in changing the landscape of Britain. After the devastation of the Second World War, the socialist Labour government, swept to power in a landslide election, saw that the railways would be essential to rebuilding the country. The US government was to recognise the importance of investing in infrastructure as well as to feeding and keeping free the people of Western Europe through the Marshall Plan. In Britain this was the job of the government, which, along with other essential industries such as coal and steel, took over the railways, worn out and war weary like the populace, though they were.

By the 1960s the state, not private industry, had made a vast investment of £1.2 billion in replacing steam with electric and diesel locomotives, while the network of rail lines had been rationalised, the amount of rolling stock reduced and the workforce cut from wartime levels. However, investment in the railways and the service they provided to state and private sectors alike came to be regarded as losses. This mindset also affected the view of other strategic areas such as the state-owned (and rescued) airline, the ferry services to mainland Europe and Ireland; the National Grid supplying power to homes and industry, the gas supply, the General Post Office telephone system, Royal Mail postal service and so on. Framing investment in these as losses provided part of the rationale for the privatisation of publicly owned assets and services at knock-down prices often set on the self-serving advice of very large-scale institutional investors. This intervention by government was driven by neo-liberal beliefs. It was intended to engineer a property and share-owning democracy under the flag of popular capitalism; creating a nation of small investors was in part aimed at curbing state control. Instead, it both resulted in weakening what little influence taxpayers and voters had over the economy and failed to spread private ownership or investment. Ownership of stocks and shares in Britain, like other forms of wealth, is concentrating in fewer hands. According to the Office of National Statistics, UK individuals owned 11.5% of the value of the UK stock market at the end of 2010, down from 16.7% in 1998. Nor have taxpayers been freed from spending on the industries whose ownership they have lost. Aside from paying fares, guaranteed – by the state – to rise at rates higher than inflation, taxpayers also subsidised the UK's private train operators to the tune of £4 billion in 2013. To add insult to injury, the operators then paid their shareholders dividends of £200 million. The

Office for Rail Regulation has called the way the UK's railways are now run '*the economics of the madhouse*'.

The government – our representatives – should be responsible for infrastructure investment: not just transport infrastructure but education and health, as well as energy and electronic communications. All these make the economy work, connect and grow. Yet, government has lost sight of its vital role in making infrastructure happen, because 'it is too expensive', missing the point that investment increases growth and generates government revenue. This does not have to mean the state paying for it all, but government certainly needs to create the environment for genuine investment. True, building new infrastructure and rehabilitating existing works are costly. Projects must compete with other needs in the budgets of revenue-strapped federal, state, and local governments. And the return on investment in infrastructure can take many years – beyond the planning horizon of many elected officials – so the temptation is strong to delay infrastructure maintenance. However infrastructure is an investment that brings returns over five, ten, twenty or fifty years.

The relationship between infrastructure development and economic growth has not gone unnoticed by the world's two most populous countries, China and India, which have a combined population of almost 2.5 billion. The experience of these two rapidly growing nations illustrates how different the paths to growth can be. Living standards in China, as measured by GDP per capita, overtook those in India more than 15 years ago. Since that time the Chinese economy has grown nearly twice as fast as India's, and its GDP per capita is now more than double India's. Investment in infrastructure is recognised as one of the main ingredients of China's success. China's most visible infrastructure investment, however, has been in roads and highways. By 2020 China plans to build 55,000 miles of highways, more than the total length of the US interstate system, which was 46,385 miles in 2004, according to the Federal Highway Administration. The Chinese are also building 8000 miles (12,900 km) of high-speed rail line and have plans to double that in under a decade, whereas the whole of Europe has only 4148 miles. Currently, the UK operates 68 miles of high-speed rail and even when the new route from London to Birmingham comes into full operation in 2026, this will only double that.

There are other forms of transport and other examples of intellectual stagnation breeding economic stagnation, such as the constant vacillations over the future of London's airports. The UK government said in 2012 that it wanted to defer the decision to expand London's airports until after the election in 2015, but nearly a year later there is still no decision. For 50 years, governments of one stripe or another have been sitting on a proposal to build a major airport in the estuary of the River Thames east of London that could grow without causing urban upheaval. The prevailing wind in the UK comes from the southwest. Heathrow's location west of London ensures that incoming flights pass over the capital and their frequency is such that planes appear from the ground to be on one another's tails. London's main airport has two runways; Amsterdam's has six, built on reclaimed land.

There is a lot more than transport that is crumbling and not keeping up with the demands of today and the needs of tomorrow. Schools, university, public leisure and recreational facilities are all suffering from reduced budgets due to short-sighted views and a lack of radical thought as to how all this could be funded and effectively pay for itself from the increased national and local wealth that would result.

Throughout history, transportation has been the facilitator of trade and the engine of the industrial world, yet this perceived wisdom is being ignored to the detriment of economic growth. If we want economic growth we need to invest in infrastructure especially transport and it has to be available to all. Though it is not just inadequate infrastructure that has been slowing economic growth, it has been the policies of government that have had a significant negative effect. So unless there is a bold strategic and radical vision on economic policy and infrastructure development, we are going to be confined to the slow lane, which benefits no one. And as has been demonstrated, even with good economic growth the benefits can go to the few, not the many.

1.3. Government isn't working (for us)

Our democracy has been damaged; the widening gap in economic inequality has disenfranchised many who are not able to participate in the opportunities that their country should be able to offer. The rise and rise of the super-rich has turned our democracies into plutocracies: societies ruled and dominated by the small minority of the wealthiest citizens. At the same time, money from big business is poured into lobbying and electoral campaigns. We have strayed a long way from government of the people, by the people, for the people.

Our liberal democracy has been undermined by big money and political polarisation. Governments are becoming dysfunctional. In the USA, particularly, the government has come to a halt on several occasions thanks to intransigence over budgets and spending. In 2010, in the UK, the lack of an outright majority for one party led to the first coalition government since the Second World War. It failed to act with a sense of urgency or clear direction and was antithetical to stimulus initiatives and focussed instead on austerity measures that mainly hit the poor. An election in 2015 put the Conservatives into power by a narrow majority promising more – much more – of the same. But in recent decades both the US and UK governments have lacked any clear agenda for sustainable and socially just structural change. Their purpose should be to sow the seeds of prosperity, to cultivate them and harvest the benefits for all. Yet their policies are making matters worse for the majority, and the problem is partly down to tax.

Tax codes have become increasingly complex, as have the ways of avoiding taxes. Governments still raise most of the revenue from taxes on incomes. In the UK, over 43% of government revenue comes from taxes on incomes including National Insurance. As its name suggests, National Insurance was introduced in the UK in 1911 as an insurance scheme to which workers and employers contributed to cover for illness and unemployment. It was later expanded to cover retirement pensions and other benefits. Successive governments have undermined the concept and it is now treated openly as a tax. In the USA, the cost of health insurance, while not a tax, adds significantly to employers' costs. Domestic property taxes (Council Tax) in the UK have to be paid by both homeowners and renters so are just another tax that falls harder on the less well off. The UK also has a sales tax, Value Added Tax, paid by the end-user, which has a disproportionate impact on the poor. The concept of taxes on wealth and higher tax on higher incomes seems to be side-lined. 80% of British Income Tax payers earn below £32,000 and yet still have to pay Income Tax which actually adds so little to the government revenue. It is not worth causing so much hardship for such a small return. Yet there are no effective taxes on the wealth accumulated by the few. Capital Gains Tax and Inheritance Tax account for just 1% of UK tax revenue. If Stamp Duty (a tax on property transactions) is included as well, then it rises to just 3%. Austerity programmes have hit hard but, by definition, the wealthy are protected. Huge numbers of low-paid workers are still below the poverty line and receiving state benefits. In effect, taxpayers are subsidising wealthy shareholders and low wages. So very clearly the government is not working for us, the majority.

In his book *Public Revenue without Taxation*, my father, Dr Ronald Burgess, showed that there is a more equitable and efficient way of funding government. His argument rests on a widely accepted definition of tax: '*a compulsory contribution to a public authority irrespective of the exact amount of service rendered to the taxpayer in return*'. It follows that, if what the taxpayer is required to pay is in direct relation to services rendered, then it is not a tax: it is a payment for services rendered, just like any other transaction and indeed a much more palatable process than the current system.

So, if all 'tax' could be in direct relation to the services and benefits received from the government, then the payments to the government from the people would not be a tax. Instead they would be getting what they paid for. This could be achieved by using the value of land, the natural resource that is in limited supply, as the tax base. The price of property already includes the value of these public amenities, but it is necessary to distinguish the value the land from the value of any building or other improvement on the site. The former is a publicly created value and the latter is privately created. To tax the building and improvements is to penalise private investment, but to 'tax' the value of the land is to collect for the public purse what has been created at public expense.

This is equitable, but there is a further benefit: as improvements to public infrastructure and local services are automatically translated by the market into higher land values, this will trigger higher contributions to the public purse from the land owners who benefit in proportion to the benefit received, as valued by the market. This is a virtuous circle: the more services provided, the higher the land values and the greater public revenue. This concept will be examined further to see how such system could be implemented and its significant impact on rampant inequality.

This principle could and should be extended to more areas of local and national revenue collection. While it has been shown that sufficient public revenue could be raised without taxation, tax could still be a useful economic management tool, in which case, with current levels of inequality, it may still be necessary to keep some taxes for the time being. But contrast this model with what we do now.

Too many are in what is described as the poverty trap. It's bad for them and bad for the rest of us. Because employers are subsidised to pay low wages through the system of in-work benefits, there's less money moving through the economy and consequently less flowing into the Treasury. Broadly, it is estimated that it is not worth coming off welfare benefits in UK unless the job pays more than £15,000 per year. The policy of successive governments has been to cut welfare budgets to save money; austerity measures have meant more people need more welfare; there is less scope to meet this need. Initiatives to increase growth and provide more work that would have alleviated the pain for those most hard-pressed, have been eschewed. But if we took bold moves to increase income for the lower earners it would also create more opportunity for those currently in poverty to break out of it, and it would boost consumer demand. Increasing both the number and the value of jobs would reduce the welfare budget so that government could focus funds on growth and wealth creation. Win-win instead of lose-lose-lose.

Talk of cutting back on government, reducing its role, and therefore decreasing taxes, misses the point that government is there to provide a service to its people. We, all of us, are the people. We elect a government to provide what we cannot provide for ourselves, individually or as a local community on a small scale. Government is not there just to legislate and regulate or only act as a protector of the individual against others or outsiders. What services it should provide and to what extent, we decide. Others may differ, but in my view, it makes sense for the government to provide healthcare, welfare, education, infrastructure, law and order, defence and international relations. Its primary roles should be to ensure opportunity for all and to minimise inequality in line with basic human rights. This is neither a recipe for the 'Big Government' so despised by right-wing libertarians nor for 'rolling back the state' to the point where every other activity would be beyond its remit. It is simply a question of resetting our priorities. Narrowing the wealth gap and abolishing the democratic deficit that it creates are all part of the same process. We tell ourselves we live in a democracy with freedom and opportunity for most if not all. Yet we see policies directed and influenced by those with wealth while the poor and the powerless are marginalised and disenfranchised; this is not democracy but plutocracy, a society dominated and run in the interests of the wealthy.

The idea of tackling poverty and empowering the poor instinctively worries some people who think it might lead to swarms of the discontented tearing down the gates of their mansions, invading their holiday islands or tossing them through their penthouse windows. Why should it? If anything, putting even greater distance between haves and have-nots is far more likely to end messily. In 2008, then Australian Prime Minister Kevin Rudd called today's new rich *'the children of Gordon Gekko'*, referencing the character in the movie *Wall Street* who said, *'greed, for lack of a better word, is good'*. Between them a class of fat cats and wide-boys backed by political zealots brought about the Great Recession of the early 2000s, ruined countless lives and – against all natural justice – did very nicely out of it. There has been no let up in the eye-watering salaries, golden handshakes and 'bonuses' that help create the wealth gap.

The multi-billionaire owner of luxury jewellery Cartier, Johann Rupert who has amassed a fortune of around $7.5 billion from brands including Cartier, Chloe and Vacheron Constantin commented in June 2015 that the thought of the poor rising up and overthrowing the rich keeps him awake at night. He added that he fears that such a revolution will mean the middle classes won't want to buy luxury goods in the future for fear of exposing their wealth. *'How is society going to cope with structural unemployment and the envy, hatred and the social warfare? We are destroying the middle classes at this stage and it will affect us. It's unfair.'* It seems the harsh reality may be starting to sink in to the 1%.

New York-based, Insite Security, specialising in personal security for wealthy individuals as well as executives in multinational corporations has seen a 40% annual increase in demand for work on panic rooms in 2015. Founder, former lawyer and US secret service agent, Christopher Falkenberg told *The Financial Times* that *'Fears of inequality have heightened concern among people on Wall Street and those in hedge funds. Inequality is an issue. People are concerned for their safety from activists or criminals targeting the affluent.'*

For some the remedy appears to lie in the enlightened self-interest, even philanthropy. Take Bill Gates and Warren Buffett, two of the wealthiest men in the world. On a March day in 2010, they sat in a diner in Carter Lake, Iowa, and hatched a scheme to ask America's billionaires to pledge the majority of their wealth to charity. Buffet decided to donate 99% of his, saying, *'I couldn't be happier with that decision.'* Even bearing in mind how much they will have left in the bank when all is done, this is about as generous as it gets and it chimes with a long tradition of benefaction amongst the super-rich in the USA.

J. Paul Getty made his first million dollars by the age of 24. By the middle of the last century he was one of the richest men in America and by any measure he was both shrewd and successful. He said:

> No matter how many millions an individual amasses, if he is in business he must always consider his wealth as a means of improving living conditions everywhere. He must remember that he has responsibilities toward his associates, employees, stockholders and the public.

I have no doubt this was honestly meant but in a democracy we all have these and similar responsibilities. Our duties and rights are, or at least should be, the same. Philanthropy on the industrial scale practiced by Gates, Buffett et al, is the privilege of the 0.1% who have acquired countries' worth of wealth or the even more infinitesimal number who choose to exercise it. There is nothing wrong and a great deal right with people contributing to worthwhile causes to alleviate misfortune, help cure disease and spread happiness. We should all be in a position to do so in our own right or through the people we elect. Something is very wrong if plutocrats are setting the social agenda.

The US property billionaire and Presidential candidate Donald Trump may have some questionable and outrageous views but in 1999 he came up with an interesting idea. The national debt has always been a burden for most countries. The high cost of servicing it comes out of the current account every year but it goes no way to reducing the debt. At the turn of the century, Trump proposed a plan to pay off the US national debt with a one-time 'net worth tax' on individuals and trusts worth $10 million or more. A 14.25% levy on such net worth would raise $5.7 trillion and wipe out the debt in one fell swoop. The value of the individual's principal home would be exempt, deducted from the net worth total. At the time, he calculated that eliminating the national debt in this way would save the Federal Government $200 billion a year in interest payments. He proposed to earmark half the savings for middle class tax cuts, and the other half for Social Security. Trump, whose own net worth was then estimated at $5 billion (it's slightly less now), said, *'personally this plan would cost me hundreds of millions of dollars, but in all honesty, it's worth it.'* He predicted that debt elimination combined with his tax cuts would trigger a 35 to 40% boost in economic activity, with more business start-ups, more jobs, and more prosperity. *'It is a win-win for the American people, an idea no conventional politician would have the guts to put forward.'* It went nowhere, which is no surprise, but what is particularly shameful is that it took a plutocrat to propose it in the first place.

When wealth captures government policymaking, the consequences include the erosion of democratic governance, the pulling apart of social cohesion and the vanishing of equal opportunities. The Oxfam report

Working for the Few highlights one of the potential effects of the plutocracy and the wealth gap as irreversible 'opportunity capture' by the wealthy: this is where the lowest tax rates, the best education, and the most effective healthcare are all claimed by the children of the rich, creating cycles of advantage that are transmitted across generations. As US Supreme Court Justice Louis Brandeis famously said, *'we may have democracy, or we may have wealth concentrated in the hands of the few, but we cannot have both.'*

One of the demands of Britain's mid-19th century Chartist movement was that Members of Parliament should be paid an annual salary of £500, so that any adult male who was qualified to stand and was elected, could afford to serve without needing to be independently wealthy. Today, MPs are a mix of committed people who have given up their jobs, others who combine being a paid representative with another career (often the law or multiple company directorships) and career politicians whose entire life and income revolve around Westminster. Their basic salary is £67,000 a year but they also receive expenses to cover the costs of running an office, employing staff, accommodation in London and their constituency, travel between the two and sending out letters. They receive a pension when they retire and a one-off payment if they lose their seat. Small parties that are not in government are given a helping hand in the form of 'short money' (in the House of Commons) and 'Cranborne money' (in the Lords). All of this is designed to 'keep them honest'.

When these arrangements are seen to be abused there is a scandal. In a case that caused outrage and amusement in equal measure in 2009, Tory MP Sir Peter Viggers was forced to retire when *The Daily Telegraph* revealed that he had claimed £30,000 for gardening, including £1645 for a floating duck house. MPs have to sign a register of interests but they can quite legitimately take on outside work. In 2012 the *Daily Mail* calculated that some were earning 13 times their public salary from second jobs, including a former environment minister paid £140,000 by green companies for a 51-hour month. MPs are often accused of being remote and disconnected from 'real life' and, if earning ability alone could make this true, many probably are. Some are also remote from Parliament because they are actually working elsewhere.

Like their US counterparts, British MPs are subject to lobbying by interest groups, big business, party backers and powerful individuals. In 2012, the multi-millionaire Conservative co-treasurer Peter Cruddas resigned after being filmed asking a donor for £250,000 for his party, to fix up a meeting with the Prime Minister. In 2010 the *Sunday Times* and Channel 4 TV uncovered the influence-peddling of three former Labour ministers including Stephen Byers who was secretly filmed saying that he was like a 'cab for hire' at up to £5000 a day. While in some countries these 'extramural' activities would be considered a perk of the job and the amounts involved piddling, what it demonstrates is a mindset contaminated by greed and contempt for voters. The two go hand-in-hand. No wonder we are loosing trust in politicians.

It is fair to say that while the UK and America share common problems in this area there is a difference in scale. One of the most notorious lobbying scandals in the USA blew up in 2006. A group of lobbyists led by one Jack Abramoff were accused not only of giving gifts to politicians and making enormous campaign donations in return for votes, but also of ripping off their clients, mainly Native American casino interests, to the tune of $85 million. Significantly, Abramoff was jailed for conspiracy, fraud and tax evasion. Somewhere along the way the idea that tens of millions of dollars were involved in exercising influence over legislation, seems to have been overlooked. Perhaps one reason is that politics has always been an expensive game. Somebody had to pay for all those trains that candidates took to using for whistle-stop campaigns, starting with William Henry Harrison in 1836.

From George Washington onwards, barely a handful of US presidents, such as Abraham Lincoln and Harry S. Truman, have been non-millionaires, or the equivalent, either on assuming office or in later life, the richest of all being John F. Kennedy. In either country, being an ex-minister or former congressman or woman will not harm your chances of a comfortable retirement. But if it helps to be rich to be in power, in a plutocracy the super-rich do not have to be in government to shape laws or alter policy. The super-rich can deal at arm's length through lobbyists or at closer range, around the dining table, aboard the super-yacht or each winter in the Swiss Alps at the World Economic Forum, an annual event hosted by a foundation whose 1000 members are mainly global corporations with yearly revenues exceeding $5 billion.

I was impressed by the American constitution when I first studied it at school. I liked its clear and ordered approach compared to the British mish-mash of laws collected over the centuries. I admired the consensus politics in America. In the British system the Government and opposition benches of the Houses of Parliament are the length of two swords apart, just in case debates get a bit rambunctious. Both houses are plagued by a confrontational system, tempered by quaint rules that, for example, forbid members from calling one another liars, but will allow them to say they have been '*economical with the* actualité' (French scholars look away now). I remember talking to a Conservative MP back in the early 1990s who saw his main role as keeping the 'socialists' out; foolishly, I had assumed it was to serve his constituents, whatever their beliefs.

If my picture of US politics was ever entirely true, things have certainly changed: the left and the right in America are now so at loggerheads that the Government has been paralysed repeatedly by budget disputes and constant blocking of proposals. This meant that significant pieces of legislation like the Affordable Care Act were watered down in order to please all factions as well as the men with the money.

Even before Obamacare (which still leaves many without healthcare), efforts to improve healthcare provision has been going on for a long time but get bogged down in trying to make health insurance more affordable, rather then making healthcare available to all. This is a classic case of the government not working for us but working for those that provide health insurance and medical and pharmaceutical services. A similar plan for healthcare was proposed by Harry S. Truman six decades ago and has been attacked ever since as 'socialist'. The World Health Organisation calculates that the US has the highest health spending in the world, equivalent to 17.9% of its Gross Domestic Product (GDP), or $8362 per person (more on this later). US politicians, the health care 'industry' and pharmaceuticals companies however, are determined that Americans would rather 'go private' and spend twice as much per head on healthcare than submit to the semi-Communist tyranny of a system like the UK's state-funded National Health Service, which, horror of horrors, is free at the point of delivery. The British government that brought in the NHS almost 70 years ago did so through sheer weight of numbers after a landslide victory in which wartime coalition leader – and aristocrat – Winston Churchill was thrown out of Downing Street. The British were sick and tired both of the 'Giant Evils' identified by the Liberal William Beveridge – want, disease, ignorance, squalor and idleness – and the country's class system. The NHS is the holy cow of British politics; a great example of the government working for us, support for it is the equivalent of motherhood and apple pie, despite the fact that its introduction was bitterly resisted and subsequent governments have tried to 'marketise' it, ready to hand it over to big business.

In Britain there is not much scope for the government working for us in the short term even though the ruling Conservative Party has moved from serving (or self-serving) the land-owning aristocracy to the centre ground. After a General Election with no clear winners in 2010, the Conservatives formed a joint administration with the minority Liberal Democrats (which was formed in 1988 by the merger of the Liberal Party and Social Democrats). At times the coalition had a bumpy ride, even as the junior partner in the coalition, the Lib Dems, managed to get some of their policies enacted and put a brake on what they would see as the worst excesses of the Conservatives whose instinct is to cut taxes for the rich and slash benefits for the poor (which they still did). The coalition demonstrated that is was possible to have an alternative to two-party confrontational politics of the type that has stymied progress on either side of the Atlantic. However, due to a clear lack of direction, the coalition did not achieve the much needed, bold reforms; it was really just business as usual, with the same structural problems still there and unsolved.

But if the government is not working, would the opposition fare any better? In Britain the opposition Labour Party seems to have lost direction and lack a consistent, cohesive message, resulting in it loosing the 2015 general election. Then with massive popular support far left-leaning outsider Jeremy Corbyn was elected leader but with many dissenting Members of Parliament. Despite his radical views and his determination to bring change, it appears his management and communications skills leave a bit to be desired. He has however done a massive service to the nation by bringing the belief that change is possible, business as usual needs to end. It now needs a bold visionary leader to pick up on this strength of feeling in the electorate and turn it into reality for the betterment of all.

And in thanks for their contribution for government the Lib Dems were reduced to not much more than a handful in the House of Commons in the 2015 General Election, with very little clout to achieve anything, for the time being at least. Similarly the Green Party and the UK Independence party did also not make much ground.

And even the lawmakers believe that the government isn't working. John Dingell is the longest-serving congressman in US history with over 60 years in office. In February 2014 he announced his retirement. He said the institution he once revered was riven by acrimony and marked by lack of productivity. He had grown frustrated with the law-making process; he had run out of patience with Washington's divided, confrontational politics. Aside from partisan animosity, Dingell despaired of the corrupting influence of money and the increasing cost of running for election. He recalled when Democrats and Republicans actually worked together, now they were against this or against that and he did not hear what we are for or what they would be willing to compromise on. Dingell said he always sought compromise during a career working '*with – not under, and not for – 11 presidents, from Eisenhower to Obama*', adding that this is not a Congress that is working, but it could be and should be. '*The problem comes when disagreement is expressed through venomous name-calling, mindless vitriol, and* ad hominem *attack,*' says the American political economist and commentator Robert Reich.

> Hatefulness too often blinds us to what we hold in common; it makes it impossible for us to listen to opposing views; and it serves as cover for the powerful and privileged who would rather divide us than have us join together for the common good.

The best ideas come from listening and talking. Those with a lifetime of experience can understand how things have changed for the worse, though.

Summary

The facts are staring us in the face, yet governments still fail to act decisively. It is not just bad, it is getting worse, inequality is becoming more extreme, poverty destroys lives, economic progress is still 'fragile' and so many are disengaged from democracy that the plutocrats retain control in their own interests. So we know the problem: what do we do? It is time for a radical rethink.

CHAPTER 2

Radical Rethink

W E LIVE IN what purport to be a democracies, but how can it be truly democratic when wealth – and its concomitant, power – is allowed to concentrate into so few hands and governments do precious little, decade after decade, to help the struggling democratic majority? How can we think there is a fair society when we are forcibly taking away hard earned income from lower wage earners, so limiting their choices and making life more difficult? Particularly as, at the same time, so many are allowed to accumulate so much.

Allegedly it was Albert Einstein that defined insanity as doing the same thing again and again and expecting a different outcome. The reason that this absurd problem has not been fixed is simple: the same old policies have been applied year after year. No wonder we are losing trust in our politicians. A glimpse at the bland UK 2015 election campaign demonstrates the point. None of the major parties had a clear, holistic strategy on the core economic and social justice issues, or a way to tackle the unnecessary misery of so many. In the USA, meanwhile, there are constant threats of government shutdowns, threats to cut Medicaid and Medicare budgets and undo Obamacare, and constant bickering while the President tries to move the agenda forward – still with no clear message and strategy. As the 2016 presidential election unfolds, the focus is on the personalities and fund-raising, with very little on the policies that will actually improve life for the majority of Americans.

Our governments seem to be wandering in the dark, going from one crisis to another, averse to pushing through any progressive policies that would benefit the majority. More and more legislation is added to the statute books and yet we are still not making real advances on the key issues, just papering over the cracks. There seems to be no clear strategy for solving problems and creating a better life for all. The old ways are not working; they have lost their relevance to the 21st century as vested interests and traditional thinking get in the way. Now is the time for a bold vision. We cannot go on making the same mistakes; structural reform cannot be resisted any longer. If changes to income and wealth concentration do not happen very soon, the warnings that the 'pitchforks are coming' and that political earthquakes will erupt, will become a reality.

The key component of this change is you; none of us can sit back and wait for others, we have to come together if change is to happen. This means decisive action to create a better life for all. As prosperity improves, individuals and families need to make wise choices and act responsibly if we are to feel the fresh air of freedom. All this is possible, providing there is a radical rethink in the approach and an open mind to the initiatives required.

That is how we will move From Here to Prosperity.

In the next chapter, I outline the Agenda for Progressive Prosperity around three key interlinked policy areas. Before we examine these, let's look at how we could move from Austerity to Prosperity and the tools that we can use to build that future, hopefully by evolution, though the need is urgent, or we face a revolution.

2.1 Austerity to prosperity

'Prosperity is more than just the accumulation of material wealth, it is also the joy of everyday life and the prospect of an even better life in the future.' That is how the Legatum Institute, which produces the annual Prosperity Index covering 142 countries, describes prosperity. Prosperity is a state of well-being, peace and happiness.

Extreme economic inequality, persistent poverty, slow economic progress and damaged democracy are stumbling blocks. They leave us directionless. Lewis Carroll, author of Alice in Wonderland said, 'If you don't know where you are going, any road will get you there.' The challenge now is choosing which route we take to Prosperity. I believe the best path for that is with dialogue and consensus. The partisan policies of the past need to be put aside. Dialogue is essential, particularly with adversaries, if we are to better understand each other's goals and identify common ground. In times of war, we put aside party politics and pulled together. While we are not (yet) at war over it, wealth inequality is a form of conflict, if only with ourselves. The policies I outline will benefit everyone, whatever their political affiliation.

Politicians can be too timid, too scared, too worried about re-election or keeping the other party out to really push radical policies such as the reduction in Income Tax for lower earners and the raising of the minimum wage to a real living wage. Having apparently put the Great Recession behind us, lessons should have been learned and our nations be moving on with renewed confidence and healthy economic growth but we are not. We were plunged into an extended period of unnecessary austerity (except for the 1%); Government laws and regulations still increase by the day; tax codes remain horrendously complicated, and regulations for business continue to get more onerous. Government needs to re-examine its purpose. The issue is not that we need less government, but that we need better government to meet the needs of all the people, for both those that voted for the political 'rulers' and those who did not.

Some of the initiatives I am proposing here have been mooted in the past. For example, the contribution to public revenue based on the location value of land (or what some may call Land Value Tax) was originally proposed at the end of the 19th century. Other socially just ideas have been ignored but remain valid. For example, the concept that a tax based on personal and corporate wealth, has been proposed on many occasions, recently by Thomas Piketty. Governments are too scared to propose this for risk of alienating wealthy backers and voters. As we all help create the wealth it seems to make sense that it should be reinvested for the good of all stakeholders. So I have now put together some fair, just and logical proposals to bring greater equality and more opportunity, in a simple, positive and practical Agenda for Progressive Prosperity that takes a holistic strategic approach to achieving prosperity.

What is prosperity?

Let's take a closer look at what makes up prosperity. Certainly prosperity means more than just more money. It could safely be assumed that most people in the world would aspire to a state of prosperity and it could therefore be considered a good thing to try to achieve for mankind. However, it could be estimated that out of a population of seven billion only a very few nations or individuals have achieved a sustainable state of prosperity. In this book, we will focus on the more tangible elements;

I will leave others to go deeper about the meaning of life, the search for enlightenment and love!

It seems logical that in order to achieve prosperity we need consistent and manageable economic growth but it comes at a price. In his book *Prosperity Without Growth* (2009), author and economist Tim Jackson argues that *'prosperity – in any meaningful sense of the word – transcends material concerns'* and he goes on to summarise the evidence showing that, beyond a certain point, growth does not increase human well being. He proposes a route to a sustainable economy, and argues for a redefinition of 'prosperity' in light of the evidence on what really contributes to people's well being. *'It is the clearest message from the financial crisis of 2008 ... that our current model of economic success is fundamentally flawed.'* He believes that for the *'advanced economies of the Western world, prosperity without growth is no longer a utopian dream. It is a financial and ecological necessity.'* I would agree that the current economic model is fundamentally flawed and that prosperity is about well-being, but I believe a better plan would be to seek prosperity with socially responsible economic growth. Economic growth is the wealth creator; the challenge is to make sure that the greatest number enjoys it.

Here's my take on 10 key components of prosperity. I think it about covers everything but their relative importance will vary for different people.

1 Health
2 Financial security
3 Wealth
4 Success
5 Doing good
6 Opportunity
7 Freedom/choices
8 Hope
9 Happiness
10 Love

1 Health: This is simple. Unless you have good health then you cannot fully participate in the benefits of prosperity. It is not simply about access to medicine when needed, or even medical research. It is also about having school playgrounds where our children can build the foundations of physical and mental health through play, interaction and exercise; creating a healthy and diverse food culture; caring for carers; effective, transformative social services and decent, respectful provision for housing and looking after the elderly. Health is the right and responsibility both of the individual and of the community as a whole.

2 Financial security: Maybe prosperity is just a feeling of financial security; indeed this would be a very important goal for most people. But the term is relative, so we cannot really create a clear definition of what 'financial security' is, it will be different for everyone. It could mean just being able to pay all the bills each month or owning your own home outright. The current culture is the opposite, tolerating job insecurity, exploitation and usury.

3 Wealth: Having wealth undoubtedly gives a feeling of prosperity. Wealth consists of money and assets that you own and these assets have value such as your home or other property, pension plan, shares etc. In general, you can only accumulate wealth if you have more than sufficient income to live off and are careful and thrifty. Some wealthy people have worked hard, are talented or just got lucky. That is fine. But those on lower incomes have to spend all their money just to live and are unlikely to save and acquire wealth. They are disqualified. It is the system, not the individual that is at fault and allows these levels of inequality. It needs to be fixed. However, I find no correlation with significant wealth and happiness!

4 Success: To many, the goal is success and money is its yardstick. Though true success is about being challenged and stimulated, and being surrounding by good friends and family who you can trust and who you know will look after you when you need support (and vice versa). It may be, too, that you have strong faith that carries you through and is the cornerstone of your moral code. It would seem the benefits of having a good and steady income are self-evident. Significant financial success achieved by some can breed greed which is bad for us all.

5 Doing good: Give and you shall receive, has been a message of many faiths over the centuries. Academically described as pro-social behaviour, actions such as making charitable contributions, buying gifts, volunteering one's time, and so forth and pro-social expenditures in particular can make us happier than personal expenditure. In their book, *Happy Money: The Science of Smarter Spending*, Elizabeth Dunn and Michael Norton outline research demonstrating that people derive more satisfaction from spending money on others than they do spending it on themselves. This spans poor and rich countries alike, as well as income levels, regardless of the size of our bank accounts. Investing in others can make individuals feel healthier and wealthier, even if it means making yourself a little poorer to reap these benefits. Apparently the benefits of giving emerge among children before the age of two, and giving as little as $1 away can cause you to feel more flush.

6 Opportunity: In 1931 James Truslow Adams defined the American Dream as, '*life should be better and richer and fuller for everyone, with opportunity for each according to ability or achievement,*' regardless of social class or circumstances of birth. Indeed the idea of the American Dream is rooted in the United States Declaration of Independence, which proclaims that '*all men are created equal*' and that they are '*endowed by their Creator with certain inalienable Rights*' including '*Life, Liberty and the pursuit of Happiness*'. Right now, too many people are excluded from opportunity because of family poverty, lack of education or poor health. Most of those born in poverty stay in poverty and even when the opportunity is there, too few know how or indeed believe they can seize it.

7 Freedom: Freedom is one of the greatest components of prosperity. As Martin Luther King said in 1963: '*Let us not satisfy our thirst for freedom by drinking from the cup of bitterness and hatred.*' It is a wonderful feeling but it comes with responsibility. If we are to progress to prosperity we must take responsibility for our actions on a personal, family, community and national level, and indeed as one people sharing a planet. If we want business freedoms, then we must act responsibly. If we want religious freedom then it comes with the responsibility of tolerance for other faiths. If we want the freedom to live in peace then it comes with the responsibility of respecting personal territory, national sovereignty and international agreements, including upholding the role of the United Nations. If we want basic freedoms as detailed in the Universal Declaration of Human Rights, we must make sure all signatory countries honour it. If we become wealthy, we must honour the responsibility we have to the community that enabled us to become so.

8 Hope: One of the reasons that governments consistently fail to turn hope into reality is that political platforms are built on isolated policies not on a holistic approach with a clear vision for structural and fundamental reform. Vision with substance is required and practical initiatives with outcomes that benefit the majority, not just the elites.

9 Happiness: Surely happiness is the main goal in life. Happiness means many different things to many people, plus it is difficult to quantify and compare, though generally we know when we have arrived at happiness even if it is short-lived. One attempt at rating happiness has been devised by the Happy Planet index. The 2012 results show the extent to which 151 countries across the globe produce long, happy and sustainable lives for the people that live in them. The overall index scores rank countries based on their efficiency, how many long and happy lives each produces per unit of environmental output. Costa Rica comes out on top with the UK at number 42 with 47.9 points and USA at 105th place with 37.3, the world average is 42.5.

10 Love: Is love all you need? Love is nevertheless linked to the feeling of well-being and prosperity. When we care so little about one another that we allow such extreme levels of man-made hardship to exist and not act, where is the love?

Measuring progress to prosperity

'Are we nearly there yet?' Many parents will have heard this cry from the back seat of the family car. Right now, the answer is *'No! We have only just started the engine.'* There are some hopeful signs, though. In September 2014, the US Census Bureau revealed that there was a statistically significant decline in poverty in 2013. It is the first since 2006, and only the second since 2000. The numbers remain a major concern, however: 15% of Americans lived in poverty in 2012; 14.5% in 2013, that's more than 45 million people. The waste of human potential is staggering and the urgency of our campaign undiminished. An essential element of any campaign is measuring its success in order to devise tactics that bring results in the shortest time. We want to close the wealth gap, to increase fairness and spread prosperity so we need to measure our progress towards social justice and its sustainability. Traditional indicators – economic growth, wages, disposable income and employment levels – will not tell enough on their own. Indeed, they may not even be the right ones to use. How will we know if we are getting there? Is life really getting better? How can we tell? What are the milestones we need to reach? What are the key elements to improving life? Better education, environment,

healthcare, housing or working hours? Does progress mean the same thing to all people or in all countries and societies?

For many years, the rate of growth of the economy the Gross Domestic Product (GDP) was the surest indicator of a nation's economic strength and the well being of its people. The US Commerce Department reported on 26 September 2014 that the economy grew at a 4.6% annual rate in the second quarter of the year. At first hearing that sounds good but other indicators are going in the opposite direction. For instance, median household income continues to drop, as almost all the gains from growth go to the top of the income and wealth tree. Robert Reich suggests on his Facebook page that:

> America should stop regarding GDP growth as the most important indicator of the economy, and substitute a more important number: median household income. If that number is heading downward, as it has been since the late 1990s (it's now a full eight percentage points below what it was in 2007, adjusted for inflation), we're in deep trouble, and getting deeper.

The wrong indicators are being used for the feeling of progress and being bandied around by politicians as evidence of their success. But wait!. We are now in a multi-stakeholder economy where the rewards of our work in wealth creation are not being shared in any reasonable proportion. So what might work? Let's just look at some of the measurements that may be relevant:

1 World Economic League Table
2 Prosperity Index
3 Good Country Index
4 OECD Better Life Initiative
5 UK Personal Well-being Report

1 World Economic League Table: This uses the traditional method of measuring and comparing the wealth of countries by Gross National Product (GDP). While this is still a measure, many believe this does not give a true picture especially when it comes to prosperity, quality of life and human happiness. World Economic League Table (WELT) is produced by the Centre for Economics and Business Research (Cebr), the economics consultancy. Topping the 2014 league is the United States followed by China, Japan, Germany and the United Kingdom. But in the next few years it is expected to be China, United States, India, Japan, and

Brazil, with the UK dropping to number six, though would become the largest economy in Europe.

2 Prosperity index: Measuring prosperity of countries is a different matter and has been undertaken by the Legatum Institute with their Prosperity Index of 142 countries. Traditionally, a nation's prosperity has been based solely on macroeconomic indicators such as a country's income, represented either by GDP or by average income per person (GDP per capita). However, as Legatum says: *'most people would agree that prosperity is more than just the accumulation of material wealth, it is also the joy of everyday life and the prospect of being able to build an even better life in the future.'* Legatum claim the Prosperity Index is distinctive in that it is the only global measurement of prosperity based on both income and well-being.

The ranking is based on a variety of factors including wealth, economic growth, education, health, personal well-being, and quality of life, using 89 different variables, grouped into eight sub-indexes, which are averaged using equal weights. The eight sub-indexes are:

- Economy
- Entrepreneurship & Opportunity
- Governance
- Education
- Health
- Safety & Security
- Personal Freedom
- Social Capital

Norway tops the list in the 2014 rankings followed by Switzerland and New Zealand. Twenty-seven of the top 30 countries are democracies. The USA ranks 10th and the UK ranks 13th.

3 Good Country Index: While an individual may do well by doing good, how about a country? How good is a country? Or how much does it contribute to the greater good. The Good Country Index ranks 125 nations based on how much they do for others globally in seven areas: science and technology, culture, international peace and security, world order, planet and climate, prosperity and equality, and health and well-being. The ranking was created by merging 35 data sets produced by organisations like the UN, WHO, and UNESCO over a period of nearly three years, according to *The Economist*. A balance sheet was created for each country to show at a glance whether it is a net creditor to mankind, a burden on the planet, or something in between. Ireland came out top followed by Finland and Switzerland. The UK was seventh and the USA 23rd in the overall rankings. One of the seven rankings on the balance sheet was prosperity and equality. Again Ireland first and this time Switzerland second and Finland third. The UK got in at nine and the USA right down at 53!

4 OECD Better Life Initiative: The OECD (Organisation for Economic Co-operation and Development) has been working to identify the best way to measure the progress of societies – moving beyond GDP and examining the areas that impact people's lives. In 2011, the culmination of this work was presented in the OECD *Better Life Initiative*, collecting data from its 34 member countries. This focuses on developing statistics to capture aspects of life that matter to people and that shape the quality of their lives. This allows for a better understanding of what drives the wellbeing of people and nations, and what needs to be done to achieve greater progress for all.

While The UK and USA cannot be compared in size there are a number of interesting comparable indicators:

In the UK, the average household net-adjusted **disposable income per capita** is $25,828 a year, more than the OECD average of $23,938 a year, but as regards the gap between the richest and poorest, the top 20% of the population earn nearly six times as much as the bottom 20%. In the United States, while the average household net-adjusted disposable income per capita of $39,531 a year is higher than the UK, the gap between the richest and poorest is even higher with the top 20% earning approximately eight times as much as the bottom 20%.

In terms of **employment**, over 71% of people aged 15 to 64 in the UK have a paid job, above the OECD employment average of 65%. Some 76% of men are in paid work, compared with 66% of women. People in the United Kingdom work 1,654 hours a year, less than the OECD average of 1,765 hours. In the USA, 67% people aged 15 to 64 in the United States have a paid job. Some 72% of men are in paid work, compared with 62% of women. People in the United States work 1,790 hours a year. Around 11% of employees work very long hours, higher than the OECD average of 9%, with 16% of men working very long hours compared with 7% for women.

In terms of health, **life expectancy at birth** in the United Kingdom is 81 years, one year higher than the OECD average. Life expectancy for women is 83 years, compared with 79 for men. In the United States life expectancy at birth is almost 79 years, one year lower than the OECD average of 80 years. Life expectancy for women is 81 years, compared with 76 for men.

Having a good **education** is an important requisite for finding a job. In the United Kingdom, 77% of adults aged 25-64 graduated from secondary school, higher than the OECD average of 75%. The USA was well ahead with 89% of adults aged 25-64 have earned the equivalent of a high-school degree.

Voter turnout, a measure of public trust in government and of citizens' participation in the political process, was 66% during recent elections in the UK. This figure is lower than the OECD average of 72%. Social and economic status can affect voting rates: voter turnout for the top 20% of the population is an estimated 73% and for the bottom 20% it is an estimated 50%, a broader difference than the OECD average gap of 11%, suggesting there is room for broader social inclusion in the United Kingdom's democratic institutions. Only 1% higher turnout in the USA at 67% during recent elections; voter turnout for the top 20% of the population is an estimated 75% and for the bottom 20% it is an estimated 53%, so like the UK there is in fact even more room for broader social inclusion.

In terms of **satisfaction,** people in the United Kingdom are less satisfied with their lives than the OECD average (76%), with 74% of people saying they have more positive experiences in an average day (feelings of rest, pride in accomplishment, enjoyment, etc.) than negative ones (pain, worry, sadness, boredom, etc.). While Americans are very slightly more satisfied with their lives than the Brits, with 75% of people saying they have more positive experiences in an average day than negative ones.

While the USA and UK are in a close range on this sample of indicators they are both ahead of the OECD average on income, education and employment and both a below average when it comes to levels of satisfaction, though UK has a higher than average life expectancy while the USA is below average. However it is not just OK to be higher than average than a group of 34 countries, we really need to aim for a good quality of life, so there is much work to be done!

5 Personal Well-being report (UK): When the concept of measuring the nation's well-being was launched in the UK in 2010, Prime Minister David

Cameron quoted Robert Kennedy, speaking 40 years earlier, as saying that, while GDP had its purpose, '...[it] *measures everything except that which is worthwhile'*. Measuring national wellbeing matters because it challenges the dominance of wealth and consumption as indicators of 'success', and it underlines the importance of relationships and the capabilities of individuals.

The Office forNational Statistics (ONS) in the UK now produces estimates on personal well-being. The 2013/14 report suggests year-on-year improvements in reported well-being since 2011/12, when ONS started to collect the data. Below is a summary:

- Over this three-year period, there have been small but significant improvements in average personal well-being ratings in each UK country, and across all four measures of wellbeing.
- The proportions of people reporting the highest levels of personal well-being have grown since 2011/12 for each of the four measures. The greatest gain has been in reduced anxiety levels. The proportion of people in the UK reporting very low anxiety grew between 2011/12 and 2013/14.
- There were also reductions in the proportions of people in the UK rating their wellbeing at the lowest levels for all of the measures.
- In 2013/14, people in Northern Ireland gave higher ratings for each aspect of their personal wellbeing on average than those in any other UK country. This has been the case in each year since ONS began collecting the data.
- In 2013/14, people in London reported lower personal well-being on average for each of the measures than the equivalent UK averages, but since 2011/12 London has had improvements across all the average measures of well-being.
- Since 2011/12, average ratings of personal well-being have improved significantly across all measures in the West Midlands. The region also had the lowest average anxiety rating of any English region in 2013/14.

While much of this is a step in the right direction, it is only to be expected as a country moves out of recession (extremely slowly). However, the survey also revealed another example of how some government policies may be working against peoples best interests. It showed that among stay-at-home parents, 83% rated their sense of worth as high or very high, significantly above the average. This led the group, Mothers at Home Matter, to comment that the figures showed that government policies encouraged more parents to work full time, which could cause more harm than good.

However this survey can be a fundamental and valuable measure of movement towards our goal of personal well-being, or in another word, prosperity. A lot more could have been and needs to be done to speed it up, so more people can live fulfilled lives.

Platform for prosperity

There needs to be a platform on which to build the prosperity programme. For the USA there is the Constitution but this is still open to interpretation despite the clear, righteous intentions of the founding fathers. It is a bit more difficult for the British with no written constitution, just volumes and volumes of laws and precedents. It goes back to the Magna Carta of 1215 considered the first bill of rights in Britain. The road to democracy was further paved a few years later when the first modern parliament was set up by Simon de Montfort who now has a university (from which I graduated) named after him in his home town of Leicester, and in 1689 Parliament passed a Bill of Rights. The first 10 amendments to the US constitution are packaged as a Bill of Rights. However, the most up to date document of human rights on a global scale is the Universal Declaration of Human Rights (UDHR) adopted by the United Nations General Assembly in 1948.

So what is the ideological basis for the actions that need to be taken and the policies that need to be implemented to make progress on the road From Here to Prosperity? In order for the changes I propose to be appropriate, sustainable and fair, a foundation is required on which we will build a policy agenda, our moral compass and guiding force. If, as I hope, we can build a broad-based movement for progressive prosperity, this will be our reference point and inspiration for our manifesto. To get mass appeal, a non-partisan approach to prosperity is needed, a way forward that will appeal to all the electorate, an approach that we can all agree on. We could go back to nature, natural law, or just look at 'self-evident truths' or make value judgements on what social justice really means. However, in my view, the work has been done for us in 1948 with the UDHR.

There are five areas to consider when building a platform for prosperity:

1 Natural Law
2 Self evident truths
3 Social justice
4 Value judgements
5 Human rights

1 Back to Nature: In searching for a basis of better policies maybe the laws of man should be rejected and go back to nature. Could natural law be a basis for government? Natural law is the theory or belief that certain rights exist independently of any government's granting them, such as those encompassed in the Universal Declaration of Human Rights. For example, the US Declaration of Independence was an assertion of natural law – the right to be free, the right not to be taxed without representation. If you believe you are entitled to these rights by virtue of the fact that you are alive and human, you believe in natural law. Natural law, or the law of nature, is a system of law that is determined by nature, and so is universal. Thus natural rights follow from the nature of man and the world.

Generally, whenever a group rebels against their government and asserts rights that the government hasn't granted them, they are making a claim of natural law. Many children, for example, appeal to a sense of fairness when faced with parental authority, and most people around the world agree that murder is a severe violation of natural law.

This is compared to positive law, which is the theory or belief that all law comes from the government or lawmakers. Basically, you have no rights that are not granted to you from the government, and no action is inherently right or wrong under the law unless there is legislature or court-created law that says so. Basically, murder isn't illegal because it's 'evil' or bad, it's illegal because there's a written law in the books that says so.

So natural law could give us a basis for developing a policy agenda? I would say it gives us a framework and a reference point but does not answer what policies we should put in place.

2 Self evident truths: The sources and interpretation of the US Declaration of Independence of 1776 have been the subject of much scholarly inquiry. The Declaration justified the independence of the United States by listing colonial grievances against King George III, and by asserting certain natural and legal rights, including a right of revolution. Having served its original purpose in announcing independence, references to the text of the Declaration were few for the next four score years! Abraham Lincoln made it the centrepiece of his rhetoric (as in the Gettysburg Address of 1863), and his policies. Since then, it has become a well-known statement on human rights, particularly its second sentence:

> We hold these truths to be self-evident, that all men are created equal, that they are endowed by their Creator with certain unalienable Rights, that among these are Life, Liberty and the pursuit of Happiness.

This has been called *'one of the best-known sentences in the English language,'* containing *'the most potent and consequential words in American history.'* The passage came to represent a moral standard to which the United States should strive. This view was notably promoted by Abraham Lincoln, who considered the Declaration to be the foundation of his political philosophy, and argued that the Declaration is a statement of principles through which the United States Constitution should be interpreted. It provided inspiration to numerous national declarations of independence throughout the world.

3 Social justice: Social justice is the ability people have to realise their potential in the society where they live. 'Social justice' is generally used to refer to a set of institutions, which will enable people to lead a fulfilling life and be active contributors in their community. The goal of social justice is generally the same as human development. The relevant institutions can include education, health care, social security, labour rights, as well as a broader system of public services, progressive taxation and regulation of markets to ensure fair distribution of wealth, equality of opportunity, and no gross inequality of outcome.

While the concept of social justice can be traced through ancient and Renaissance philosophy, such as Socrates, the term 'social justice' only became used explicitly from the 1840s. But the current tax policies of many countries are not socially just and penalise the worse off with higher rates of tax than the well-off.

If we evaluated the proposed policies against our social justice meter, Income Tax would not rate as fair. Why do we take away hard earned income so that those in the 75% are paying a greater percentage of their income in tax than the top 5%? Is it fairer that the wealthy pay more towards the cost of government as they have more than enough to live on by virtue of their wealth? We must not forget that many, but not all, wealthy people achieve wealth through their own hard work and developed talent. The problem comes when it gets to extremes and deprives the majority of economic freedom. If Income Tax were reduced or even abolished, it would be easier for more people to accumulate their own wealth.

Many calls for social justice go way back. The Magna Carta Libertatum or The Great Charter of the Liberties of England was sealed on 15 June 1215 under oath by King John at Runnymede, on the bank of the River Thames near Windsor in England. Magna Carta was the first document imposed upon a King of England by a group of his subjects, the feudal barons, in an attempt to limit his powers by law and protect their rights. The charter is widely known throughout the English-speaking world as an important part of the protracted historical process that led to the rule of constitutional law in England and beyond. The 1215 charter required King John to proclaim certain liberties and accept that his will was not arbitrary. For example, accepting that no 'freeman' (in the sense of non-serf) could be punished except by due process of the law, a right was recognised that still exists under English law today, as well as in the legal systems of many other nations.

There are certain self-evident truths, undeniable values, a natural way that will give us the wisdom to tread the path towards prosperity, values that no one could dispute.

4 Value judgements: We can, of course, create our own set of values to guide us through the economic and political policy-making. Normative economics expresses value judgments about economic fairness, or economic outcomes, or goals of public policy ('what ought to be'). This is as distinct from positive economics ('what is'). So we could say that the cost of bread should be a certain amount in order to give wheat farmers a living wage.

A moral compass is needed, an inner sense which distinguishes what is right from what is wrong, functioning as a guide (like the needle of a compass) for morally appropriate behaviour. We also need policies that are morally based and established on natural law and social justice. This can provide a yardstick against which to measure the ideas. However when a new idea is suggested, there are always the 'aah buts', but history tells us that when social change is morally right, slavery, women's rights, civil rights, change happens, though it may take a while, it may take mass demonstrations and persistent lobbying, but it will happen.

Robert Reich said that when he was Secretary of Labor in the Bill Clinton administration in the mid-nineties, they considered a no smoking at work bill but thought there would be too much resistance so it was dropped. Now it is accepted behaviour.

Our politicians should not be afraid of proposing radical policies that we believe are morally right but may be considered initially unworkable. Necessity is the mother of invention; we can find a way to make it happen.

5 The Universal Declaration of Human Rights: The Universal Declaration of Human Rights, which I have already referred to a few times, makes our goals very clear as it enshrines natural law with social justice. The UDHR, adopted by the UN General Assembly on 10 December 1948 at the Palais de Chaillot, Paris, was the result of the experience of the Second World War. Much of this was due to the leadership and determination of Eleanor Roosevelt, the widow of former President Franklin D. Roosevelt. With the end of that war, and the creation of the United Nations, the international community vowed never again to allow atrocities like those of that conflict to happen again. But sadly they are still happening though thankfully not on a world scale as in the two world wars.

It is worth noting that:

Article 1 states:

All human beings are born free and equal in dignity and rights. They are endowed with reason and conscience and should act towards one another in a spirit of brotherhood.

Article 2 states

Everyone is entitled to all the rights and freedoms set forth in this Declaration, without distinction of any kind, such as race, colour, sex, language, religion, political or other opinion, national or social origin, property, birth or other status. Furthermore, no distinction shall be made on the basis of the political, jurisdictional or international status of the country or territory to which a person belongs, whether it is independent, trust, non-self-governing or under any other limitation of sovereignty.

It would seem strange then that the civil rights movement, particularly in the US, had to push for these universally agreed truths to be accepted, and then they had to be put into law to enforce them. Even stranger is that they are laid out in the Declaration of Independence but some states decided to reverse this and bring in segregation.

It seems, however, that many countries are still not upholding these principles. It is as much about a change in attitude as it is about following through on commitments.

It is worth restating the preamble to the Declaration:

Whereas recognition of the inherent dignity and of the equal and inalienable rights of all members of the human family is the foundation of freedom, justice and peace in the world,

Whereas disregard and contempt for human rights have resulted in barbarous acts which have outraged the conscience of mankind, and the advent of a world in which human beings shall enjoy freedom of speech and belief and freedom from fear and want has been proclaimed as the highest aspiration of the common people,

Whereas it is essential, if man is not to be compelled to have recourse, as a last resort, to rebellion against tyranny and oppression, that human rights should be protected by the rule of law,

Whereas it is essential to promote the development of friendly relations between nations,

Whereas the peoples of the United Nations have in the Charter reaffirmed their faith in fundamental human rights, in the dignity and worth of the human person and in the equal rights of men and women and have determined to promote social progress and better standards of life in larger freedom,

Whereas Member States have pledged themselves to achieve, in co-operation with the United Nations, the promotion of universal respect for and observance of human rights and fundamental freedoms,

Whereas a common understanding of these rights and freedoms is of the greatest importance for the full realisation of this pledge,

Now, Therefore THE GENERAL ASSEMBLY proclaims THIS UNIVERSAL DECLARATION OF HUMAN RIGHTS as a common standard of achievement for all peoples and all nations, to the end that every individual and every organ of society, keeping this Declaration constantly in mind, shall strive by teaching and education to promote respect for these rights and freedoms and by progressive measures, national and international, to secure their universal and effective recognition and observance, both among the peoples of Member States themselves and among the peoples of territories under their jurisdiction.

It seems to me that the UDHR is a solid basis on which to build our policy platform that will move us towards prosperity.

2.2 Tax as a toolbox

Oxfam in its October 2014 report on inequality entitled *Even it up*, commented that *the tax system is one of the most important tools a government has at its disposal to address inequality.* It went on to show how data from 40 countries demonstrated the potential of redistributive taxation and investment by governments to reduce income inequality that had resulted from market conditions.

Tax has long provided the toolbox for government when it comes to managing the economy. But these tools are rusty and no longer fit. You can't just apply WD-40 and loosen everything up! Most of the taxes imposed on nations have been making matters worse, effectively taking from the poor and giving to the rich. The way that most governments have collected revenue in the past is actually part of the economic problem, as it causes inflation and stunts economic growth. A radical change in how public revenue is raised could have a significant effect and make many things possible. The primary role of taxation is to raise revenue for the common good. Tax should not be seen as a weapon to redistribute financial resources, but rather as a tool to create a system whereby redistribution is unnecessary; a system whereby those who work, gain the full benefit of their labours and enjoy the wealth they have helped create, instead of a few accumulating disproportionate amounts. Currently, with the focus on taxes on income rather than wealth, tax is playing a major role in moving financial resources the wrong way, from the poor to the rich. It is time for a new set of tools in the toolbox, to fix the problem, once and for all.

Nobel Laureate Joseph Stiglitz makes it very clear that he sees reforming tax as a way to promote growth and equality as outlined in his October 2014 paper for the Roosevelt Institute. In his summary, he states:

> reforms to corporate and personal income taxes will be essential in restoring economic vitality. Examples include implementing financial transaction taxes; increasing corporate tax rates while incentivizing investment and closing loopholes; increasing taxes on rent-seeking; reforming estate and inheritance taxes; and making personal income taxes more progressive. All reforms must be made with the understanding that deficit reduction in and of itself is not a worthy goal. Rather, taxation must be reformed to help grow the economy, improve distribution, and encourage socially beneficial behaviour on the part of firms and individuals.

There are some who want to see tax for all reduced significantly and at the same time reduce the role of government to a sort of night watchman role. However, in order to move towards prosperity, a government is in a unique position to create the right environment for everyone to prosper, not just a few individuals.

The big problem with current tax is that it limits personal choice, increases pressure on households by reducing disposable income and consumption options. For business it increases costs and therefore prices to consumers, as well as reducing job opportunities. So it distorts the economy causing, inflation and unemployment. Such problems with current tax systems have been elaborated at length in many learned papers and reports – I am more interested in finding the answers that work.

Clearly government is getting its revenue from the wrong places and by the wrong means. If the government was more enlightened, it would radically change the tax system and help progress towards prosperity. For most governments the majority of revenue comes from taxes on income and a lesser extent on consumption, so consumers get stung at both ends. Many of the 75% in the middle can be paying 50% of their income, or more, in income and sales tax, whereas some very rich are only paying a small percentage in taxes on their income or indeed their wealth pile – Warren Buffet famously commented how strange it was that he was paying a lower percentage on his income than his secretary.

The single biggest step a government can take towards prosperity is to change the tax base. The way most governments raise the bulk of their revenue is out-dated, outmoded and morally wrong. The answer has been staring at us in the face for decades and there have been books written, speeches made and groups formed that push new ideas, but still we follow the same old path, close to the cliff edge. We are taking taxes from people who can't afford it, in the sense that it reduces their disposable income below the level that enables them to lead a fulfilled life, reducing their choices, restricting their freedom.

As will be outlined later, reforms to the tax system can reduce the costs to business. This would enable businesses to pay living and fair wages, allow more investment in people and production, encourage the creation of more jobs and put more money into people's pockets so they can decide how they spend it. They may choose to save and build their own wealth or spend their earnings, thereby creating more jobs.

Avoid it if you can

No one likes paying tax, particularly Income Tax. Many people go to such great efforts to avoid paying income taxes that a huge service industry has grown up to support this, with the same companies coining it on both sides of the equation by advising Government of how to frame tax laws, while devising ways for their clients to circumvent them. Tax collection is so arranged that the honest, the hard working and the compliant, subsidise corporate and individual greed.

I am not about to defend tax-dodging, but it is not surprising that almost all of us would want to maximise our income and minimise our tax expenditure, whatever our earning power. Nor is it a shock that the higher you are up the income scale, the more opportunities there are to do this. I think this is explained by the fact that most people feel the tax system is unfair and that they have little control over how their money is spent. But we don't need to evade taxes to be free of Income Tax altogether – legitimately. This could be done quite simply by switching the tax base from income earned to the value of land. Money is mobile. Land is fixed and can't be hidden so no one can avoid paying their due. Land has a value because we all need somewhere to live and work. If a percentage of that value were paid annually to the government instead of Income Tax, you would still benefit from rising land values as the population grows and the economy expands. When, however, you are taxed on income, the money you have earned from your time and effort, and that is rightfully yours, is taken away. We part with it reluctantly, though it is in fact taken from us compulsorily. Income tax has been likened to theft. In the UK, tax freedom day, the point at which average earners have settled their tax bills and start working for themselves, is June 2: half way through the year. If we based our tax system on the wealth we already own, tax freedom day would be New Year's Day.

And just think what it would be like if the tax paid by companies on profits was seen as a contribution by them to funding education or healthcare, two key requirements of any productive workforce. Imagine if there was a league table of those companies that contributed the most. If they were seen as good citizens, more socially responsible, they would be more inclined to pay their dues, instead of hiding them or going off shore. Why not combine this with tax breaks for being good companies, so that if a company had good education and training programmes, paid living wages, and provided other benefits, then it could reduce its payments to the government? That seems fair.

The costs of running a company would be greatly reduced by eliminating Income Tax, payroll tax and insurance and social security payments, thereby cutting the cost of employing staff. Get rid of all anti-market tariffs and put a levy on bottom line profits and you would still leave the business with the funds for future investment. Profits could increase significantly (wealth to be shared), inflationary pressure would be reduced, and the incentive to move profits offshore would diminish so that government would have a more forecastable and secure revenue.

Left the country

A big problem for many governments is the amount of potential tax revenue that seems to go overseas or is not repatriated from foreign operations. In order to remedy this constant headache international action and coordination is required. In 2011 ActionAid first revealed that 98 of the UK's biggest companies, most of which operate in the developing world, are also using tax havens. In 2014, the IMF published a new policy paper, entitled *Spillovers in International Taxation*, looking at the effects that one country's tax rules and practices can have on others. This clearly shows that tax havens are a cause of poverty, particularly in developing countries according to the Tax Justice Network, an independent international network which maps, analyses and explains the role of tax and the harmful impacts of tax evasion, tax avoidance, tax competition and tax havens. The Tax Justice Network has estimated that offshore wealth of some $10 trillion belongs to 92,000 of the planet's richest individuals, representing not the top 1% but the top .001% – that is 1% of 1%! Further, they have said that 'capital flight' out of Africa, for example has amounted to some $1264 billion, just one measure of wealth flowing into tax havens.

Then there is the argument that if there were high taxes for the rich in countries like the UK and USA, then the most wealthy would leave the country and take their business elsewhere. This is fallacy as even for the wealthy, family and cultural values can still be strong. If it is just down to money, and accumulating even more, then good luck and goodbye! The whole non-domicile and overseas residential farce could be minimised if countries worked together on international agreements to align tax arrangements and where tax is due, instead of trying to be an attractive tax option for international business. Is this a job for the United Nations?

A key issue here is to whom should the tax be paid? In the UK, many foreign-owned (especially US-owned) companies such as Amazon, Google and Starbucks are paying very little UK corporate tax even though they have substantial operations on which, if they were UK-owned, they would be paying Corporation Tax. These companies argue, however, that they are contributing significantly to UK tax revenue as they create jobs for many people who pay income taxes, sales taxes and all the other taxes. In addition they collect VAT on behalf of the UK government. So clearly a code of conduct needs to be agreed as to how much is fair to be paid to the 'host' country and how much is returned 'home'. Switching taxes to land values would greatly simplify this.

Facebook paid just £4,327 in tax on its profits from UK operations in 2014 and it was within the law. Companies profits are the wealth that we all help create, a tax on profits provides one way of making sure that those that created the wealth, share in the wealth. So at a 20% Corporation Tax rate that would mean that Facebook was delivering about £21,635 in profit from UK operations. Globally, Facebook showed a profit of $2,940 million on revenue of $12,466 million, that's a profit margin of 23% profit. So on a like for like basis (based on Corporation Tax they actually paid) their UK revenue would be: £94,065 ($144,333). I don't think so!! In fact that is a lot less than just one UK advertising agency I know spends with Facebook annually. In 2013, Facebook UK revenues were £233 million, so if in line with company growth of 58% they would now be £368 million in 2014 so could expect a profit of around £84.6m in the UK alone, so a resultant Corporation Tax of £16.9 million might be a reasonable estimate. Now I know that there are allowances and deductibles and also the Facebook UK needs to make a contribution to the corporate overheads, but this is pushing it a bit far! Especially when the Facebook's 362 UK employees received bonuses totalling £35.4 million, an average of nearly £100,000 each. Clearly Facebook is not facing the facts, just cooking the books at the expense of everyone in UK.

There has been a lot of comment about 'inversions' in the USA where US companies are in fact leaving potential US tax revenue overseas when it is claimed to be due to be paid to the US government. In August 2014, it was reported that Microsoft was currently sitting on almost $29.6 billion it would owe in US taxes if it repatriated the $92.9 billion of earnings it is keeping offshore, according to disclosures in the company's most recent annual filings with the Securities and Exchange Commission.

Like many issues there has been a lot of talk but so far no bold, decisive and fair proposals on the table.

High cost of collection

Collecting taxes under the current system is very expensive and is liable to abuse and avoidance. In 2011 the Laffer Center estimated that that cost of tax collection alone in the USA was $431 billion: 30 cents on every dollar paid in taxes. Businesses, large and small, hire teams of accountants, lawyers, and tax professionals to track, measure, minimise and settle tax liabilities. In addition there is the cost of in-house time as well as government costs. Like taxes themselves, tax-compliance costs change people's behaviour. Taxpayers, whether individuals or businesses, respond to taxes and tax-compliance costs by changing the composition of their income, the location of their income, the timing of their income, and the volume of their income. So long as the cost of changing one's income is lower than the taxes saved, the taxpayer will engage in these types of tax-avoidance activities. The National Taxpayers Union estimated in 2009 that the income-tax industry employed *'more workers than are employed at the five biggest employers among Fortune 500 companies – more than all the workers at Walmart Stores, United Parcel Service, McDonald's, International Business Machines, and Citigroup combined.'* Simplifying the tax code should be a top priority.

In the UK, the cost of collecting £100 in Income Tax is £1.16 and that is just the government cost, the tax collection industry is much smaller in the UK than in the US pro rata on size of population. Most Income Tax is collected monthly via employers on the Pay As You Earn scheme (PAYE). However, the UK Taxpayers Alliance noted that these 2009 costs of collection had hardly changed since 1958 despite huge improvements in technology and communications. The Institute of Economic Affairs says the cost of tax collection in the UK is almost £20 billion pounds per annum (about 2% of government budget), and estimates that the cost of tax-related red tape to businesses could be reduced by about £5 billion.

So we have out-dated tax systems that do not meet the needs of the 21st century and tax is both difficult and expensive to collect. It's time for a change, but why tax anyway?

Why tax?

The tax system in the UK has evolved over more than two centuries. Income tax was first introduced to fund the war against Napoleonic France in 1803. The National Insurance system dates back to 1911, before the First World War. VAT was introduced in 1973, but it was preceded by Purchase Tax, which operated from 1940. Profit taxes of various forms have been in place since the 1950s, with Corporation Tax introduced in its current form in the 1960s.

All sorts of different ways of raising funds have been deployed at some time. In the UK, from the 12th to the 17th centuries, Land Tax was one of the many ways in which money was raised from the population. There were Lay Subsidies, a tax levied on things such as goods and crops, and sometimes on land and buildings. There was a minimum value before taxation. In the 16th and 17th centuries there was a variety of taxes on land, buildings, goods and wages. There were poll taxes in the 14th, 17th and 18th centuries. From 1662 to 1688 there was a Hearth Tax, and a Window Tax from 1696 to 1851; servants, horses, dogs, sheep, carriages, silver plate, game, coats of arms, uninhabited houses and even hair powder were all taxed at one time or another. In 1798 the Land Tax became a fixed annual charge and many people purchased an exemption from paying it. Income tax began in 1799.

Before 1776, the American Colonies were subject to taxation by the United Kingdom, and also imposed local taxes. Property taxes were imposed in the Colonies as early as 1634. The United States Constitution, adopted in 1787, authorised the federal government to lay and collect taxes, but required that some types of tax revenues be given to the states in proportion to population. By 1796, state and local governments in 14 of the 15 states taxed land. Delaware taxed the income from property. By the American Civil War, the principle of taxation of property at a uniform rate had developed, and many of the states relied on property taxes as a major source of revenue. Tariffs were the principal federal tax through the 1800s. The first federal Income Tax was adopted as part of the Revenue Act of 1861. Income, estate, gift, and excise tax provisions, plus provisions relating to tax returns and enforcement, were codified as Title 26, also known as the Internal Revenue Code. This was reorganised and somewhat expanded in 1954, and remains in the same general form. In 1913, the 16th Amendment to the United States Constitution was ratified, permitting the federal government to levy an Income Tax on both property and labour.

While tax was originally levied on the population to wage wars (and it still is!), it has now extended to cover a range of other activities, namely:

1 To raise revenue for public services such as education, health, welfare, defence, law and order.
2 Tax has also been used as a tool to redistribute wealth but, as noted, it has been used extremely ineffectively and has only made matters worse. It is in fact taking money from the 'new insecure' and giving it to the wealthy. For instance, Income Tax on the lower paid ends up in the pockets of landowners via the increase in land values consequent upon public expenditure on infrastructure projects paid for out of general taxation. Business subsidies are another case in point.
3 Regulation of the economy. While this use, in my view, is valid, it would not need to be used nearly as much if the economy was in good order and well managed and there was less inequality and less cyclical boom and bust activity. It is a question of getting our house in order and all the repairs done properly, so that it will not need constant maintenance.

When asked in 1978 if we can run a country without Income Tax, celebrated economist, Milton Friedman said:

There's a sense in which all taxes are antagonistic to free enterprise ... and yet we need taxes. We have to recognize that we must not hope for a Utopia that is unattainable. I would like to see a great deal less government activity than we have now, but I do not believe that we can have a situation in which we don't need government at all. We do need to provide for certain essential government functions – the national defence function, the police function, preserving law and order, maintaining a judiciary. So the question is, which are the least bad taxes? In my opinion the least bad tax is the property tax on the unimproved value of land, the Henry George argument of many, many years ago.

Public revenue without taxation?

'In this world nothing can be said to be certain, except death and taxes.' So said Benjamin Franklin in 1789. Well it could only be death! Do we need tax at all?

My father, Ronald Burgess was a learned economist; he lectured and wrote many papers on a range of issues and wrote a book published in 1993 called *Public Revenue without Taxation*. In order to show how this idea would work he had first to define taxation, which he took as a '*compulsory contribution to a public authority irrespective of the exact amount of service rendered to the taxpayer in return*'. The corollary of this is that a payment to a public authority that is in direct relation to the services provided is not a tax (e.g. Congestion Charge or proposed road pricing payment schemes). At one time taxes were raised for specific projects, for example, the Road Fund Tax in the UK charged annually on motor vehicles was to cover cost of building and maintaining roads. This cost is nowhere near covered by the revenue from this tax, which is still a very small amount. What is now collected just gets lost in the government pot. There could be a case to significantly increase the 'duty' on vehicle usage to cover the cost of road building and maintenance, which would not be a tax but a charge to use the road system.

Industrial countries need ways to stimulate their economies without stoking another inflationary boom. Ronald Burgess argued for a reappraisal of the way in which public revenue is raised on the grounds that present taxation methods are essentially inflationary. He demonstrated that the injustice of taxation is unnecessary when the fundamental law of the market place is allowed to take its course, with those who use and benefit from public outlay bearing the cost of the services they enjoy. People have become so accustomed to being taxed that they take it for granted that government has to raise its revenue by taxation and usually think of Income Tax. Historically this is not true, nor is it in principle.

My father refined Alfred Marshall's distinction between the public and private value of land to reveal an alternative, peculiarly public source of revenue, determined by market forces. There is a direct correlation between what is paid and the public services received, so it is not a tax as defined. He developed Keynes's General Theory of Employment to show that:

> taxation is a primal cause of both inflation and unemployment. Regardless of this, the freely elected governments of contemporary trading economies – with the acquiescence of electorates — persist in raising the major part, if not all, of their revenues by means of taxation. The immediate cause of such action by governments, and for the compliance of their electorates, is ignorance of any acceptable alternative method of raising sufficient public revenue.

He also pointed out that, because governments fail to collect their revenue from this publicly created source, they have to take it from the private property of the taxpayer, infringing his or her property rights and leading to distortions of the economy: not only inflation and unemployment, but also to tax havens, flags of convenience and the black economy.

This work was published over 20 years ago, the main difference now from then, is the huge increase in economic inequality, which urgently needs to be addressed. The move to a sustainable economy with greater social justice is entirely possible but may take a while to come to fruition. First we need to address the structural problems that are messing up our society and causing unnecessary hardship.

Reform of the revenue

Whatever your view on taxation, where it comes from and where it is spent, almost everyone agrees that in most countries the tax system is grossly unfair and needs reform. Nowhere is this more true than with property taxes which in both the UK and USA and undoubtedly other countries are based on out-dated valuations often over 20 years old. The last big wave of tax reform in the UK took place in 1980s when Conservative Margaret Thatcher was Prime Minister. Since then there has been relatively little reform and restructuring, both businesses and individuals are struggling to deal with an increasingly anachronistic and dysfunctional tax system.

Britain's bosses think the tax system is not 'fit for purpose' and must be overhauled if companies are to pay their 'fair share' of tax. The Annual CEO Survey by consultancy PwC noted that almost three quarters of UK bosses believe the present tax system is unfit for the 21st century, and efforts to reform it will be in vain. The PwC survey also revealed though that that 75% of CEOs questioned said that paying a 'fair share' of tax was important to their company.

In an article in the *Daily Telegraph* in August 2014, Andrew Sentance, a senior economic adviser to PwC and a former member of the Bank of England Monetary Policy Committee proposed that a serious overhaul of the UK tax system should be high on the agenda for the government in power after the 2015 election. He reminded us that the world has changed and so should the tax system, it should be fit for the 2020s and beyond.

He thinks we should tax earning less and spending more. The government is heavily reliant on income taxes, which penalise the proceeds of economic success – income and employment – and create a significant gap between what an employer pays out and what the employee receives in their pay packet. He notes that National Insurance is a particularly heavy burden on average and lower earners. It is levied on earnings over £111 per week (£5,772 per annum) and is charged at a combined rate of nearly 26% – an employer 'contribution' of 13.8% plus 12% paid by employees. This is a higher rate than Income Tax (20%) and cuts in at a much lower earnings level.

Second, the taxation of various forms of spending is uneven and based on out-dated concepts. Value Added Tax (VAT) is levied at 20% – but only on about half of household expenditure. Many items, which are deemed 'essential', are zero-rated, including food, children's clothes, books and public transport. There are many anomalies. Caviar is zero-rated because it is a food, whereas other essential items in the household budget carry the full burden of VAT. A printed book is zero-rated but the equivalent eBook or audio book carries 20% VAT. None of this makes any sense in the modern world and a thorough review is overdue. He suggests a more rational system of VAT with fewer zero-rate exemptions could yield more revenue over the longer term – creating scope for tax reductions elsewhere in the economy.

So, while Andrew Sentance's comments are refreshing and he is undoubtedly a learned specialist in tax, he does not go far enough; his comments are still based on the old thinking that most government revenue has to come from income taxes and sales taxes. We need new thinking. Why do we have income taxes at all? There are other ways that are much more beneficial to all, sustainable and future proof.

Andrew Sentance goes on suggesting a third area much in need of review is the way businesses are taxed.

> Corporation tax is levied on company profits, but businesses pay many other taxes – including National Insurance and business rates. These other taxes fall particularly heavily on smaller businesses. While we need to ensure that large and successful businesses pay their fair share of corporation tax, it is also important that we do not stifle smaller, dynamic and entrepreneurial businesses with other taxes.

He is right that we do not want to overload small business with taxes., Goodness me, I know this only too well having had my own businesses for 30 years. However, a comprehensive method of sharing the wealth generated by larger firms through contributions to government revenue would in fact seem fair.

He also suggests rightly:

Environmental taxes must also be overhauled. The environmental taxes currently in place – such as the Climate Change Levy, Air Passenger Duty and the Landfill Tax have been introduced on an 'ad hoc' basis. Motorists pay very high rates of duty on petrol and diesel but other activities that cause environmental harm are lightly taxed – if at all.

Current environmental taxes are absolutely too low compared to the impact they cause and streamlining into a levy based on impact is the more sensible option. It is also urgent, as we cannot go on destroying our atmosphere at the current rate .

Sweeping reforms of the tax system are needed to improve Britain's economic performance and living standards, according to a wide-ranging study chaired by Sir James Mirrlees, a Nobel laureate and professor of economics at the University of Cambridge. The review published in November 2010 showed the UK tax system was costly and inequitable. *'It discourages saving and investment, and distorts the form they take. It favours corporate debt over equity finance. It fails to deal effectively with either greenhouse gas emissions or road congestion.'* He said it was *'undeniable that some of the proposed changes would be politically difficult'*. But sticking with the current system involved complexity, unfairness, and significant economic costs. The review said: *'We cannot forever succumb to the tyranny of the status quo.'*

The review sought to identify the characteristics of a good tax system for an open developed economy in the 21st century. It concluded Britain's tax system is ripe for reform in ways that could significantly improve people's welfare and the performance of the economy. It highlighted some key issues and scope for reform but still missed making a radical recommendation. The review set out a comprehensive set of proposals for tax reform. The key principles that underlie the proposals is that the tax system should:

- Be designed as a whole, in conjunction with the benefits system. The system as a whole needs to be green and to be progressive. The way taxes (and the benefit system) fit together matters very much.
- Seek neutrality. Tax systems that distort people's behaviour by treating similar activities differently without very good reason – as the UK system currently does – create inefficiency, complexity and opportunities for avoidance. Those exceptions, to deal with the costs of smoking or pollution for example, should be limited and carefully designed.

- Achieve progressiveness as efficiently as possible. That means relying on the rate schedule of personal taxes and benefits – rather than inefficiently distorting the tax base – to achieve redistribution. It also means designing that rate schedule carefully to minimise the extent to which the tax system reduces employment and earnings.

This learned review still missed the opportunity for a radical proposal of moving the tax base away from income and more focussed on wealth. The review did however state the economic case for a Land Value Tax, which is simple and effective. Why, then, do we not have one already? Why, indeed, is the possibility of such a tax barely part of the mainstream political debate, with proponents considered marginal and unconventional?' (Mirrlees Review, *Tax by Design*, Chapter 16)

These calls for reform in the UK are similar in context to those in the USA where the tax system is even more complicated and burdensome, especially given the three levels of federal, state and local taxes.

All these learned comments from respected individuals and organisations and still no serious proposals for change, just a little tinkering here and there which adds to the complexity. The tax system or, as I would prefer, the public revenue system, provides a very practical toolbox to encourage significant and sustainable economic growth, increase incomes of lower earners and those in poverty and generally create the opportunity of a better life for the majority. Of course a strong work ethic, high productivity, great education, a high standard of health and welfare provision, integrated updated infrastructure and a compassionate approach to our fellow human beings, all play an important role in moving us From Here To Prosperity.

2.3 Revolution or evolution?

So little has been done to improve opportunity for the majority and what has been done has had so little impact. The level of inequality has got severely worse especially in the last 20 years; the writing is now on the wall. We are close to a tipping point where unless we act and act boldly, all hell will break loose to the detriment of all. So let us heed the warnings, we can wait no longer.

In January 2015 Economist Intelligence Unit (EIU) predicted political earthquakes could be in store for Europe. It said the rising appeal of populist parties could see some winning elections and mainstream parties forced into previously unthinkable alliances. It said that Europe's had a *'crisis of democracy'* with the gap between elites and voters. There is *'a gaping hole at the heart of European politics where big ideas should be,'* low turnouts at the polls and sharp falls in the membership of traditional parties are key factors in the phenomenon.

The United Kingdom is *'on the cusp of a potentially prolonged period of political instability,'* according to *The Economist* researchers. This was reflected in the election in May 2015 when although the centre right Conservative won 330 out of a 650 seats (with no need for a coalition as in the previous five years), a very slim majority of 10 seats, 50.8% of total seats. The popular vote tells a different story with only 37% of voters proactively voting Conservative, but then only 66% turned out to vote, which means three quarters of the electorate did not vote for the party that now forms the government. This is no clear mandate for a government. It was a very disappointing campaign with no bold ideas, no clear vision and no real answers to the underlying extreme inequality problems in the UK. In the end, fear, uncertainty and doubt decided the result. Half the country will be feeling disappointed, disenfranchised and in need of answers.

The EIU further cited elections with potential for unpredictable results in Denmark, Finland, Spain, France, Sweden, Germany and Ireland. *'There is a common denominator in these countries: the rise of populist parties. Anti-establishment sentiment has surged across the Eurozone (and the larger European Union) and the risk of political disruption and potential crises is high.'* Its analysis is that populist parties and movements – of the left, the right and the indeterminate – are moving into the space that has opened up between the old political parties and their traditional social base. Opposition to governance from Brussels, immigration and austerity are key themes and rallying cries for many of these parties.

Meanwhile, alongside the rise to prominence of populist movements, there has been an upsurge of popular protest in many parts of the world in recent years. It has swept through Europe, the Middle East, North Africa and Latin America in recent years. Other regions such as Asia and North America have been less susceptible, although have not escaped entirely. The EIU estimates that significant protest movements surfaced in more than 90 countries during the past five years – in the main, it says, led by young, educated, middle class individuals who resent their political leaders and who prefer Twitter and other social networks to the traditional political soap box.

Similarly in the USA, where there is a rigid two party system, there are calls for a new party or a new political movement. There are parties within the party with the right wing Tea Party and factions within the Democratic Party like the Fiscally Responsible Democrats. There only seems to be one independent voice, that of presidential nomination candidate Senator Bernie Sanders of Vermont. He constantly speaks his mind and is not afraid to give his opinion on the key issues, standing up to the big money politics of the main parties. Polls having been showing that his views resonate with the American people and reflect the mainstream, not the wacky left. Within the Democratic Party Senator Elisabeth Warren is one of the few candid members of Congress calling for radical reform. Former Secretary of State and presidential candidate Hillary Clinton, at the time of writing, seems to have very little to say and certainly nothing new and exciting on the way forward. While several Republicans have indicated the wish to run in the 2016 presidential nomination, they appear to be a field of samey, mainly white men with no strong vision or bold leadership qualities. So unless there is a strong uniting force in the USA, there is likely to be an on-going period of instability with little or no progress being made on moving forward to a sustainable growing economy and a fair society. Unless, of course, we, the people, act now.

So what is the right thing to do? Let us heed the warnings that unless we act on inequality, the pitchforks will be on their way. However, history can help us. Let's look at the past and see how determination and mass movement has bought real change. Bernie Sanders has made it clear that voting is not enough, it needs people to follow through with their convictions with a movement for change even after a new president is elected, then change may happen. To bring real change bold compassionate leaders with a clear vision are needed that do not let themselves be sat upon by the big money of politics dedicated to maintaining the status quo.

The pitchforks are coming

Revolutions arise from inequalities. The condition, which leads up to all revolutions, is the desire of the many for equality, albeit as Jacques Mallet du Pan observed, '*revolution devours its children*'. That was certainly the case during the French Revolution when onerous taxes on the lower and middle classes enhanced the lives of the wealthiest aristocrats. The American Revolution was also about unfairness: '*no taxation without representation*'. Taxes were levied on the colonies by Britain but there was no formal representation in the British parliament, which decided what those taxes should be. The rest is history!

The top 1% may have the best houses, access to the best education, the best doctors, and the best lifestyles, but there is one thing that money doesn't seem to have bought: an understanding that their fate is bound up with how the other 99% live. Throughout history, this is something that those at the top often learn too late.

And then there is the loss of trust in politicians. The electorate questions their values, integrity and decision making capability. Martin Sheen, the British actor who has on several occasions played the role of former Prime Minister Tony Blair, speaking at an election rally in February 2015 commented that:

> In today's political climate, where politicians are careful, tentative, scared of saying what they feel for fear of alienating a part of the electorate; where under the excuse of trying to appear electable, all parties drift into a morass of bland neutrality; and where the real deals, the real values we suspect, are kept behind closed doors – is it any wonder that people feel there is very little to choose between? So when people are too scared to say what they really mean, when they're too careful to speak from their hearts, when integrity is too much of a risk, it's no surprise that people feel disengaged with politics.

Disillusioned with both ineffective government and the unequal economy, people increasingly ask whether capitalism, as we practice it, is worth the costs. We see this in movements such as Earth Day and Occupy Wall Street. In many parts of the world – from the Arab Spring countries to Brazil, Turkey, Venezuela, and Ukraine, frustrated publics are taking to the streets.

Even the 1% is getting scared. Amazon early investor and billionaire Nick Hanauer admitted in an article in June 2014:

> If we don't do something to fix the glaring inequities in this economy, the pitchforks are going to come for us. No society can sustain this kind of rising inequality. In fact, there is no example in human history where wealth accumulated like this and the pitchforks didn't eventually come out. You show me a highly unequal society, and I will show you a police state, or an uprising. There are no counter examples. None. It's not if, it's when.

He added:

> At the same time that people like me are thriving beyond the dreams of any plutocrats in history, the rest of the country – the 99.99 per cent – is lagging

far behind. The divide between the haves and have-nots is getting worse really, really fast. In 1980, the top 1 per cent controlled about 8 per cent of U.S. national income. The bottom 50 per cent shared about 18 per cent. Today the top 1 per cent share about 20 per cent; the bottom 50 per cent, just 12 per cent.

Many super-rich may live in fear of the mob. One dog may bark at you but it's more likely that a pack will attack you. And so it can be in human society. What we might not do as individuals, we may do as part of a group. People may lose control of their usual inhibitions, as their mentality becomes that of the group. There have never been peaceful riots. Riots are by definition violent in nature. A riot is simply violent group behaviour. The larger the group, the greater the amplification of that group behaviour. If the individual behaviour is peaceful, demonstrated by Martin Luther King and Gandhi, the group behaviour is peaceful and orderly. If the group behaviour is violent, the larger the group the more magnified the violence. To win the confidence of the majority, we must always be on the side of respect and peace.

An early warning on the looming uprising is the Occupy international protest movement against social and economic inequality, quickly spread throughout the world. Its primary goal is to make the economic and political relations in all societies less vertically hierarchical and more flatly distributed. Local groups often had different focuses, but among the movement's prime concerns was how large corporations and the global financial system control the world in a way that disproportionately benefits a minority, undermines democracy, and is unstable. While not succeeding (yet) in bringing about social change, the movement was a symptom of this simmering, underlying unrest. However it did have some support in the establishment. Los Angeles City Council became one of the first governmental bodies in the United States to adopt a resolution stating its informal support of the Occupy movement. In October 2012, the Executive Director of Financial Stability at the Bank of England stated the protesters were right to criticise and had persuaded bankers and politicians 'to behave in a more moral way'. One of the issues of its perceived lack of success was that it was not organised or coordinated well. In fact, Professor Reich tells the story of being invited to speak at the Occupy camp in Oakland, California, only to arrive and to be told that he could not speak. 'Why is that?' he asked. The answer was, 'Because the anarchists don't want you to'!

But we have not heard the last of these movements and it clearly demonstrates how many people can be mobilised and how much general support there was for the movement. The real issue is having an organisation and a clear picture of the goal you want to achieve, not just protest. To avoid revolution, the rich need to use reason and common sense. The current situation is not sustainable and it is in everyone's interest, rich included, to bring change peaceably.

History lessons

At many times in human history there are tipping points for change. That's what happened in the 1960s after the world had settled down from the shocks of the Second World War. Now 50 years later we face another tipping point. Looking back to the Sixties (which I can!) we can see how much social change has taken place, civil rights, gay rights, role of women, air travel, plus the huge technological advances so that we now have instant access to people and information around the world from our desks, laps and pockets. However one thing remains, there is an even greater amount of inequality in the world, inequality of income, wealth, education, housing and opportunity. There has been progress in some emerging countries but in the more developed countries the situation has not improved. We seem to be returning to a Victorian age when a few people owned the capital, the labour, the land and they called the shots.

There have been many moments where radical social change has happened; looking back it is difficult to believe we allowed such behaviour. But social attitudes evolve, we must always make sure it is for the better. There are many examples where positive change happened, it was long time coming but it did come. It only happened through hard work, determination and against all odds, but the final push was when the people really showed their strength of feeling. Let it be a lesson to us all. History has shown us that the despair over the exclusion of large sections of the population from the fruits of their labour can quickly heat up to boiling point, with disastrous consequences. Many people, in particular the lower paid, feel short-changed by their employer, or by society as a whole – that their work is not being properly valued. This is over and above the frustration of those who are unable to find paid work that is rewarding and fulfilling, or indeed any paid work at all.

Perhaps not many people will make the connection between net take home pay (after tax), and its effective purchasing power in terms of the real goods and services that it can purchase, most of which will include a further element of tax collection in the final price paid by the consumer. If the effective rate of taxation is a high percentage of GDP, then that is reflected in the price of everything. In this way, the effect of payroll taxes on the lower paid is compounded at every turn. A reduction of payroll taxes is therefore a very effective way of raising living standards, as it increases the effective purchasing power of net take home pay.

There are several historical examples of social change from the old order, which now seems morally corrupt, to the new order. Looking back it is difficult to believe the old order existed, but change is gradual. The common thread with each of these examples is that there are movements, which developed a groundswell of popular support and captured the attention of the legislators who eventually took action. It then seems wrong that we ever allowed the old morally unacceptable order to exist.

Extreme inequality is not new. The most ironic thing about rising inequality is how completely unnecessary and self-defeating it is. It has been with us for a long time, there are times when equality has been better, but there are times like now when it is at an extreme not seen since the 1920s. Henry George observed this and documented it in his 1879 book *Progress and Poverty* which sold over three million copies. He was struck by the apparent paradox that the poor in New York, a long-established city, were much worse off than the poor in the less developed California. He argued that the reason was because a sizeable portion of the wealth created by social and technological advances in a free market economy falls into the hands of landowners, and that this accumulation of unearned wealth is the main cause of poverty. George considered it a great injustice that private profit was being earned from restricting access to natural resources while productive activity was burdened with heavy taxes, and equated such a system with slavery. He proposed that government levy a tax on the value of the land itself to prevent private interests from profiting from mere ownership, but that all improvements made to that land should remain the untaxed property of investors. He inspired the economic philosophy that became known as Georgism, whose main tenet is that people should keep all they create, but acknowledge that everything found in nature, most importantly land, is the property of all humanity for which a rent is payable for exclusive use.

Even Theodore Roosevelt, the first great Republican progressive, elected President in 1901 fought his campaign on the issue of 'trust-busting' and talked freely about *'malefactors of great wealth'*. After serving his two terms he went on to form the Progressive Party, which contributed to splitting the Republican Party.

In the 1932 Presidential campaign, Franklin D. Roosevelt outlined his ideas for the New Deal when he spoke at the Commonwealth Club of California in San Francisco, the oldest and largest public affairs forum in the United States, founded in 1903, of which I am a member but only in recent years!

> It seems that things are in a rut, fixed, settled, that the world has grown old and tired and very much out of joint. This is the mood of depression, of dire and weary depression. A glance at the situation today only too clearly indicates that equality of opportunity, as we have known it, no longer exists. … Clearly, all this calls for a re-appraisal of values … The day of enlightened administration has come.

He noted that a recent study of the concentration of business showed that economic life was dominated by some six hundred corporations, who controlled two-thirds of American industry. Ten million small business-men divided the other third. He forecast that:

> … if the process of concentration goes on at the same rate, at the end of another century we shall have all American industry controlled by a dozen corporations, and run by perhaps a hundred men. Put plainly, we are steering a steady course toward economic oligarchy, if we are not there already.

Well, if not then, we are certainly there now! We know that 400 Americans control the same amount of wealth as 150 million, half the population.

Roosevelt's new social contract between government and individuals was set out to guarantee new rights – and new powers for government. The contract requires government to protect the individual against the *'princes of property'*. Each right corresponds with new assurances, backed by a federal government program. First: *'Every man has a right to life; and this means that he has also a right to make a comfortable living.'* Second: *'Every man has a right to his own property; which means a right to be assured, to the fullest extent attainable, in the safety of his savings.'*

FDR's New Deal sought to stimulate demand and provide work and relief for the impoverished through increased government spending and the institution of financial reforms. These programs focused on what historians call the '3 Rs': Relief, Recovery, and Reform. That is Relief for the unemployed and poor; Recovery of the economy to normal levels; and Reform of the financial system to prevent a repeat depression.

So, we have been here before!

Radical change is possible and despite whining and complaining, these fears are usually ungrounded and when radical social change happens it opens up huge new opportunities. This was demonstrated during a debate on climate change in House of Lords in the UK. Concerns were raised about the negative impact on the economy of extensive measures. Lord Puttnam, the former film producer (of *Chariots of Fire* and many others) reminded Parliament that exactly 200 years before, the same body had debated the abolition of the slave trade. And at that time, everybody in UK believed that slavery was an abomination and that it was a moral catastrophe that had to be abolished. But the question was, how soon and how could it be done because slavery represented at that time 25% of the GNP of Great Britain. It was the principal source of energy for the entire British Empire and it was thought that if it were abolished outright, the economy would collapse. But after a year of debate, Parliament made the moral choice and abolished the slave trade overnight – literally. And instead of collapsing, the British economy exploded, as thousands of entrepreneurs rushed into that space to create new forms of energy, mainly mechanical ones in an era we now know as the Industrial Revolution, which was the greatest epic of wealth creation in the history of mankind. And the abolition of the slave trade had exposed all these hidden inefficiencies that were associated with not cheap but free labour. Indeed this is likely to be the same with climate change as some say it will put up costs whereas it is a huge opportunity to innovate and generate economic growth.

Though the final decision on slavery was quick, it was a long time coming. It is worth noting a bit more background on the slave trade as well as the significant victory on votes for women and the still ongoing struggle for the self-evident freedom of civil rights.

Slave Trade: It was back in 1787 that the Society for the Abolition of the Slave Trade was founded in Britain. It was a further 18 years later in 1805 that a bill for abolition passed in House of Commons but was rejected in the House of Lords. Then two years later in 1807, on 25th March, the Abolition of the Slave Trade Act abolished slave trading in the British Empire. But that only affected the trading in slaves, it did not end slavery completely. It was another 27 years before the British Slavery Abolition Act of 1834 came into force, abolishing slavery throughout most of the British Empire. This freed nearly 800,000 slaves but even then it was not until 1843 that it was abolished in territories controlled by the East India Company and Ceylon, which then became part of the British Empire. So in Britain and its empire that was 56 years from the start of the movement to the complete abolition. It was not until a further 19 years later in 1862 that the United States abolished slavery.

Slavery is an inhumane abomination against all understood and agreed principles of human rights. Today, in addition to criminal activity such as people-trafficking and enforced prostitution, we have a different type of legal slavery, where the poorest 20% continually struggle to break free. Then there is the wage slavery of those in the middle, whose earnings are not increasing in real terms, whose costs are mounting and who, still pay inordinate amounts in taxation, which restricts their freedoms. Slavery today is the lack of freedom and opportunity (as well as pain and suffering). We have far too many that do not benefit from the freedoms enjoyed by the top of the income and wealth scale, and it is increasingly harder to break out and escape up the ladder; the rungs are missing.

Votes for women: In the UK, during the latter half of the 19th century, a number of campaign groups were formed in an attempt to lobby Members of Parliament and gain support for votes for women. Seventeen of these groups came together in 1897, to form the National Union of Women's Suffrage Societies (NUWSS), which held public meetings, wrote letters to politicians and published articles. After a considerable number of protests, rallies and civil disobedience, it was not until The Representation of the People Act, 1928 that the voting franchise was extended to all women over the age of 21, granting women the vote on the same terms as men, 31 years after the NUWSS was formed. It takes time to change the political will, it now seems absurd and harsh that women were ever excluded in the first place! The battle is far from won. Women still suffer pay and opportunity inequality both of which will be tackled as part of the Agenda for Progressive Prosperity.

Voter registration: This remains an issue in the United States, largely reflecting its 19th-century origins. It has not kept pace with advancing technology and a mobile society. At a time when government budgets are significantly strained, the antiquated paper based system remains costly and inefficient according to a Pew Research Center Study in 2012. The study found that 24 million registrations – one in eight – are no longer valid or accurate, more than 1.8 million deceased Americans are listed as active, 2.75 million Americans have active registrations in more than one state and 12 million records contain an inaccurate address. A registration system rife with such inaccuracies could drastically alter the results of elections. A study of the 2008 election estimated that 2.2 million eligible voters were turned away because of flawed registration data. The voting age population was 235.2 million in 2012. In addition there is the accusation of gerrymandering of election districts, which is still causing controversy. Today, while we have a universal adult franchise, many people are still excluded from democracy as a result of the political agenda that reflects the money behind it. The rise of the plutocrats means the decisions are made by the few in favour of the few.

Civil rights: Civil and political rights guarantee equal protection under the law. When these rights are not guaranteed, or when such guarantees exist on paper but are not respected in practice, opposition, legal action and even social unrest may ensue. This was particularly true in the USA. The 15th Amendment (1870) to US constitution provides that '*the right of citizens of the United States to vote shall not be denied or abridged by the United States or by any State on account of race, colour, or previous condition of servitude*'. However many southern states went against this and passed their own laws on wide-ranging segregation, the so-called Jim Crow laws, from around 1880. They ranged from petty but humiliating bye-laws through state legislation that denied non-whites the vote, to the segregation in the armed forces brought in just before the First World War. Harry S. Truman proposed civil rights legislation immediately after the Second World War and in 1954 segregation was abolished in public schools, in the teeth of opposition. Partly in response to an example of this opposition and the infamous Little Rock school incident (where nine African American students were prevented from entering the school at which they had enrolled), Dwight D. Eisenhower brought in the 1957 Civil Rights Act. Although this aimed to increase the number of black voters, the punishment for denying them their rights was negligible. Meanwhile in 1955, Rosa Parkes refused to give up her seat to a white person on a Montgomery, Alabama bus. This was a trigger for more determined action, which culminated in 1963 with the March on Washington where Martin Luther King made his *I have dream* speech. When the 1964 Civil Rights Act and the 1965 Voting Rights Act finally eradicated the Jim Crow laws, it was some 85 years after the first had been introduced. Dis-crimination persists, but radical change does and can happen; it needs determination, mass support and action to win through. Even now, despite the first black President, discrimination, exclusion and racism still exist.

Freak out

History suggests that when inequality gets so bad there is the danger of disruption and revolution. Change can occur often just in time, when inspirational, determined leaders are able to inspire a movement of the masses and a signal gets through to government that it must happen and happen fast. If the old answers and the same way of doing things hasn't worked, what will? We need to think differently, to change our approach.

I heard Steven Levitt and Stephen Dubner talk at the Commonwealth Club in San Francisco in 2014. They related a story from their book *Think Like a Freak: How to Think Smarter about Almost Everything*, which suggests we can solve our problems more effectively by examining our approach to them. One of the case studies they talked about to illustrate the point is that of Takeru Kobayashi, an unknown first-timer at the *Nathan's Famous Fourth of July International Hot Dog Eating Contest* in 2001. He hit a new record by consuming 50 hot dogs when the previous record was just 25 hot dogs in 12 minutes. According to Levitt and Dubner, his success had little to do with physical prowess, and everything to do with his mental strategy.

> If you think like a freak, there are at least two broader lessons to be gleaned from his approach. The first is about problem solving generally. Kobayashi redefined the problem he was trying to solve. What question were his competitors asking? It was essentially: how do I eat more hot dogs? Kobayashi asked a different question: how do I make hot dogs easier to eat?

His system involved breaking the dogs in half, dunking the buns in water, and eating the meat and bread separately. Not only did he ingest faster, but also he saved valuable seconds that might have been spent chewing and drinking water.

Now, while the thought of gorging on hot dogs is quite bizarre, if not a little disgusting, it shows that the way to win through and get results is by fresh thinking. And that's what we need for our political, economic and social systems. The old thinking is that the answer to fixing the budget deficit is to raise taxes and cut expenditure. A fresh view says raise revenue from those with the ability to pay not from those that are already squeezed, then devise a public revenue system where revenue increases with growth so there is a constant source of finance to build the infrastructure and provide the services an economy needs. This is not pie in the sky but a practical answer, which is completely viable, as we shall see later.

Bold policies

There have been numerous books, report, articles and TV and radio programmes on the problems of extreme inequality, slow economic growth and damaged democracy. They have one thing in common, a lack of bold strategic policies that will fix the problem.

The Commission for Inclusive Prosperity was convened by the Center for American Progress and chaired by former US treasury secretary Larry Summers and Ed Balls, the then UK shadow Chancellor of the Exchequer. It presented its 164 page report on 15th January 2015, it contained very few fresh ideas on the answers to the problems addressed. The transatlantic cooperation proposed five key policy areas that needed to be developed to deliver inclusive prosperity:

- Raising wages: full employment in an economy where work pays.
- Educational opportunity for all.
- Measures to support innovation and regional clusters.
- Greater long-termism.
- International cooperation on global demand, trade, financial stability, and corporate tax avoidance.

That was it! Talk about stating the obvious! This could have been a great manifesto for a political campaign but it lacked boldness and vision, just saying what could be done, not how it could actually be done. The *New York Times*'s analysis suggested it amounted to '*the first draft*' of an agenda for Hillary Clinton's presidential campaign. But where was the strategy, the detail on the specific initiatives that would be required and how it would be implemented?

Once again, this report is not about deconstructing the problem with radical and common sense answers but, instead, about proposals that will lead to more and more regulations to compensate for the partial or complete failure of current measures.

Don't just take my word for it; Christine Lagarde, the managing director of the International Monetary Fund said a mix of bolder policies were needed to make sure that the 'new mediocre' doesn't become permanent. She urged action in a speech ahead of its annual meeting in October 2014, including an easing of austerity, job creation programmes and higher spending on infrastructure – to boost growth. She urged that the pace of consolidation and composition of fiscal measures – tax and public spending should support economic activity to the greatest extent possible, suggesting lower payroll taxes to encourage firms to hire and for higher public investment.

> There is some economic recovery but as you all know and as you can feel … that growth is not enough to respond to the challenges that the world is facing. We believe that the clouds can be pushed back, provided that all policymakers actually aim higher, try harder, do it together and are country specific.

Traditionally Robin Hood's idea was to take more from the rich and give to the poor. But actually today we are effectively taking from the poor and giving to the rich. Lower income families pay Income Tax and National Insurance/payroll taxes plus taxes on consuming, why? They can't afford it; they do not have enough for their basic needs. So they receive benefits from the state. This means the government is taking from the people and subsiding companies for paying low wages. Surely it is better to pay higher wages, a living wage, then the government does not need to provide so much benefit. Of course, this is then followed by the cry from businesses, that increased wages will cut the number of jobs, as it will put up the costs for a business, indeed it does but only at the expenses of profits, which once distributed tend to go to the richer members of society. As we know, increased wages means increased consumption which increases growth and benefits all (or rather can do if managed well). I know it is tough for a small business, I have been there for 30 years, though my staff were typically professionals on higher salaries but still trying to make a margin was a constant challenge.

Yet these lower earners still get stung with payroll or income taxes and as their earnings rise, it is all pretty pointless as it slows growth and wealth creation. However consider, if we also abolish payroll taxes for employer and employee, this would reduce business costs and contribute to profit. This will be looked at in more detail later and also how the shortfall in government budgets can be made up by other more equitable means.

Bold moves and new thinking are needed to get rid of all these taxes as there are other ways in which public revenue can be raised, as outlined in *Public Revenue without Taxation* by Dr Ronald Burgess, or indeed by more equitable contributions from those with the ability to pay.

Creeping communism?

It seems a big concern in the USA is that too much involvement of government smells like a socialist state. This is particularly true when it comes to the concept of universal healthcare which is the norm in most European states, even those with more right wing governments.

Dr Ben Carson, Republican presidential candidate and the former director of Paediatric Neurosurgery at Johns Hopkins University and Hospital, as well as author of bestseller *One Nation*, drew a parallel between Obamacare and *'socialised medicine'* and cited Communist leader Vladimir Lenin's support for government-run health care as the *'keystone to the establishment of a socialist state'*. Dr Carson said that Obamacare *'was never about healthcare. It was about control,'* and making all Americans *'subservient to the government'*.

This opinion does seem a little strange. It's ironic that people who iden-tify themselves as opposed to socialism would consider Lenin a reliable authority. Even Democrats refer to 'socialised medicine'. It is reminiscent of the McCarthy era politics where people where scared of communism creeping in, and 'Reds under the bed'. A universal national health service with no cost at the point of access is more about a civilised society caring for its people than about socialism. Why are so many Americans scared of such great and more simplified service? The Canadians, north of the border, are not.

Man has a natural tendency to want to work and improve himself and his family. The need to work and develop collective enterprise is not second nature: it *is* nature. Working is what the hunters and gatherers did, then farmers learnt to cultivate the land to yield more food, and it is the same today.

Communism is a political and economic ideology built around the common ownership of the means of production. This concept goes against man's natural tendencies to create his own territory, that he feels is his, where he will feel secure and comfortable. Communism in its purest form does not work, but then neither does capitalism, in its purest form! The answer is not in the extremes.

An electable government needs to have broad appeal, not be in the extremes, though it still needs sound principles. When Tony Blair became Leader of the Labour Party in 1993, he put forward a case for defining socialism in terms of a set of values, which were constant, while the policies needed to achieve them would have to change ('modernise') to accommodate a changing society. This key belief in public ownership was embedded in Clause 4 of the UK Labour Party constitution in 1918.

> To secure for the workers by hand or by brain the full fruits of their industry and the most equitable distribution thereof that may be possible upon the basis of the common ownership of the means of production, distribution and exchange, and the best obtainable system of popular administration and control of each industry or service.

He proposed a new statement instead of Clause 4:

> The Labour Party is a democratic socialist party. It believes that by the strength of our common endeavour we achieve more than we achieve alone, so as to create for each of us the means to realise our true potential and for all of us a community in which power, wealth and opportunity are in the hands of the many, not the few, where the rights we enjoy reflect the duties we owe, and where we live together, freely, in a spirit of solidarity, tolerance and respect.

Although the Labour Party had defined itself as a socialist party, it was no longer a party of labour, that is, just of those who only relied on income from their work, not their wealth. It moved from an extreme principle to a more compassionate approach embracing a wider section of society and so got elected in 1997 after 13 years in opposition. It now describes itself as a democratic socialist party not a social democratic party! In the UK there has been the Social Democratic Party (SDP), which was formed in 1981 by breakaways from the Labour Party, but fizzled out when it merged with the Liberal Party in 1988. Coincidently, countries with a clear social democratic agenda are the happiest, based on the OECD report (outlined previously), significantly in Northern Europe with Denmark, Finland, and Netherlands making the top three.

So let's not be afraid, let us look at the issues in a fresh light, not in a partisan way, let us not be scared of increasing government involvement, let our demands be for better government rather than just smaller government. Government is not the problem: it is in fact the answer but it is up to us to make the changes and keep pushing, learning from what has happened in the past and move on.

Leading the team

Fresh ideas and bold leadership are not something you can legislate for; it is not something you can buy. However you can buy the same old ideas overseen by weak timid leadership! To make strides in social progress, it takes great leaders, charismatic leaders who also have substance and can deliver. Effective leaders have a vision that is shared with the people and with a background, personal story that resonates with their followers.

Unfortunately great all-round leaders do not come along very often, so it is much better to pick a team. Tony Blair and Gordon Brown were a great team complementing each other's skills, but Brown really wanted the top job and is understood to have made life difficult, so eventually the dream team collapsed. Brown may have been great person, very caring and determined (I am told by those who worked with him) but he was not a great leader.

There is so much political advertising where the message is how bad the other candidate is, not how good you are. Real leaders don't do this. There have been great politicians, concerned and driven people involved in great work for the community and the nation, but there have been very few good leaders. A leader's vision needs to say *This is where we are going*, and to be able to take the people with them. By all accounts, Winston Churchill was a good leader in time of war, he was determined, and he made powerful, strong speeches, which pulled the country together behind him to defeat the enemy against all odds.

> We shall defend our island, whatever the cost may be, we shall fight on the beaches, we shall fight on the landing grounds, we shall fight in the fields and in the streets, we shall fight in the hills; we shall never surrender.

Privately, he had real concerns about the ability to achieve this but pressed on to achieve his vision and that of the British nation and its allies.

Some leaders had great insight and got to the heart of the problem, like Franklin D. Roosevelt with his New Deal and his fifth cousin before him, Theodore Roosevelt, in the progressive era. Some great leaders never give up and win through, like Winston Churchill. Some leaders are determined and resolute in their beliefs such as Margaret Thatcher. Some leaders are great as they show compassion, humility and a great connection with the people, leaders like Nelson Mandela and Mahatma Gandhi.

Some leaders are inspiring, eloquent and realistic with an inclusive approach, like Martin Luther King, who in his 1963 '*I have a dream*' speech said it is not about revolution but about working together for fairness as these truths are self evident, '*We must forever conduct our struggle on the high plane of dignity and discipline. We must not allow our creative protests to degenerate into physical violence.*' When talking about the black and white he added:

many of our white brothers as evidence by their presence here today have come to realise that their destiny is tied up with our destiny. They have come to realise that their freedom is inextricably bound to our freedom. We cannot walk alone. And as we walk we must make the pledge that we shall always march ahead. We cannot turn back.

It is the same for rich and poor today.

In my career, I advised many CEOs on how they could build their company by better communicating their message so that it was understood and acted on, whether it be to customers, suppliers, partners, employees or who ever, I would always say you need to have a vision. Being a CEO is not only about managing a business, or about refereeing a game, it is about leading from the front and being sure to bring the team with you, because it is also about working as a team. Leading a company in my opinion is not about maximizing profits for the shareholders but it is about maximizing stakeholder value! So to craft the message you need to have a vision; that vision should be simple well thought through and inclusive. It should not be arrogant and aggressive or too competitive. On many occasions I have known companies, which say their goal is to blast the competition out of the water, and will be blind in their determination to achieve this. I can recall on more than one occasion when arrogant companies have been the ones that have been sunk. It is about doing our best, not just better than the others.

Yes, when you break this down it is about being better than the competition. Many a time in a pitch for a new campaign for a potential client, my company was against two to five other agencies, our objective was to be the best. Though this did mean eliminating the competition by presenting the best option for the client, we would never do this by rubbishing the opposition, by putting them down. That is the politics of a coward who has no policy. We win by having the best strategy and best ideas that meet the needs of the client, though as we all know, one of the most important points is chemistry, you have to like each other to work well together. So too in politics, great leaders need to be good team players if we are to make progress.

In *Lessons From The Top*, based on a lifetime of interviewing the great and the good, from Bill Clinton and Margaret Thatcher to Angelina Jolie and Dolly Parton, journalist and TV presenter Gavin Esler wrote: '*You cannot be a leader unless you have followers. And you cannot have followers unless you communicate with them, leaders have been telling stories ever since Jesus.*' He notes that there are three particular 'stories' that any successful leader needs to tell. They are: *'Who am I? Who are we? Where is my leadership going to take us?'* Margaret Thatcher's *'Grocer's daughter from Grantham'* was the classic 'who am I' story. Many of the most successful leaders (though not necessarily the best leaders), of modern times have had a great 'who am I' story to tell. It didn't necessarily need to have much to do with who they really were. George W. Bush, for example (certainly not a great leader, but a successful one in that he persuaded Americans to elect him to the highest office in the land not once but twice) was a member of America's East Coast elite: his grandfather a senator, his father successively head of the CIA, vice-president, then president. But none of that would have played well with the voting American public, so he managed to sell himself as 'Dubya', the good ole country boy from Texas. Bill Clinton pulled a similar trick. When he first met Clinton, Esler says, it was before he had even run for the White House. *'He told me "I'm just a boy from Hope".'* Hope, Arkansas, that is.

Being able to identify the 'Who I am ' and 'Who we are' (in which a leader identifies what the group he or she belongs to stands for) stories are necessary conditions for leadership, Esler says, because, if a leader can't tell them, he or she can't succeed. Gordon Brown is a good example of that. *'He had a great personal story to tell,'* Esler says. *'All he needed to do was to say "the reason I don't come across on TV is because I'm blind in one eye from playing rugby, and can't see much out of the other". But he never told that story.'*

So if change is to happen, the leader must have a bold vision and the leadership skills that can convince all to follow.

Summary

As we have seen, we have been in the situations before when there has been extreme inequality, excessive poverty, slow economic progress and where the very rich are in control. On many occasions this has resulted in revolution or war and in others there has been significant initiatives to correct the situation only to find that over the years we have slid back to the bad old days. Now we have another chance to create lasting change. Maybe we can be a bit smarter, maybe we will tackle the key structural problems to create a compassionate socially responsible society which makes fairness its key goal. Let's hope so, and let's not mess it up. We have the tools available, we have the experience, we know where we are going.

We can move from Austerity to Prosperity using the tax system as a toolbox to build that future, hopefully by evolution, but it needs to be urgent, or face a revolution. The Universal Declaration of Human Rights provides a strong set of aged values on which to build a policy platform with a common sense approach based on the principle of '*income for me/wealth for we*'.

In the next part of the book, over the next three chapters, I will outline an Agenda for Progressive Prosperity built around three key interlinked policy areas, which will bring significant benefit to everyone without hurting anyone.

PART II

The Agenda for Progressive Prosperity

'Let us not despair but act. Let us not seek the Republican answer
or the Democratic answer, but the right answer.
Let us not seek to fix the blame for the past.
Let us accept our own responsibility for the future.'

John F. Kennedy, 1958

T HE GROUNDSWELL of feeling that 'something' needs to be done is rising. There has been the warning that the pitchforks are coming and political earthquakes are rumbling. The stark details of excessive levels of inequality have been well documented and more appear every day. Politicians are starting to realise that this is a core issue. The evidence is overwhelming, there are the massive stockpiles of wealth in the control of a few that should be fuelling the fire of the economy and easing the hunger of the needy, but instead they are lying idle on the balance sheets of corporations or in the assets of the super rich and the vaults of the banks.

This chronic condition is bad for everyone, rich and poor alike. With such a high concentration of wealth in so few hands, it means this money is not in circulation, it cannot be used to the buy goods and services that create jobs for many people. For the wealthy, their wealth is under threat as more people are less able to buy the goods on which fortunes had been built. A very wealthy person who earns 1000 times as much as a low income earner cannot consume 1000 more meals, shoes, shirts, cars etc. So that accumulated wealth does not create more jobs and ease inequality.

It is not about being Robin Hood and taking from the rich and giving to the poor. It is about creating an economic system where high levels of inequality do not arise in the first place, where everyone has the opportunity to participate in prosperity. If the capitalist system is to be retained with its beliefs in private property and profit, then it needs to be a socially responsible capitalism that works for all, not just the few.

The stories about the evils of inequality and poverty makes it is increasingly obvious that this is a crime for which we are all responsible. But it is no good just to say how bad it is; or accept that it is too difficult to fix, we have to say this is the action required. We are a democracy and therefore have no right to make life unnecessarily hard for the majority of the people. To bring change, there needs to be a clear and concise manifesto of practical policies that can be implemented with comparative ease for the benefit of all – a manifesto that not only expresses a clear vision but also charts a defined course. It is no good complaining about low pay, austerity polices or reduced public services unless we have ideas that can make life better. This book is only the beginning. My proposed manifesto is called an Agenda for Progressive Prosperity. It contains initiatives that will bring real change for the majority of people. And it is simple and short.

The Agenda for Progressive Prosperity is a bold but common sense agenda to create a sustainable future and greater social justice. Prosperity does not just mean more money or wealth: it is about the quality of our lives. Progressive Prosperity is based on the principle of 'income for me, wealth for we'. If we work hard as individuals, we should be fairly rewarded and should keep what we earn. As members of the community, we all also play a part in creating collective wealth and this should be shared more equitably by all of us and not be siphoned off by a tiny fraction of our number.

The Agenda for Progressive Prosperity will benefit all society. If certain policies are put in place, the other ills can be solved as a result. On the financial side, it will put more money in the pockets of the poor and lower-income groups, which is not only good for them but it is good for everyone as it means more consumption, more growth, more jobs and more wealth created for the benefit of all. Sure, the better off will be paying more back to society, but such proposals are only likely to affect the top 10% on the income and wealth scale to varying degrees and, to a greater extent, the 1% and the 0.1%. But such people already have a very good lifestyle and the impact on them will be minimal and unthreatening. Having to pay an additional contribution to society may result in some having to sell some of their assets but it is a long, long way from causing any detrimental effect on their personal well-being.

More money circulating in the economy creates more jobs more growth, more scope for wealth creation and a more prosperous society. Similarly the increased emphasis on investment in infrastructure, transport, energy, communications, education and health will result in a much better environment in which to do business with a better educated and skilled workforce and a more healthy one too. In addition such investment particularly in education will enhance enjoyment of life. This Agenda is also good for the rich and the super rich, once we all understand the future of the human race depends on our ability to create a fair and just society. However the mean and greedy are going to be seriously disappointed.

So we all have a choice, make change happen or not. My answers are clear, simple and above all practical. They can be summed up in three areas of public policy that we need to act on to bring significant change and move us towards prosperity for the majority.

- Change the way we raise public revenue so that it is fair, sustainable and benefits everyone.
- Change the economic system so that it reflects the contribution of stakeholders not just shareholders.
- Change the focus of government expenditure to invest in opportunity: infrastructure, education, health and welfare.

CHAPTER 3

Turnaround Taxation

We can take the first major step toward minimizing economic inequality by raising government revenue from the wealth we create together, instead of taxing incomes from our work.

THIS SIMPLE SHIFT in the source of public revenue would provide an immediate and substantial relief to millions of people trapped on low incomes and in poverty without jeopardizing the functioning of the economy or government. Indeed, the idea sounds seductively simple – easily summarised by the approach: '*income for me*/*wealth for we*' – but the idea has far-reaching consequences. We should keep what we earn individually; we should share what we create together more equitably.

Let's be clear what we mean by 'income' and 'wealth'. Income is what we each earn from paid work. Many people earn less than or only just enough to get by (after they have paid income taxes). Others earn a lot more and they can save and accumulate wealth. Being wealthy by definition means we have enough to live on, as this is what we have saved or invested and it is generating a further income for us. This is also called unearned income. It may be just our house or at least the part that is not mortgaged, it may be shares in a business, it may be cash in the bank or bonds or a second home, it may be our private pension pot. Those who have hardly enough to live off are excluded from the wealth community and can't break out, even though they may strive hard to escape and climb the ladder.

Those that have some wealth can go on to accumulate more. For instance, if you have some savings you can make a down payment on a house, which even with modest rises in land values will bring a good return, and then if you need a loan for a car you can use the house as security. If you have no savings or access to funds you are barred from such opportunities. It is now so hard to save enough for the deposit on a house which, together with the rising price of property, means that many remain in rented accommodation for longer, and pay a higher percentage of their income towards housing costs and have nothing to show for it. Whereas many who own a house are in fact accumulating more wealth while living in it than the mortgage is costing them, so becoming net savers. In some cases the house price it going up more annually than the salary they earn, it happened to me for a few years!

As we have seen, calls for the reform of the tax system are long overdue. Properly managed, the tax system can provide a powerful tool to create greater equality and reduce poverty without negatively interfering with the economy as it does now. As President Franklin D. Roosevelt said in 1936: *'Taxes shall be levied according to the ability to pay, that is the American principle.'* That sounds like a wise principle that could be applied to most nations. As wealth implies you already have enough to live on, then the most just way to raise public revenue is from wealth (both personally and from companies) and it would not interfere with the free market of the everyday economy. This will require change of mindset as we have for so long associated the word tax with Income Tax; it need not be this way. Yet today, governments get the vast majority of their revenue from Income Tax and other taxes relating to income, and very little from wealth. Raising revenue from taxes on income and sales reduces disposable income and puts up costs, distorting the economy, interfering with the market and slowing economic growth and therefore reducing the opportunity to build wealth.

Government is collecting its revenue by inappropriate (and unfair) methods. It takes large proportions from those people with limited means and small proportion from those people who have a good helping of income and wealth. Those who benefit from good fortune resulting from hard work, gifted talent, and determination or by being born into a family with wealth are in a better position to contribute more. Most people have no choice, they are trapped, they can't escape from poverty and if above the line, they are being hit with shrinking or static wages and rising costs. Their income is being taken away involuntarily and reducing their choices, reducing their freedom.

There is a toolbox of taxes available to rebuild our economy, bringing benefits to all. The problem is we have been using the wrong tools, so with the right tools we can make change happen, we need a set of spanners that actually fit!

Shifting the public revenue base from income to wealth is not only morally right, it is practical and it will raise sufficient funds to meet current levels of government budgets as well as provide much needed capital for major public investment. The main issue is political will as we are currently ruled by a plutocracy who decide the political agenda, but later in the book we will look more closely at how we can convince this elite that it is in everyone's best interest to make changes.

To bring about this shift of the base from income to wealth, three areas for immediate action are proposed:

1 Abolish taxes on income for the majority of people, giving the squeezed middle more disposable income
2 Introduce a contribution to public revenue based on wealth, as a way of sharing the wealth we all helped to create, thereby putting more funds in circulation, in turn leading to more jobs
3 Replace current property taxes and introduce a charge to landowners based on the public value of land. This will realise the return on investment in the community by the community and so sharing in the greater wealth created

Let's now look at these points in more detail. The key point is we can afford it. The funds are there. The books will be balanced.

3.1 Income for me

What you earn should be what you get, the income you receive should not be taxed or have any amount taken away involuntarily. This enables you to decide how you spend your income, you have choices, and this gives you more freedom. This concept should appeal right across the political spectrum and offers us a real opportunity to unite warring ideological factions and bring benefit for the greatest number. Of course, an immediate reaction is that that sounds a truly great idea, but if the government gets most of its revenue from Income Tax, how can an economy possibly afford to do this without drastic cuts in government services? Well, I will show you how.

First, we have to wake up to reality. Bill O'Reilly, the Fox News presenter and self-styled voice of the right, posted on the Fox News website in November 2014:

> Did you know that about 70 per cent of all American workers earn less than $50,000 a year? Did you know that? I didn't know that. That means the folks are struggling. They are living in a very insecure way. They have little savings and if they get sick it's a disaster. Educating their children? A huge financial burden. As is saving for retirement. So priority number one is to stimulate the economy so that workers make more money.

Well, yes, Bill, 70% of Americans do know that (just as the 80% of Britons earning under £32,000 know how hard it is). He goes on to suggest raising the minimum wage. Great, there maybe some areas of common ground. Let's build on it! But then he blows it by suggesting cutting corporate Income Tax to 20% as he suggests it will create more jobs (Note: According to Nielsen TV data through mid-January 2014, the average age of Fox News viewers is 68-years-old). This diatribe clearly reflects the knowledge, or lack of it, of a large part of the electorate, who think traditionally that cutting taxes on profits will trickle down to create more jobs and that significantly cutting Income Tax is not feasible as we should all pay Income Tax. In fact part of the problem is educating people in how the economy works and what policy options there are. Many do not have a clue and acquiesce in accepting the status quo of Income Tax. No, stop! There is another way: it need not be like this. The media is a key source of information but many prefer media that are superficial or show a distinct political bias. However the media are not the key problem, unnecessary hardship is.

Our time is precious, we are on this earth for a limited time. We all need to work to live and provide for our ourselves and our families. As you have earned your income from the time and effort you have put in, you deserve to keep it. You then make the choice as to how you spend it. You could spend it all as you have a family to support. You could save some so you can put down a deposit to buy a house. You could invest some in other assets or redecorate your house, or buy a car. Most people would be careful and make sensible decisions, although there will always be some people who may spend their money frivolously.

An enterprise that cannot pay fair wages does not deserve to succeed. That doesn't only apply to large firms but also to the small ones. Remuneration needs to be fair, at all levels. There is now such a wide disparity of income with the difference between top salaries and the ordinary worker growing significantly by the year. So if you are a high earner, say in the top 10%, then it would be right that you pay some contribution out of your income as part of your contribution to the community. Maybe once income inequality has reduced to more acceptable levels then Income Tax could be further minimised, but that time is not now. In addition we will also need to take into account income in terms of gifts of assets like shares as part of a remuneration package. There could also be a case for greater adoption of performance-related pay, and that performance need not be just financial: there could be socially responsible elements too which could be treated more favourably as regards tax.

Some degree of inequality is inevitable. The aim is not for all to be on the same wages! It is to reduce the current levels of extreme inequality caused by an out-dated and structurally unsound economic system. Greater wealth and financial security is a prime motivator for all to have an incentive to better ourselves, get educated and see a possibility of achieving rewards through diligence and hard work. That opportunity must be real and available to all, not like now when the majority are excluded. In line with this, it must also not be worthwhile to maintain a welfare mentality, just living off benefits and not bothering to find or hold down a job. It is not good for the individual and his family and it is not good for society, we all want a sense of purpose and we all want to give and care for our families and friends. Salary scales must be within sensible limits. It is not about a minimum wage, but a living wage, for all and having opportunities for all to earn bonuses, additional income and a stake in the wealth of the business that employs you.

The transition away from government revenue from taxes on personal income could be phased in over a four-year period so as to smooth the shift to a fairer and more effective public revenue system and maintain balanced government accounts. There are three stages to this plan, which will significantly boost the disposable income of the majority of the population, minimise hardship and usher in a period of sustainable growth:

Stage 1: Immediate action, abolish Income Tax for the majority

Abolishing Income Tax for lower earners would significantly raise wages; think what a boost that would be to the economy! Plus this would be further enhanced by the raising of the minimum wage to an acceptable living wage, which is covered in more detail in the next chapter.

In the UK, Income Tax represents only 25% of government revenue then when you add in National Insurance, it rises to 43% of revenue. The majority of taxpayers are at the lower income levels. In the UK, 81% of Income Tax payers are earning below £32,000 per year (the average income in the UK is £26,000) but they contribute only 8.5% (£55bn) of total government revenue. Abolishing Income Tax for those earning less than £32,000 pa would give 25 million people up to 15% extra disposable income, but only reduce government revenue by 8.5%. This amount is small enough for it to be possible to make up the loss with a more progressive and fair approach to raising revenue from those more able to afford it. Such a move could be implemented fairly easily and quickly by raising the tax threshold from £10,600 to £32,000. This dramatic cut would also mean that those earning over £32,000 would automatically get £32,000 tax-free. That would defeat the object and give a huge boost to higher earners. There would have to be a sharp progressive rise in taxes on income over the threshold so that, although there could be some marginal benefit to ease the transition for goodwill and to make the move more politically palatable, the benefit would not be significant. The top 20% will see their tax rates based on income adjusted and be more progressive to take into account the new threshold. I would want to shift any increases in income related taxes right to the top end.

A reporter for Bloomberg New York reminded me that those on low incomes don't pay Income Tax anyway as under the current welfare benefits system, many low earners are receiving tax credits to top up their income. While tax credits are clearly very helpful in alleviating a dire situation, it would be far better if they did not have to pay Income Tax in the first place. It seems ridiculous that we are taking it away with one hand and giving it back with another. What a waste of time. Bureaucracy could be simplified by putting a stop to shifting money around. It is not taking from the rich and giving to the poor, it is taking from the poor and then giving some back to the poor!

So in the UK, taking 80% of people out of Income Tax would put £55 billion back in their pockets and into the economy to circulate and create jobs as well as enable savings. The UK government currently spends £30 billion on top ups with child tax credits and working tax credits. According to the Treasury, about 4.5 million families (out of a total of 18 million, 25%, one in four) received child and working tax credits in 2013-4, nearly 70% of whom were in some form of employment. While some people may still need support, the vast majority will now be able to 'fend for themselves' and not have to ask for welfare, which most people dislike but are forced to take advantage of due to distressed but common circumstances.

After the General Election of May 2015, the new Tory government sought £12 billion in welfare cuts. This is completely unnecessary and is a further example of trying to solve the outcome not the source. If 80% of people were not paying Income Tax, then there would be an automatic reduction in welfare spending. Instead this government seems to prefer to be seen as villains by most people rather than as champions for higher incomes! So with this Income Tax cut and the adoption of a true living wage (based in needs not an arbitrary minimum wage) maybe 50-60% of the budget on wages top up would not be required. So the net effect of these policies could be a reduction in government income of £35-40 billion.

In the United States, total government (federal, state, local) revenue was around $6 trillion in 2015. 37% comes from Income Tax and 25% from social security taxes. That's 62% or $3.7 trillion (Source: usgovernment revenue.com based on federal and local data). It is estimated that the bottom 50% of earners, those earning below $36,055 only contribute 2.8% to Income Tax revenue (Source: Kiplinger.com based on government data 2012). If on the same basis they contributed to social security taxes at the same 3% rate; this would mean a total (Income Tax and Federal Insurance Contribution) of $111 billion which is just 2% of all government revenue or around 4% of federal revenue. So half the population is suffering great hardship due to income related tax deductions that have very little impact on government revenue. Currently an individual earning $40,000 per year will pay over $7,000 in Income Tax and Federal Insurance Contributions that is 17.5% of their income. Such a simple bold move would bring huge benefit to 70 million Americans by giving a pay rise of up to 15% and yet make such a small difference to government revenue.

In fact, surprisingly, Prime Minister David Cameron promised in June 2015 an end to what he called the *'ridiculous merry-go-round'* of taxing low earners then handing them money back in benefits. He said it was wrong to treat *'the symptoms of the social and economic problems we face'*, while *'ignoring the causes'* of low pay. He argued the UK should be a *'lower tax, lower welfare society'*. Despite this appealing talk, there is still no statement about how and when real lower taxes for the lower paid will happen, just timid gestures to raise the threshold a very small amount. This is politics today: say what people want to hear, but not how or when you are going to do it: all talk and no action!

It took newly elected Conservative MP and current Mayor of London, the affable, comb-challenged Boris Johnson to warn David Cameron against '*hacking back*' on benefits for low-paid workers until companies '*cough up*' more money and increase their pay. He said that private firms that fail to pay the living wage and force their staff to rely on tax credits to top up their pay were '*scandalous*'. He is right. Historical note: Boris Johnson and David Cameron were at Oxford University together and both members of the Bullingdon Club, the notorious elitist boys club said to be the inspiration for the film *The Riot Club* where members held expensive, gluttonous, private functions and got insanely drunk and destructive.

I am sure the abolition of Income Tax for lower earners will bring the same benefit in many other countries too. This revenue could easily be made up from other more equitable sources. So why is this simple policy not acted on when it will do so much to improve the life and opportunity for so many?

The significant increase in wages for lower earners means that more things become affordable particularly the essential items whether this be childcare, housing (action is still required to reduce these costs as covered later) or nutritious food, so there is less need for taxpayers money to used in subsidies. While some low earners may still need welfare benefits due to special needs, it could be expected that the demand on the welfare budget will be meaningfully reduced. When the income you receive is taxed or have any amount taken away involuntarily, it means you decide how you spend your income, you have choices, and this means you have more freedom. This concept offers us a real opportunity to unite across traditional political lines to tackle the concentration of wealth through the abolition of Income Tax, initially for lower earners.

Once the initial reductions have taken effect, then the next stage would be to reduce Income Tax for the rest, leaving only about 10% of earners paying some Income Tax, which would be significantly progressive above that figure. In the UK it would mean those earning over £32,000 and in USA those earning over $50,000. This group of people often includes young professionals and skilled workers keen to get on but who are currently hampered by the tax burden, often increased by student loan paybacks. We are already seeing the side effects of the false economy of the student loan concept in the reduction of spending power and the anxiety of graduate workers. It would be better to make higher education free, it would be cheaper and keep more spending power in the economy. My daughter has only just paid off her student loan, nine years after graduating. She is one of the lucky ones; there are so many who carry the burden on for years, which is bad for the economy as it stunts demand. Making changes for this group is not just being kind to the individuals, it is actually good for society as we have seen that this group is not spending as much as it could because it has less real disposable income. It is a strong middle class that will make the economy grow which in turn will strengthen the middle class; it is all just common sense. The second stage will need to be phased in over a few years as it represents a much larger proportion of government revenue and other methods will need to be in place to generate additional revenue.

Stage 2: Reduce payroll taxes

The second stage of this plan would be to reduce those annoying deductions from earnings, effectively Income Tax by another name. Currently these taxes are extremely regressive and put a huge burden on the lower paid with little change as salaries increase. While the initial intention of such taxes was to cover health and social security, they have now lost that direct link and for practical purposes all goes into the same pot. Implementing this initiative at the start of the transition to the new public revenue system could be too costly. Indeed the boost to the economy, individual and families would be so great that it could overheat. However, this initiative remains part of the plan to be implemented within a four year period, once the Income Tax reduction has taken effect.

In the UK, National Insurance raises £110 billion, that's about 17% of government revenue (compared to £167 billion from Income Tax). So the 80% who contribute only 8.5% of government revenue through Income Tax are likely to be contributing a much higher percentage in national insurance. This could be as much as £60-80 billion, so the cut would be more 'expensive' to implement. However the contribution is split between employer and employees. I would propose eliminating the employee contribution first for the lowest earners, so significantly increase the threshold at which it becomes due. Then eliminate for employers, as it is an unnecessary restrictive cost that minimises margins for business.

Having abolished Income Tax for the lower earners, Income Tax could be abolished for all. Well, not quite, no one likes paying Income Tax but they are less fussed about paying insurance and social security so I would rebrand Income Tax as social insurance. So those at the top end, instead of paying Income Tax would make a contribution to a social insurance scheme to cover health and welfare. For instance in the UK, National

Insurance is an Income Tax by another name, but instead of folding National Insurance into Income Tax, it could be done the other way round. Abolish Income Tax and just have National Insurance, which directly goes to pay for the welfare system.

At the current levels of inequality it is not practical to continue to levy this on the lower paid, instead it will only be applied to higher paid. So there would be no Income Tax only insurance contributions, which seems a very fair way of making provision. This is much more than semantics, it is about principle and the purpose of taxation. It is socially just and therefore is more likely to be accepted as a fair contribution rather than the tiresome burden of involuntary Income Tax. Once a more acceptable level of economic inequality has been reached, there could be a case to have progressive form of National Insurance contributions for all those working as it is prudent to save for a rainy day or when not able to work. This still leaves the employers contribution, which we will review later.

Stage 3: Realign sales taxes

In an ideal world, sales taxes do not seem justifiable as they are the same for all. In most countries essential items such as food are excluded so the impact on the poor and lower earners is minimised. However there is a strong case to review this and in fact put more basic items on the no tax list but at the same time increase the tax level on non essentials and luxuries.

The scope to reduce sales taxes is limited and is not so much of an urgent item for reform in this agenda. In the UK, Value Added Tax (VAT) is a European Union requirement. In the USA, individual states set the sales tax so it is considered a valuable local revenue stream though some states choose not to levy sales tax at all. As sales taxes varies in different states this means all prices quoted are less tax, so the price you see is not the one you pay there is always a bit more!

Taxes on consumption are regressive. In November 2014, the *Daily Telegraph* printed research by accountancy firm BDO showing that British taxpayers typically pay £3,844 a year more to the government over and above income related taxes. When VAT was put up to record 20% in 2011, the UK Chancellor of the Exchequer, George Osborne claimed that '*If you look at the population and how much they spend, then VAT is progressive... Income tax and National Insurance would have a more damaging impact on poorer people in our society.*' Not sure how he worked that one out, as the Office for National Statistics said that the poorest fifth of UK households pay significantly more in VAT as a percentage of their disposable income than the richest fifth. He is looking at it from a rich person's perspective: the rich spend more, therefore they pay more VAT in absolute terms, while the poor person spends less and therefore contribute less in VAT.

Setting a zero rate for VAT on all but non essentials and luxury goods would lift a huge burden from the majority of the population. VAT was first introduced in France in 1954 but is now paid in around 120 countries, turning millions of shopkeepers, taxi drivers and the like into unpaid tax collectors and, it is argued, contributing to inflation in the process. Legend has it that VAT was introduced because the French had made Income Tax evasion both an art and a national pastime. It was levied by the local mayor and based on appearances. Supposedly, one reason so many small French towns are shabby but still have wonderful restaurants is that no one wanted to show off their wealth with a freshly painted house or new roof; traditionally they would take their money to the next town and spend it on long lunches instead. True or not, other countries ended up with both Income Tax and VAT, the worst of both worlds. While finding ways to pay as little Income Tax as possible is seen as fair game, VAT is unavoidable.

Income tax has been regarded as a punishment for enterprise or hard work, an imposition and a disincentive. From one perspective Income Tax is seen either as an attack on self-reliance and the work ethic or simply as something to avoid. From the other perspective Income Tax is viewed as progressive but only if it is applied on a sliding scale: a flat rate of Income Tax is anathema and as unfair as indirect taxes such as sales taxes.

Any reductions in Income Tax or VAT would have to be meaningful cuts. Before the 2015 UK General Election Prime Minister David Cameron promised his party that '*with us, if you work 30 hours a week on minimum wage, you will pay no income tax at all. Nothing. Zero. Zilch.*' I should certainly hope they would not pay Income Tax. It would be absolutely disgraceful to charge Income Tax on someone being paid £6.50 per hour, £195 per 30 hour week. The poverty line for a single parent with one child is £220 per week (Households Below Average Income (HBAI), UK government survey 2009-2012). The Trades Unions Congress responded with analysis of the tax and benefit policies the Prime Minister had announced which revealed that a family with two children and 30 hours work at the national minimum wage will suffer a net loss of £320 a year. As usual, the Conservatives' proposals were '*a charter for handouts to the wealthy and punishment for the working poor,*' said TUC General Secretary Frances O'Grady. There is a difference between balancing the books and skewing them in favour of the wealthy!

Summary

Cutting income and payroll taxes for the lower income earners will give the majority of the population a huge financial lift, reduce reliance on welfare and bring more opportunity. This will increase economic growth, boost spending in the economy, create more jobs especially for unskilled work, giving more opportunity for those below the poverty line to move up. Initially the impact will be less as the disposable income of some families may not change dramatically as they are currently being topped up by welfare. The reduction of income related taxes will lay a solid foundation for a sustainable economy and greater social justice.

These policies could be phased in over a four-year period to ensure a smooth and effective transition to a more equitable way of raising government revenue. It would allow enough time for other methods of raising taxation to take effect to compensate for the reductions. Income tax abolition could be implemented immediately but it may not be possible to eliminate the payroll taxes for lower earners until the new revenue kicks in.

3.2 *Wealth* for we

The wealth of a country is not created just by entrepreneurs, shareholders and landowners but by the real stakeholders: the majority. We are all the wealth creators.

- We do the work
- We take the risks
- We grow demand
- We increase the jobs
- We create the wealth

This is why a fair economic system needs to ensure that all those who create the wealth, share in it. To me the key issue is the moral argument that we all create the wealth and therefore it should be shared more equitably. The tax system can be a tool to achieve this. The secondary issue is how the government can raise more revenue if it reduces income related taxes for lower earners and switches the tax base away from income, which has been traditional for so long and has caused so many of the problems we all face today.

Once you have wealth, you have choices, you have freedoms; you are in a position to financially contribute to society to make it better for all. We should all have an opportunity to share in the wealth that we all create, but it is currently accumulated by the few.

If everyone had an opportunity to share in the wealth they created, they would be able to accumulate wealth and feel more secure about their future. If you have wealth, you can afford to take some risks, invest in the future like a college education for yourself or your children (in the new shared economy, tuition would be free but you still have to live!) or put a deposit on a home, extend your home, eat healthily, keep fit or take the family on holiday. The quality of life for many would be improved even with just a little wealth.

There is a big difference between creating wealth and accumulating wealth. We can accumulate wealth by buying assets especially those that rise in value. In order to buy assets, you have to have money; you have to have enough money to live off so that you have some left over to buy the assets! Under the current system this then entitles you to be the beneficiary of any increase in value of that wealth asset even though the increase in value has nothing to do with your effort and has in fact been increased as a result of the work of others. In my view it is great if there is the opportunity to accumulate wealth, it is not great if it is only available to a few and it becomes extreme amounts. Indeed it would be OK to accumulate a lot of wealth, if there was no poverty and the squeezed middle did not suffer such hardship, but it does not work like that.

I know what is like to be an entrepreneur having had my own business for 30 years. It is not easy and the constant concern can be stressful, especially when you have a family to support. I used to think no one else really cared enough about the business as I did, it was just a job to them, and so it was right that I should earn more than them. The thing was I often earned less, as the funds were not there and had to keep the business going. Looking back it seems the most successful businesses are those where there is a good team at the top and particularly a good number two so the CEO can spend more time thinking and less time doing. While the entrepreneur has the vision, it always works better with a committed team who have a stake in the business or, as they say, 'skin in the game'. The wealth needs to be shared at company level as well as a national level. The same applies to society at large: if we all had a stake in the wealth created we would feel more engaged, more committed and more prosperous.

Pope Francis, the leader of an estimated 1.2 million Catholics representing 17% of the world's population, has called on rich people to share their wealth:

> Just as the commandment 'Thou shalt not kill' sets a clear limit in order to safeguard the value of human life, today we also have to say 'thou shalt not' to an economy of exclusion and inequality. Such an economy kills.

It is important to define wealth. It could be anything from a dollar in a savings account to the world's richest person, Carlos Slim, with an estimated fortune of $53.5 billion (just ahead of Bill Gates and Warren Buffett). Most of the super-rich have their wealth in company shares which have increased in value. They will have sold some of these to buy property and other assets, both those that appreciate in value like property, artworks and some that depreciate like cars and yachts! Alan Sugar, or as he is now known Lord Sugar, was the founder and former boss of Amstrad, a very successful British consumer electronics company and now the host of The Apprentice TV show. I had the pleasure of working with Sir Alan managing the Amstrad PR campaign in the 1990s. Alan made a fortune from the sale of his company but has gone on to make a further fortune in property and aviation. Once you have wealth it is every easy to accumulate more wealth. I have known many clients who took their companies public, made some good money and went on to make even more. This is partly because once you have wealth, you can take a longer term view, afford to take bigger risks and stick the course until you get a profit, instead of having to worry where the next salary payment is coming from and how you are going to pay the mortgage. The potential of financial success is a great driver. The problem we all have is when it is accumulated in such vast amounts by so few, allowing greed to set in.

Creating wealth is the key to the success of economy. A vast amount of wealth has been created but it has been accumulated by a very small number of people. The concentration of wealth causes a power shift, the wealthy control how their wealth is used, whether it is for practical business purposes, philanthropic or social enterprises or indeed greed or political purchase so that the political decisions always favour the wealthy. If the wealth we all created was more equitably spread then more people could enjoy the benefits of prosperity.

There are two main ways that wealth can be created:

1 Land
2 Labour

1 Land: Wealth is created by the rising value of resources such as land, because land is fixed in supply and scarce. Land value is actually generated by the community whether that is a neighbourhood, town, city-state or nation – by the collective social, economic and political activities and decisions of the community. After all a country is just an area of land surrounded by an agreed border. Land value arises due to the benefits of the site and hence the demand for a particular location for living, working and leisure space. If the community decides to improve the convenience of an area by building a road or rail service, or indeed schools, hospitals, leisure amenities paid for out of public funds, the effect is to increase the value of all the surrounding land. This added value is created by the community and has nothing to do with any action by the landowners. Under the current system, most of the benefit from the increase in the value of the land goes to the landowner and only a portion goes to the public purse when the land is sold in the form of Capital Gains Tax. This represents an opportunity to generate public revenue from what is rightly the public value rather than the current system, which means all gains from public effort to go to private benefit.

2 Labour: Wealth is also generated by profits of enterprises when they effectively have more money coming in from sales than the cost of labour and capital together. Creating profit is a good thing as long as it is not achieved at the expense of underpaid and undervalued workers. It is how that profit is used that is the issue. Every company needs profits to invest in growing the business. Increasing profits adds to the value of the company whether it is a private or public company and that profit goes to shareholders, which are indeed a different group than the stakeholders. While most companies' value or wealth is reflected in the level of their profits and balance sheet, there are many companies that have made little or no profits but still have a considerable value. This is typically seen with tech companies that receive amazing levels of investment in return for shares in the company giving these companies surprisingly high valuations, yet they have still to make a profit. Some of this value, particularly with online business, is in customer accumulations, having thousands or millions of users is valuable to an acquiring company or potential shareholder because you can sell more 'things' to this expanding user base. Any contribution to government revenue from company wealth should be based on both the profits and the value for the company. This is comparatively easy to do if the company is a public company as there is a publicly quoted share price and market capitalisation. It is different but not too hard to measure corporate wealth even for private companies once they are beyond the start-up stage.

Accumulating wealth is fine as long as it is not at the expense of those who contributed to creating it. Traditionally a tax on wealth has just been on capital gains from the sale, not the value of the assets as a whole. Yet the asset may be creating more value but not contributing to the oiling of the economy and to economic activity that would benefit the majority of people. It therefore seems right that there should also be a levy on the actual wealth not just the gain as these funds are urgently needed to benefit the majority not just the few. These funds should be invested on behalf of the nation in infrastructure, education and health all aspects that help build a strong nation for today and tomorrow, the sustainable future. The current system means that gains from accumulated wealth are effectively lying idle (until sold) and not making a contribution to society as a whole or building what a nation needs to be strong successful and sustainable.

So the contribution to public revenue will shift from income-based taxes to those based on wealth. The loss from income-based taxes will be more than made up by revenue from more equitable methods. The phases of implementation will be interlinked so that by the end of the transition, the government books could be balanced. Not only will the deficit disappear but a surplus could be achieved which will enable even more resources to finance the future, which will in turn bring an increased government revenue.

In order to ensure wealth is shared more equitably and to shift public revenue away from income and more onto wealth, a public revenue contribution based on personal wealth needs to be established above a certain threshold, this would affect only a small percentage of those with wealth. However at the same time as a counter measure for good will and to make politically palatable, the taxes on capital gains could cease.

So there two areas for action:

Stage 1: Introduce Personal Asset Contribution
Based on the principle that we all create the wealth but it is currently accumulated by a few, then a convenient way of returning the public share back to the public is through taxation. This could be achieved by what has often been described as wealth tax, a contribution to public revenue based on the value of personal assets, which I would prefer to call a Personal Asset Contribution (PAC).

Professor Ronald McKinnon of Stanford University outlined the 'Conservative Case for a Wealth Tax' in *The Wall Street Journal*, January 2012. He wrote that

> there is a strong case for reforming income taxes – both the personal and corporate – to increase efficiency and generate more revenue. Because wealth will generally present a much larger tax base than income, tax rates can be kept very low and still raise substantial revenue.

He went on to describe how it might be applied:

> In order to have a fairer tax system, we should implement a new federal wealth tax in addition to the federal income tax. A wealth tax does not rely on how 'income' is defined. However, it does require that households list all their domestic and foreign assets at some designated point in time – say December 31 in the relevant tax year. Financial assets are more easily marked to market and can be netted out: assets minus liabilities, such as mortgages and other borrowing. The current prices of physical assets – houses, cars, yachts, and so forth of the assessed value of houses are available, and real estate agents have current records of home selling prices.

For one-of-a-kind assets such as yachts and art collections, historical costs would become more important as would owner self-assessment. Where does the 'conservative' element come in? McKinnon is eager to say:

> these worthy goals would be compromised if the main objective of income tax reform was seen to reduce economic inequality by hitting the very wealthy – the proverbial top one percent of the population, [but] with a large exemption of say $6 million that effectively excludes more than 95 percent of the population, a moderate flat tax, say three percent, on wealth so defined could then be imposed.

Net worth or net wealth is the total assets, savings and possessions minus the total liabilities of an individual or business. In the UK, 22% of the population have zero or negative wealth, which means their debts, negative equity in housing and so on outweigh the value of everything they own or have in the bank. The richest 1% of households has about 12% of all household wealth in the UK, the same as the poorest 55% of all households, according to the Office of National Statistics. If all the wealth of the UK were spread evenly through the population every single person would have over £150,000 each so for a family of four that would be £600,000; enough to buy a house for cash almost anywhere in the country. So what does this personal wealth look like?

The ONS categorises personal wealth for the whole of the UK population under for major headings:

- Pensions (£3,586 billion / 38%)
- Property (£3,528 billion / 37%)
- Financial wealth such as shares (£1,299 billion / 14%)
- Physical wealth – things (£1,102 billion / 11%)

The ONS calculated the total UK household wealth rose from £9.5 trillion in 2012 to £10.3 trillion in 2013. That is an increase of £800 billion: 8.4% in one year. If just half of that (4%) household wealth was paid to the nation every year that would mean £400 billion in revenue – more than half the Government's budget of £732 billion in 2014. The Green Party in the UK has proposed a tax at one to 2% on personal assets that would raise between £21.5 billion and £43 billion annually (about five to 10% of total government revenue) from those with assets of over £3 million, well within the top 1%. Thomas Piketty has proposed an annual global wealth tax of up to 2%.

In the UK, if those with personal assets over £1.5 million (this would be just the top 3% who own 26.5% of the nation's wealth) paid a 1.5% contribution based on the asset value, it could bring in revenue of £50 billion a year. If the rate was 2% this would bring back in £100 billion which in itself would cover the proposed reduction in Income Tax and National Insurance for the 80% earning below £32,000. This would put a meaningful amount of cash into circulation to boost the economy as well as increase savings and wealth opportunities for millions. No real hardship for the wealth owners who would be expecting their assets to generate an annual income of 5% anyway. So at a 5% rate, a wealth pot of £1.5 million, would earn the owner £75,000 per year. At this entry level point it would mean the owner would be paying at 1.5%, just £22,500 which would still leave a gain of £52,500 per year, twice the average wage in UK. That would seem a very fair method as everyone gains. Setting the threshold level would be a political decision, for instance it may be considered fairer to apply this proposed tax to the top 1%, that is those with over £2.8 million assets and to charge a higher percentage such as 2% or 2.5%. Such a change could be phased in over four years. Of course, the increase in asset value could be a lot more than 5% or indeed a lot less!

Thomas Piketty not only proposes combining a wealth tax but also a progressive Income Tax reaching as high as 80% to reduce inequality. This is inline with my proposal for a much higher Income Tax threshold followed by a steeply progressive Income Tax above that threshold.

When I have been speaking to people about the idea of taxes on assets, an initial reaction is: *'Oh, another tax! And I have already paid Income Tax!'* I then explained to the relieved audience that such taxes on wealth will only kick in at high level and effect a small number of people.

Stage 2: Abolish Capital Gains Tax

The issue with Capital Gains Tax is that it only realises its value when the asset is sold. To have an efficient tax on wealth it is necessary to capture that wealth while the assets are held instead of when they are sold.

The Institute for Public Policy Research, a progressive think-tank in the UK, models different approaches to new taxes and their likely effects. The IPPR is lukewarm on net wealth tax. It says that taxing asset holdings rather than returns, means that assets producing very different rates of return are taxed at the same rate, so that investments generating a 'normal' rate of return are taxed at the same rate as those producing 'above-normal' returns. It is suggested that this issue is overcome by applying a tax on capital gains. My view is that it doesn't matter if different items have different rates of return. If the proposal was to tax assets at 2% (if over a certain amount such as £1.5m or $3m), any increase in value of those assets would be reflected in the increased taxable value and so the contribution would increase. If the assets were sold, or if there was a dividend payable on assets such as shares, then that would be counted as income and, if above the agreed Income Tax threshold, would be subject to Income Tax. Or indeed there could be a variable rate for different types of assets: Property, pensions, shares etc.

In most regimes, taxes on capital gains are surprisingly levied at a lower rate than the tax on the money that was originally invested: a kind of double jeopardy tax rule. But this lower rate is one of the mechanisms that concentrates wealth and makes 'money come to money'. Income from realised capital gains, which is new (unearned) income, should be treated the same as earned income.

The IPPR also points out that:

> the case for taxing the capital gains associated with the sale of residential property is that people who treat their home as an investment benefit unfairly when selling their home relative to people that choose to invest in other assets, and particularly people who 'invest' in rental property.

This apparent unfairness is particularly acute in the UK where real house prices in some parts of the country have risen considerably, providing their owners with windfall gains that currently go untaxed, i.e. none of the gain which resulted from the increase in the public value, is returned to the community.

The IPPR also says:

> the major distortion within the UK property and wealth tax regime is in Council Tax. The current system of Council Tax means that, overall, property and wealth held by households living in larger and more expensive properties (typically older and richer people) is under taxed while households in smaller and cheaper properties (typically younger and poorer people) are overtaxed.

Council Tax is paid both by owners and renters. If it were replaced by a property tax and Capital Gains Tax, the IPPR suggests, this would have the effect of dampening the volatile housing market and making housing more affordable. In addition, the OECD said in 2011 that the introduction of a property tax in the UK and other countries would lessen the attractiveness of housing as an investment and discourage people from leaving properties empty. More on property taxes and how this can be handled more equitably in the next section.

Summary

The proposal is that the wealthy pay a very small percentage every year on the value of all their assets over certain threshold for example £1.5 million or $2.5 million. This Personal Asset Contribution (PAC) could start from 1.5% of asset value and rise progressively. This is expected to affect the top 3% of the population. While the wealthy will pay more to the government, they will still be making money every year on their assets and so still get richer but not by so much! This will cause no adverse effect on daily living standards as it will only affect those who already have a very comfortable lifestyle. At the same time it enables considerable relief to the majority of the population and contributes towards the wealth they all created being shared more equitably. At the same time, taking funds out of storage, will significantly boost the economy, creating jobs and opportunities for all by bringing more money into circulation. It will also mean that the level of public revenue is maintained but without the squeezed middle paying a damaging percentage out of their earned income.

3.3 Location, location, location!

As Mark Twain said: *'Buy land, they are not making it anymore.'* One of the ways wealth is created is from the rising value of land, somewhat misleadingly described as rising house prices. There is a distinction between that part of property values which are due to the work and investment of the occupant(s), such as draining farmland to improve yields, or building an office block, retail outlet or factory, from the value of the land itself. The former value added is the result of the work of the occupants, and, as we have said earlier, this should not be taxed. The value of the land itself, however, will also rise, not because of the work on the site, but because with a growing population and developing economy, the demand for land grows. As communities develop and towns and cities emerge, soil fertility ceases to be the main determinant of value. Instead, location becomes the all important factor in running a business and is reflected in the much higher land prices in urban centres. It is not the landowner who has created that value: it is the presence of the community. Currently we allow landowners to reap all the benefit of increased land values, which is greatly enhanced by major infrastructure improvements paid for by the taxpayer.

Henry George, the author of *Progress and Poverty* related a story of when he was out riding his horse one day in 1871. He stopped to rest while overlooking San Francisco Bay (as I often have cycling on the bike trail!). He later described the revelation that came to him:

> I asked a passing teamster, for want of something better to say, what land was worth there. He pointed to some cows grazing so far off that they looked like mice, and said, 'I don't know exactly, but there is a man over there who will sell some land for a thousand dollars an acre.' Like a flash it came over me that there was the reason of advancing poverty with advancing wealth. With the growth of population, land grows in value, and the men who work it must pay more for the privilege.

In 2005, the Institute of Public Policy Research (IPPR) released a paper, 'Time for a Land Value Tax'. In my view a Land Value Tax is not actually a tax. According to the definition used in this book and elsewhere, it is in effect a payment for services rendered to the site. The values of these services are reflected in the value of the land. The IPPR said:

> There is a growing consensus that property taxation needs reform... Land Value Taxation could help in the reforms of Council Tax, local government

finance, planning and house building, as well as promoting macroeconomic stability. Introducing any changes will require long-term planning, detailed economic and distributional analysis – and, above all, political courage. But with vision and patience a consensus is possible. Now is the time to seek it.

A Land Value Tax applies solely to the value of land itself and takes no account of the value of any structures (houses, factories, offices…) or development on the site. A property price is based on two factors: the building and the land it stands on. Whether a building is developed or knocked down and replaced, the underlying value of the land will remain the same. The value of the land only changes in relation to communications (the existence of roads, for example), access to services such as schools, sewerage, power and so on, and proximity to markets or work, as well as by the zoning put on it by the public authority. None of these has anything to do with the landowner's efforts and any increase in value is unearned.

In 1879, Henry George, propounded the idea of a Land Value Tax thus:

> We do not propose a tax on land; we propose a tax upon land values, or what in the terminology of political economy is termed 'rent'; that is to say, the value which attaches to any land irrespective of any improvements in or on it; that value which attaches to land, not by reason of anything that the user or improver of land does – not by reason of any individual exertion of labour – but by reason of the growth and improvement of the community.

What George and others have called a tax is, in reality, a means of collecting public revenue without taxation: a contribution paid to society for the benefits received by the landowner for publicly funded community services and infrastructure developments that contribute to the site's value.

A Land Value Tax thus provides a means of returning to the community, the public value created by the community. A charge would be assessed on the value of a plot of land based on the optimum permitted planning use at any time, that is on the annual rental value of each site which is the earning potential of the land and therefore the amount an individual would be prepared to pay for the exclusive use of the site for a period of time. This is fairer than assessing a tax on the capital value, or selling price because this valuation excludes any man-made improvements to the site such as houses, factories, drainage and crops. The value will ignore the size and condition of any development already placed on the site – it is only the land itself that will be valued, as if it was a vacant site. In this way, every plot of land can then be valued and a percentage rate applied to it to raise a contribution to communal funds. The key to the success of this system is that it is a graduated contribution – highest where land is most valuable and desirable relative to other land and zero where land is deemed to be 'marginal'.

I prefer a more appropriate term: Land Usage Charge (LUC) not only makes it sound more palatable (i.e. payment for which you get something in return) but is actually more accurate. In *Public Revenue Without Taxation*, Ronald Burgess, a lifelong member of the Royal Economic Society, examines alternatives to taxation proposed by the early economists, the Physiocrats, and thinkers such as Henry George and Alfred Marshall. He uses the post-War Chancellor Hugh Dalton's definition of a tax: '*a compulsory contribution imposed by a public authority, irrespective of the exact amount of service rendered to the taxpayer in return*'. My father wrote:

> In our current society we need taxes, so we must find the 'least bad tax'. Taxes on enterprise and saving are surely the most bad taxes (to coin a phrase), so it makes sense to follow the arguments of Henry George and scrap these taxes, replacing them with a tax on the rental value of land. The potential of land value taxation to simplify the system is evident, and if this were appreciated, it could lay a solid foundation for a return to economic health.

In it he draws the distinction between the 'private value' of land due to its development and the 'public value' due to externalities such as a community or infrastructure. A Land Usage Charge is raised on the 'public value' of land and is therefore not a tax, as defined by Dalton, but the price for benefits enjoyed – a price fixed by the market, more akin to ground rent.

The reason housing has become so unaffordable is not because of the increase in the price of the houses but because of the increase in the value of the land. One way to make housing more affordable for the lower income groups is for public authorities to make available unused land it owns for developers to build housing for sale or rent, as well as shared ownership. The public authorities or indeed housing associations could retain ownership of the land, leaving developers to make a margin on the building houses. The Land Usage Charge would not be payable by the residents as they do not own the land and so are not liable for property taxes. Such properties would be of less interest to speculative landlords as they would not benefit from rising values.

As an annual charge on the rental value of the land, the LUC would not be a tax on transactions and therefore not impede development. Not only would this not conflict with government action to provide a much-needed increase in house building, it could actively promote it by providing incentives for local authorities to encourage development. For example, there are currently 700,000 vacant properties and business sites in the UK. At present, they are not contributing anything to the economy: in fact they are a drag on it. However, introducing LUC would be a massive incentive for the owners to make these sites fit to live in or fit for business development, if levied regardless of the use or development on it. That is because a vacant site would still incur an annual charge. This is a simple way to raise potentially billions of new revenue and regenerate poor communities. In addition, it would promote more sustainable patterns of development by encouraging businesses (especially those who do not need to be near market but near labour and resources) to locate to less prosperous regions, as the market value of land would be lower. So if each of these vacant properties raised an average of say £10,000 under the LUC plan assuming a mix of residential and commercial property, then that would bring in an additional £7 billion per year for infrastructure projects that will in turn further increase contributions. Altoona, a city in Pennsylvania of 46,000 people, has fully implemented Land Value Tax and raised over a $1million from vacant sites where it previously only collected a $122,000. And residents benefitted too as 73% of households pay less under LVT system than they did before.

A Land Usage Charge also has the benefit of capturing the increases in private wealth that accrue through public investment. As an annual fixed rate, revenues would rise as the land's market value (and so tax base) increases. In theory, therefore, it could provide an automatic revenue stream to help fund infrastructure projects. For almost two centuries, economists on the left and right have regarded LVT as the best of all possible taxes with almost magical powers of equity and efficiency. It was conservative hero Milton Friedman's favourite tax yet promoted just as often by the left. The LUC has the advantage that you cannot move land so you cannot dodge the tax. It also creates a powerful incentive to use land to the full, thus boosting the supply of houses whereas the existing property tax regime encourages blight and either depopulation or overcrowding. Because nobody makes land (other than by reclaiming it from the sea) there are unique results when you tax it. LUC is the only 'tax' that does not distort economic activity at all. If you tax wages, you push up the price of employment as it is the employer who pays the Income Tax; if you tax capital there is less to invest, but if you tax land values, you do not diminish the amount of land available. There is a new resonance for a a tax based on land values as house prices soar in big cities creating much of the wealth documented by Thomas Piketty and others.

According to the Coalition for Economic Justice, a Land Value Tax in the UK could raise between £30-35 billion per year based on the current value of land, which accounts for 38% of the wealth, if levied at a flat rate of between 0.5% and 0.6%. They suggest that that is enough to replace the Council Tax while also giving a tax cut to all those living in properties worth less than £350,000-£400,000. At a seminar, sponsored by the Network for Social Change, held at the London headquarters of Royal Institution of Chartered Surveyors (RICS) in London 15th September 2014, economic analysis was presented suggesting that a single annual tax based on land values would be capable of producing potential revenue flows of £82 billion, sufficient to replace all existing property taxes. The meeting concluded that the technical issues often quoted as providing reasons not to switch to assessing land rather than property, namely valuation methodology and data, are not a major stumbling block to implementation in the UK context.

It could be expected that a much higher percentage of public revenue would come from the LUC source, given the average house price in the UK in 2014 was £272,000, so a charge of 2.5% of the land value might be appropriate. While some homeowners may be paying more than under the existing system, most will be paying less in income related taxes. This increases the choice of how personal incomes are spent. Given there are about 25 million homes in UK, then the LUC could raise over £100 billion from residential land (even when the charge is only levied on the public value of land) and even more when including commercial land. In order to implement this system there may need to be some transitional relief to cater for the small number of cases where people either have no earned income, retirees or are on low income but live in comparatively expensive properties. In these cases the contribution would be deferred until the property is sold.

Whether you agree with the above proposal or not, it is beyond doubt that reform of property taxes is long overdue and the valuations are extremely out of date. It is heavily weighted against the poor and the 'squeezed middle'. In the UK, the eight bands of Council Tax lead to the absurdity of people living in properties worth half the national average (around £112,000) paying half the tax of someone owning property worth £1 million or more. Like VAT rises, the Council Tax hits the poorest hardest.

According to the Office of National Statistics, the poorest fifth of households pay 5% of their household income in Council Tax. The middle fifth pay 3% and the richest fifth pay less than 1%.

According to Bloomberg, with a discount for second-home status, the Sultan of Brunei who controls a fortune worth £40 billion paid £1,942 a year in Council Tax for his mansion house in Kensington Place Gardens in London in 2012: just £32 a month more than the Council Tax paid by the Braithwaites, a pensioner couple living with their daughter and grandchildren in a rented home in Golborne Road in the same borough of Kensington and Chelsea, less than two miles away. The Council Tax also hurts those who rent or are living in part-owned social housing. They are paying tax according to the value of a property that they may not have been able to afford to buy or even rent at market rate.

The Land Usage Charge would allow the abolition of another regressive tax: Stamp Duty Land Tax. This is another example of a misnamed tax, for it is not strictly speaking a land tax but a transaction tax that is levied on the purchase of property. The valuation for tax purposes includes both the land and any buildings, and applies to both domestic and business premises. As a transaction tax it makes it more expensive to purchase new premises or to move to a new job, downsizing or moving up to meet changing family circumstances is also inhibited putting a further drag on economic activity. The LUC does not have this effect.

Henry George's theories seem to have gained more traction in the UK than in the USA where they have been pilloried for almost a century and a half. Attempts to introduce a Land Value Tax began in the UK with the Liberal Lloyd George's People's Budget in 1909. Among those campaigning enthusiastically for the tax was Winston Churchill who pointed out that

> roads are made, streets are made, services are improved, electric light turns night into day, water is brought from a hundred miles off in the mountains – and all the while the landlord sits still. Every one of those improvements is affected by the labour and cost of other people and the taxpayers…

It ran into opposition from the landed aristocracy in the House of Lords prompting a constitutional crisis, but its eventual failure had more to do with the complexity of the scheme devised for valuing land. This meant it lapsed because it had not been implemented by the time the First World arrived. A further attempt in 1931 was scuppered when Labour's Ramsay MacDonald had to abandon it to form the National Government with the Conservatives to deal with the severe economic crisis. In 2004, Martin

Wolf set out the benefits of a tax on land values in *The Financial Times*: it offers a tax base that cannot run away, unlike capital or labour; it encourages desired development; it imposes the greatest cost of holding undeveloped land where prices, and so values in alternative uses, are highest; it captures for the public purse a part of the benefits accruing to landowners from investments in infrastructure and other amenities by the public sector.

Today there is support for a 'tax' based on the value of land not only amongst the Greens but also within the Conservative, Labour, Liberal Democrats, raising the prospect that a new campaign could create a broad front, although it will not be an easily won fight. As the Green Party's Caroline Lucas observed on the second reading of her bill to introduce LVT in Parliament:

> A Land Value Tax could be a fair and progressive way to encourage both the creation of more homes, and a more efficient and sustainable use of land by making it unprofitable to sit on unused land. Over a period of time, it could help to stabilise the property market and tackle the boom-and-bust factor that contributed towards the 2008 financial crisis – discouraging disproportionate amounts of capital from being tied up in property and excessive accumulation of debt.

Unfortunately, despite increasing support for the idea amongst economists and politicians, no government has yet been willing to look seriously into the possibilities of introducing a tax based on land values. In my view this lack of initiative is because it is too much like hard work, it is too bold and it could require higher payments by the political elite.

Yet, in 2012 Conservative MP Nick Bowles, the founder of the Policy Exchange think tank, delivered the Tory Reform Group's annual Macmillan Lecture, which included a call for a 'Land Value Tax' to fund cuts in National Insurance contributions. The TRG's website added a call for LVT to replace Council Tax, Business Rates, Stamp Duty Land Tax, planning charges and Landfill Tax, saying:

> if these taxes were to remain then LVT would be burdening people with further unwelcome costs. Instead, LVT should replace those property taxes – either entirely or at the very least mostly. It would still raise sufficient revenue if pitched at the correct rate and included main homes, with exemptions for farmland, national parks, charities and pensioners' main homes. The fact that LVT would also apply to land which at the moment is not taxed at all goes to show how it would raise more revenue than the current property taxes that place a heavy burden on ordinary homeowners.

The Tory Reform Group also argued that LVT would be simple to implement *'since land cannot be hidden in an offshore tax haven and calculating the tax bill would be made easier by the fact that land values are already measured by the market, therefore compliance costs could be reduced'*. LVT would boost productivity and discourage urban sprawl:

> LVT would also be a new 'eco-tax' that discourages construction on expensive 'greenfield' areas in favour of cheaper 'brownfield sites', so limiting urban sprawl. This brings the consequent benefits of reduced commuting distances and less costly road works, which contribute to CO2 emissions and atmospheric pollution.

Labour MP and leadership contender, Andy Burnham who called a Land Value Tax *'an idea so old-Labour it can be traced back to Thomas Paine'* (an English-American political theorist and one of the founding fathers of the United States). In an article on 2010 canvassing for his leadership of the party he wrote, *'the LVT, an annual tax on the market rental value of land, would allow for the abolition of stamp duty – a tax on the aspirations of young people to put down roots and get on in life.'*

The Liberal Democrat Land Value Tax advocacy group Action for Land Taxation and Economic Reform (ALTER) argues that a Land Value Tax would make house-builders produce more and better quality housing rather than seeking to profit from speculative land value appreciation. Vince Cable, the former Liberal Democrat Business Secretary in the coalition government supported the idea at his party's annual conference in 2010 saying:

> It will be said that in a world of internationally mobile capital and people it is counterproductive to tax personal income and corporate profit to uncompetitive levels. That is right. But a progressive alternative is to shift the tax base to property, and land, which cannot run away and represents in Britain an extreme concentration of wealth.

As Robin Harding wrote in a full page article on Land Value Taxation in *The Financial Times* on 25 September 2014:

> To its advocates Land Value Tax has almost magical powers of equity and efficiency enough to revolutionise the world's property markets. After 200 years, though the beautiful idea of land value tax maybe near its moment.

Even the much praised Mirrlees Review of the UK tax system published in 2011, argued that *'the economic case for taxing land itself is very strong'*:

Taxing land ownership is equivalent to taxing an economic rent – to do so does not discourage any desirable activity. Land is not a produced input; its supply is fixed and cannot be affected by the introduction of a tax. With the same amount of land available, people would not be willing to pay any more for it than before, so (the present value of) a land value tax (LVT) would be reflected one-for-one in a lower price of land: the classic example of tax capitalization. Owners of land on the day such a tax is announced would suffer a windfall loss as the value of their asset was reduced. But this windfall loss is the only effect of the tax: the incentive to buy, develop, or use land would not change. Economic activity that was previously worthwhile remains worthwhile. Moreover, a tax on land value would also capture the benefits accruing to landowners from external developments rather than their own efforts.

As one of the key benefits of a Land Value Tax, is that it brings a return on all public investment, it minimises much public expenditure which currently ends up as private profit. For example, in London the presence of a good state school can add up to £50,000 to the value of surrounding property; the extension of the Jubilee Line to Canary Wharf, paid for by the taxpayer, increased total property prices around the new underground stations by billions. With LUC this would change: The increase in property prices would automatically be reflected at the next annual valuation as higher LUC, so that government would reap the benefit of its investment through increased revenue, making improved public services and infrastructure self-financing. This positive feedback applies to any publicly funded facilities like schools, hospitals and recreation facilities such as parks, libraries and community centres. This investment then encourages private investment in retail outlets, entertainment facilities and so on. Managed well, this can transform an area without leaving the taxpayer with a burden of debt. In most countries including the USA and UK, the property taxes are collected by the local government authorities and mostly spent locally. With LUC this principle would remain, so it could be expected that there would be an increase in local revenue, particularly if an enlightened authority focused on constructing facilities that improved the quality of life for local residents, thereby automatically increasing their revenue. This is a win-win situation.

The application of the Land Usage Charge is highly practical in the USA and there are current examples referred to earlier. Due to the three different levels of government and the complicated tax code it is difficult to analyse comparable data to make an outline financial assessment. I do know that in northern California the property taxes are considerably higher than the UK for similar specification properties and locations. They are also based on out of date valuations and hampered by the 1978 Proposition 13, which limits property taxes and annual increases.

Summary

The implementation of Land Usage Charge would make a considerable impact on reducing inequality, as the amount of charge paid is directly related to the value received and ability to pay. By discouraging the holding of land out of use, it could bring a huge and much needed increase in supply of housing which would improve affordability, reducing costs for lower income groups and first-time buyers. Housing is a basic human need and must be affordable for all. Business would then also be paying a fair cost for the use of land it occupies and on which it creates wealth.

Summary of Chapter 3

The main proposal is to shift the tax base from income to wealth, as well as to capture the increased public value of land. These proposals would contribute significantly to social justice and a sense of fairness. It fits well with the principle of '*income for me/wealth for we*' which provides us with a code of compassion that could run through the heart of society. Disposable income would increase for the majority, breaking the chains of economic slavery and releasing so many into a world of economic freedom and choices. Demand would expand to satisfy the increased spending power. Additional funds over and above current government revenue would be generated and invested in infrastructure, education and health to the benefit of us all, not just hoarded by the few.

These proposals not only have a revenue neutral effect on government income but would in fact raise more funds without any negative impact on the economy and hardship for anyone. The additional funds will allow more cash available for investment, increasing growth and opportunity both on personal as well as enterprise level. Pressure on the welfare budget would be reduced as more people retained more of their earnings in their pockets rather than having to rely on welfare. Less regulation would be required, the current tax codes would be significantly simplified to be more robust and not need constant revision to plug loopholes.

CHAPTER 4

Socially Responsible
Capitalism

**The second major step towards prosperity is the
reform of our economic system so that it reflects and
rewards the contribution made by all the stakeholders
in the creation of wealth, not just the shareholders**

Having outlined how hardship can be reduced and economic
opportunity can be significantly improved for the lower paid individuals and families, that make up the majority of the population, I would
like to turn to the engine of growth and wealth creation, the capitalist
system. The age of the profit motive being the only driving force in the
path to prosperity is over. Being socially responsible does not damage
profits; it enhances them, but ensures the profits are not excessive at the
expense of the stakeholders, so that the rewards are shared by stakeholders not just shareholders.

To build a more appealing and beneficial capitalist system for the 21st
century, the same principle should be applied to enterprises as I propose
is applied to individuals – *'income for me/wealth for we'*. To achieve this,
corporations need to be encouraged to be more socially responsible, not
by regulation but by incentives and the demands of consumers. At the
same time, companies would contribute a fair share of the wealth created
to the public purse for the benefit of all stakeholders, not just shareholders.
At the same time the ever-expanding number of market-distorting
taxes would be minimised to allow socially responsible corporations to

maximise profits. When I talk about social responsibility, I am not talking about philanthropy, making donations, helping the community or producing glossy reports, though these actions are valid. I am talking about being responsible to society, about being a 'good' business, paying living wages, respecting part-timers with family friendly schedules (in fact respecting all workers as humans, not cogs in a machine), not paying chiefs hundreds times more than the lowest paid, not polluting, providing employee share and performance schemes, training, no big political donations, investing wisely in the company and community, not paying excessive dividends to uninvolved shareholders, rewarding all stake-holders; the list could go on.

Capitalism as we know it, is not working the way it should. It has served the purpose of creating considerable wealth, but unfortunately this has benefitted the few. For most people all they get from capitalism is a job and an income which in many cases is not enough to fund a purposeful life. Capitalism has become dysfunctional; it has created huge inequalities and maintained a high level of poverty while bringing significant rewards to those in control. We have a choice: continue trying to correct it with more cosmetic regulations or make some critical structural changes to bring capitalism up to date.

Capital enables us to produce goods and services efficiently, put simply, it pays for the machines, the resources and the workplace. When put together with labour, we have a system for creating goods, which can be sold for a profit that is over and above what was paid for the labour and the capital. In this way a business creates wealth (extra money that can be put aside for further investment or sharing among stakeholders) and value reflected in the price a business could be sold for.

On the face of it, capitalism works well, but what happens is that this profit or value goes to an exclusive few, the owners of the shares in the business. While shareholders finance the capital required, there are others who helped create that wealth and value with their work. So once you have wealth, you are able to provide or lend the capital required for an enterprise, then in return you receive interest on the loan, a dividend from the profits and the potential to increase your wealth as the value of the enterprise increases. At the same time there is a risk that the value of your investment can not only go up but also down and disappear altogether. It is this element of risk that is often put forward by entrepreneurs and shareholders as the justification of potential significant returns.

Wealth accumulates wealth but if you have none in the first place you cannot join the game. Shareholders are not the only ones taking risks. The workers in a business also take risks but they only receive their salary. There are more stakeholders than shareholders, and therein lies a major cause of inequality.

Big business is not looking after the stakeholders. I am very pro-business, having founded and developed seven businesses and worked as an adviser to companies large and small, such as Acer, Autodesk, British Telecom, Fujitsu, Dell, Novell, Regus and Sage, as well as to governments, including the Republic of Ireland and the State of California. I know the struggle involved in setting up and running a small business: the focus on sales, hassles with finding and retaining good staff, balancing the books and – if you are smart – making a profit. The lesson I have learnt is that we don't want to make it tougher for small businesses by taking a percentage of their profits as public revenue before they grow and can afford it. I am, however, saying to larger businesses that they have a responsibility to the community and nation. As Paul Getty reminds us in the last of his 10 golden rules:

> No matter how many millions an individual amasses, if he is in business he must always consider his wealth as a means of improving living conditions everywhere. He must remember that he has responsibilities toward his associates, employees, stockholders – and the public.

This is a message I make no apologies for repeating.

We now live in a multi-stakeholder society. Businesses need to make a profit to survive, but they also have a responsibility to stakeholders such as employees, customers, partners, and indeed the community as a whole. Corporate social responsibility also covers many aspects of a business such as its environmental impact and the training it provides. The growing wealth gap is evidence that the shareholder-takes-all model of capitalism, in which social responsibilities are sacrificed for profit, is failing. In the same way that a free market requires competition but tends towards monopoly unless regulated through, for example, anti-trust legislation, capitalism in a multi-stakeholder society requires that the benefits of growth and development be shared widely, not concentrated into the hands of a few.

But while our current system rewards employees with a wage, the senior team is more likely to be rewarded with a salary plus bonus, and shareholders with dividends. Building a business takes the entrepreneur's adrenalin, sweat and tears, if not usually their blood, but once a business has reached a critical mass, it is time to acknowledge and reward the contributions made by other stakeholders.

In May 2014, Mark Carney, governor of the Bank of England, speaking in London at a conference entitled 'Inclusive Capitalism', warned of a breakdown in the social contract that should be at the heart of capitalism: *'Prosperity requires not just investment in economic capital but in social capital.'* Christine Lagarde, head of The International Monetary Fund went further, noting that the world's richest 85 people could fit into one London bus and that their wealth is equivalent to that owned by the world's poorest half, all 3.5 billion of them. Warning that rising inequality is a barrier to growth and could undermine democracy and human rights, she said: *'One of the leading economic stories of our time is rising income inequality and the dark shadow it casts across the global economy.'*

Let's get a few things straight: It is OK to own property; it is OK to make a profit; it is OK to build personal wealth; it is not OK to monopolise wealth, nor is it OK for tax payers to subsidise exploitative employment practices and low pay. The wealth gap and 'corporate welfare' are bad for business, bad for society and bad for democracy.

While companies need to benefit stakeholders and not just shareholders, they also need to generate sufficient income and to invest for future growth. To do this they have to pass on costs, including tax. If a tax is too high, either the customer or the business has to pay the price. When it is the former, it pushes up prices and increases the risk of going out of business; when it is the latter, it is usually the least well-rewarded and least influential members of the company who are at risk of losing their jobs. One of the most anomalous and burdensome taxes is the tax on employment in the form of payroll taxes which push up the cost of jobs for firms. This is particularly burdensome for small companies which also face taxes on profits that both restricts the funds available for investment and their ability to borrow. The Land Usage Charge (LUC) described in more detail elsewhere does not have this damaging effect because it is not a tax.

The principle of *'income for me/wealth for we'* provides a sustainable and equitable basis for capitalism in the 21st century. Companies could retain more of their income but have the responsibility to share more of their profit with multiple stakeholders, not just the shareholders. It forms the code for socially responsible capitalism, which is inclusive and works for the majority, not just the few. It would not require excessive amounts of regulation if more taxes over time were replaced with an increased rate of LUC. This would in fact significantly simplify the current tax codes and could bring benefits to all in a short time frame. By reducing the taxes that are costs to companies, margins would increase and so would profits. Companies that demonstrate good social responsibility would pay less tax. It would also mean that the taxpayer would be picking up less of the bill for low pay and we would not simply be transferring taxpayers' subsidies from bad pay to other bad practices. Just as I am recommending that lower income earners do not pay Income Tax so that they can participate in the wealth economy, the same goes with companies: the smaller ones should not be contributing to pubic revenue until they are strong and sustainable. Being a socially responsible company is very much part of the code of comprehensive capitalism, so companies that contribute measurably and materially to the wellbeing of their stakeholders need contribute less to government coffers.

To create socially responsible capitalism for the 21st century there are three key areas for action. Firstly, the establishment of a living wage as the baseline for employment. This will give a huge number of people a boost they deserve. It will also stop the crazy 'corporate welfare' where companies pay below the living wage, yet make good profits, while taxpayers top up the wages with welfare benefits, hence boosting corporate profits at taxpayers' expense. Secondly, use 'social offsetting' to ensure companies contribute fairly to public revenue from the wealth they create. Also minimise payroll taxes and other out-dated direct taxes which push up company costs, putting pressure on wages and profits. Thirdly, to work together to ensure all dues, where they are due, are paid, both nationally and internationally. Let's now look as these points in more detail.

4.1 Fair pay all the way

Work is the surest way out of poverty. But there is an increase in the working poor, those employed, full time or part time, but still below the poverty threshold. This problem could be minimised if all businesses paid the agreed living wage. This would not only benefit the individuals and their families but the economy as a whole by increasing demand and jobs growth. No one on a living wage should have any income-related taxes taken from him or her: it puts them back into poverty.

The Living Wage Foundation, a London based charity, gives many examples. Among them, Zina who works for CTS Cleaning Solutions Ltd, a family-run cleaning business that offers services from window cleaning to commercial office cleaning and building maintenance. As she says: *'The Living Wage is important. Before I worked here, I was always trying to make ends meet working several jobs. It was stressful and I took it out on my family, always cross with no time to talk.'* Peter Cooke the managing director of CTS explains: *'I grew up in a family that was impacted by poor pay and conditions, and vowed that I would always respect and value my employees: the Living Wage embodies that belief.'*

'No business which depends for its existence on paying less than living wages to its workers has any right to continue in this country.' So said US President Franklin D. Roosevelt in 1933 and yet in 2014 some 3.3 million US workers were paid the federal minimum wage of $7.25 an hour ($15,080 a year) or less. The minimum is a misnomer, a euphemism, a sop. The US Census Bureau reckoned in 2012 that the poverty threshold for a single wage is a poverty wage for many with dependents. To their shame, eight states either have no minimum or set theirs even lower and attempts in 2014 to raise the federal rate to $10.10 over two years were thwarted by Republican opposition in both houses of Congress.

It would be good to think that more companies are becoming more enlightened. In January 2015, Mark Bertolini, CEO of managed healthcare company, Aetna, announced that the company's lowest-paid workers would get a substantial raise – from $12 to $16 an hour, in some cases – as well as improved medical coverage. Bertolini said that it was not 'fair' for employees of a Fortune 500 company to be struggling to make ends meet. He explicitly linked the decision to the broader debate about inequality, mentioning that he had given copies of Thomas Piketty's *Capital in the Twenty-first Century* to all his top executives. In an interview with *The New Yorker*, he said: *'Companies are not just money-making machines. For the good of the social order, these are the kinds of investments we should be willing to make.'* Aetna has revenues of around $50 billion and employs nearly 50,000 people.

The arguments against raising the minimum wage are mainly that it would cause unemployment. *Forbes* magazine has argued this point, saying *'the best result we have from the academic literature is that a minimum wage in the 40-45 per cent region of the median wage has little to no effect on unemployment,'* but above that figure jobs are lost or unpaid benefits such as free parking are withdrawn.

Another comment made to me is that some jobs are not worth the living wage or indeed minimum wage, as it will make a business model uneconomic. If that is the case they should not be in business or should get creative and redesign their business model. Having run a business, I know you have to adjust your business model for the going rate for the role you want to fill. In my case it was professional marketing services, so we did not have people on minimum wage. In fact it was more the other way: the industry salary levels were high but we knew we had to pay that or more if we were to get good highly motivated and successful team members, so we had to ensure our business model delivered the margins to make the business worthwhile. It is the same at the lower end of earners: it is worth paying these people well, which means a living wage. The going rate for the minimum wage should be the living wage. That's it, make it work. Clearly, in companies which employ a large number of low paid staff, such as in retail and hospitality, the wage bill is higher, but I do not accept that they cannot build a working business model around a living wage. With much larger established businesses, the argument is used that it will reduce profits. Well, if that is the case, fine: the business is less profitable. If it takes it into a loss, then you need to rethink the plan. But the living wage is the baseline, there is no excuse for not paying a living wage, yet we still allow such exploitation. Excessive profits means the company has funds to pay decent wages, not just money for expansion and investment and to pay shareholder dividends. Moreover, my proposal to replace the revenue lost by raising the Income Tax threshold with a Land Usage Charge will make this easier for labour intensive industries.

In June 2015, IKEA USA announced a further major minimum wage hike bringing the average store's starting pay to nearly $12 per hour. The starting wage for any given store reflects the living cost in a particular area determined by the MIT Living Wage Calculator, which takes into account the local cost of rent, food, transportation and the like. Six months after introducing the raises, IKEA announced that it was on track to reduce staff turnover by 5% and was attracting more qualified job seekers to work at its stores. In July 2015 IKEA promised to pay its UK workforce the 'living wage', UK employees will receive £7.85 ($12.22) per hour, or £9.15 per hour in London, from April 2016. This compares with a national minimum wage of £6.70 per hour from October 2015. According to IKEA, more than 50% of its 9,000 workers in the country will see their wages lifted. The company joins around 1,600 other businesses in opting to pay the living wage, which is set by the Living Wage Foundation and is calculated according to the cost of living.

The recent raises implemented by retailers like Gap and Walmart are a response to calls for higher wages for the working poor, particularly due to the success of organisations like the 'Fight for $15' movement. They are also calculated business decisions, made in an improving labour market. As the economy recovers and unemployment falls, retailers have to compete to attract talent in a way they didn't need to during the recession and sluggish recovery.

The Office of the Chief Actuary calculated in 2013 that the average wage was $43,041 and the median wage was $28,031 a year. By *Forbes*'s estimate anything over $12,613 a year puts people out of work. The Economic Policy Institute disagrees. In October 2014, it calculated that if the minimum wage was raised to $10.10 per hour, 1.7 million Americans would no longer rely on public assistance and the projected rise in consumer spending would provide a net increase in GDP of $22.1 billion, creating roughly 85,000 new jobs. Alaska, Arkansas, Nebraska and South Dakota all voted in minimum wages that were higher than $7.25 an hour in 2014 and Seattle City Council voted unanimously to give businesses there with 500 employees or more three years to introduce a minimum of $15 an hour. A number of large local employers have attempted to have themselves reclassified as small enterprises to delay having to pay decent wages, but Seattle Mayor Ed Murray's efforts to '*make Seattle affordable to everyone*' was helped by his forming a broad-based Income Inequality Advisory Committee that included a mix of businesses, unions, and non-profit organisations.

The first state minimum wage was introduced in 1912 in Massachusetts. It was non-binding and only applied to women and children. The UK had to wait until 1998 for its first National Minimum Wage Act, which was opposed by the Conservatives and the Confederation of British Industries. It did not result in the forecast job losses. While the UK now has a compulsory minimum wage of £6.50 per hour, the obligation to pay a living wage is not enshrined in law. In 2014 the Living Wage Foundation proposed that it should be raised to £7.85, 21% more than the National Minimum Wage. The Greater London Assembly sets the rate in London. It has risen from £8.80 an hour to £9.15, but accounting firm KPMG – a supporter of the living wage – found that 22% of the working population earn less than the 2013 level Living Wage of £7.65 an hour. It said more than five million people were paid below that rate, and that women were more likely to earn less than men. The Resolution Foundation think tank reckoned that 4.8 million UK workers earned less than the living wage, equivalent to one in five employees and up from 3.4 million in 2009. One explanation could be that employers no longer fear the minimum wage, but actually welcome it because it sets a benchmark for 'acceptable' low pay. It legitimises low wages along with other abuses linked to internships and zero hour contracts. The latter, also known as casual contracts, ensure that workers are on call but employers do not have to give them work. In theory workers can turn down the work offered. The reality of 'flexibility' for many is the stress arising from precarious work, financial insecurity and problems with issues such as childcare and transport. Women are particularly badly hit. More than half (54%, according to the Office of National Statistics) of workers on zero hours contracts are female. The Social Mobility and Child Poverty Commission pointed out in October 2014 that women also make up 60% of those earning less than around £8 per hour and as the *New Statesman* commented *'it is frankly quite shocking that, on average – in 21st-century Britain – a woman still earns just 80p for every £1 earned by a man'*.

If low pay has been legitimised, no pay has also been given spurious respectability. In its 2013 annual report, the Low Pay Commission said:

> In recent years the Commission has received a substantial volume of evidence suggesting a growth in the terms 'internship', 'work experience' or 'volunteer' to denote unpaid activities that look like work and to which the National Minimum Wage should apply... We continue to receive evidence of widespread non-payment of the minimum wage for positions that appear to be work. The longer this continues the greater is the risk that extracting work from unpaid interns becomes a 'new normal'.

It was a surprise to many when George Osborne, the Conservative Chancellor of the Exchequer, in his first post coalition budget in July 2015 announced a new national minimum wage of £9 per hour by 2020, annexing the term 'living wage'. While this is too slow and not enough, it is a step in the right direction and put the concept of a living wage firmly on the political agenda. It is particularly ironic as the opposition Labour Party was only proposing a minimum wage of £8 per hour! However while the UK government labelled this the National Living Wage, it is really only a higher minimum wage as it is not based on living requirements. The Living Wage as proposed by the Living Wage Foundation is actually based on basic costs for a basic standard of living.

Wages for the squeezed middle are under constant pressure with little sign of relief. The average couple with two children saw their real income fall by £2,132 a year between 2009-10 and 2012-13 according to the Confederation of British Industries. But in November 2014, CBI director general John Cridland made it clear that it would not back any moves to enforce the Living Wage. *'The National Minimum Wage is about ability to pay,'* he said. *'The Living Wage is what people need to earn. Should companies pay the Living Wage if they are able to? Yes, I would encourage them to. Can it ever be more than an encouragement? No.'* This is particularly interesting as his strong statement comes less than a year before the government announced that a national living wage would be the legal minimum. It shows us how opinion can shift in such a short time if the pressure for change is maintained. Instead the CBI proposed measures that included an increase in the threshold at which employees pay National Insurance to £10,500 to bring it in line with the Income Tax personal allowance.

The right-wing Taxpayers Alliance demanded in 2012 that National Insurance Contributions (NIC) be rebranded as *'Earnings Tax'* to make it clear that *'its true function is overwhelmingly a tax, not an insurance scheme'*. Income Tax represents only 25% of government revenue in the UK but when you add in NIC, 'earnings taxes' rise to 43% of revenue. The CBI is keen on cutting NIC because of the £110 billion gathered each year by Her Majesty's Revenue and Customs (HMRC) about £60 billion comes from employers. Limited companies in the UK have to pay 20% Corporation Tax on profits, Capital Gains Tax on business disposals and Value Added Tax, essentially a sales tax. These are offset with tax allowances and VAT is passed on to the next person or organisation in the value chain, until it reaches the end-consumer. Its imposition is mandated by the European Union but countries have some discretion over the rate and what they levy it on.

Raising the minimum wage to $15 per hour would inject about $450 billion into the US economy each year, according to venture capitalist and reformer Nick Hanauer. It would give more purchasing power to millions of poor and lower middle class Americans and would stimulate buying, production and hiring. By not paying employees a living wage, the tax-payers are picking up the tab and effectively subsidising company profits in what has become known as 'corporate welfare'. An example of hard-pressed taxpayers subsidising Scrooge businesses to pay low wages can be found with Walmart. It employs 825,000 people in the USA who earn less than $25,000 per year, wages that leave many of them and their families below the poverty line. If the recent investment by Walmart in share repurchases of $6.6 billion was redirected toward human capital this could mean a raise of $5.13 per hour for this low wage workforce. The $3 billion spent in dividend payments to the Walmart heirs, who already control more wealth than 40% of Americans combined, would amount to a raise of $2.38 per hour for Walmart's 825,000 low-wage workers. Americans for Tax Fairness used a 2013 study by the US Committee on Education and the Workforce to show that Walmart's low wage policy costs US taxpayers an estimated $6.2 billion in public assistance including food stamps, Medicaid and subsidised housing. To pour salt on the wounds, the same company that brings in the most food stamp dollars in revenue almost certainly has the most employees using food stamps. Walmart is not alone. In 2014 *Forbes* reported that '*other large retail chains have been the focus of similar reports in recent months*'. The American fast food industry 'outsourced' a combined $7 billion in annual labour costs to taxpayers. McDonald's alone accounted for $1.2 billion of that outlay. Yum Brands came in at a distant number two, with its Pizza Hut, Taco Bell and KFC subsidiaries costing $648 million in benefit programs for workers each year. Perhaps the most effective way to achieve an end to 'corporate welfare', as this abuse is known, would be use the tax system to reward decent payers.

British clothing retailer Next once explained that the reason it paid low wages was that it had 30 applicants for every job. Next posted a 12.5% rise in profits in 2015 to £798 million. It pays its 48,417 staff an average of £11,000 per year. It says its rate of £6.70 per hour is above the legal minimum wage of £6.50 per hour. However the recommended living wage is now set at 7.85 per hour (17% more) and £9.15 in London. So Next could afford to pay all its lower paid workers the living wage. This would only reduce the profits by about 11%, injecting about £90 million into the economy instead of adding even more to the wealth pile of the share-holders. Plus many of these lower paid workers are also receiving welfare benefits and consuming taxpayers' funds (UK taxpayers pay £30 billion in welfare to low paid workers, that's one third of the total welfare benefits paid, excluding state pensions). So effectively the lower paid who pay taxes on income and consumption are subsidising the richer in the form of increased shareholder value and dividends – shouldn't that be the other way round? So urgent action on the adoption of a true living wage would bring tremendous benefit to five million people earning below the living wage, without hurting anyone.

It is not just about fair pay for lower earners; it is also about fair pay for the high earners as the exorbitantly high pay of the top earners has grown disproportionately in recent years. Excessively high pay for big business leaders is the biggest threat to public trust in business, according to a survey of members of the Institute of Directors carried out on behalf of the High Pay Centre, an independent non-party think tank established to monitor pay at the top of the income distribution and set out a road map towards better business and economic success.

Simon Walker, Director General of the Institute of Directors said:

> Performance-related pay can be a key driver of success. Companies of all sizes have policies that reward individual contributions through mechanisms such as commission and bonuses. When it comes to senior executives there are higher standards, and rightly so. Pay must be sufficiently long-term to encourage them to plan five, 10 or 20 years ahead. However, in some corners of corporate Britain pay for top executives has become so divided from performance that it cannot be justified. Runaway pay packages, golden hellos, and inflammatory bonuses are running the reputation of business into the ground. Large companies need to look closely at the role excessive pay is playing in fuelling an anti-business backlash from the public and some politicians.

Summary

So the first step towards socially responsible capitalism is to ensure fair pay throughout the pay scale. Paying below the minimum wage or discriminating on sex, ethnicity or any other contradiction of human rights is just not on. It is the same at the top end, good pay for good work, great performance, long hours and significant responsibility is fine but excessive pay is just as socially irresponsible as not paying a living wage. So there needs to be a realignment of how we calculate pay, starting at the bottom end first as that is very urgent. A capitalist system that embraces all must ensure fair pay, all the way.

4.2 Profits for people

It is the people within a company who create wealth through their diligence and hard work so as such it seems fair that they as key stakeholders should have a share of the wealth they help create. Widening share ownership to include employees' schemes is one way to achieve this. However, the stakeholders in any enterprise are more than the shareholders and the staff. An effective way to ensure stakeholder reward is for the company to make a contribution to community from the wealth created and this can be realised through the tax process. While a tax on profits is the basis of the current system, it needs considerable refinement in order to operate in an equitable way and to ensure that enterprises honour their commitment to the well-being of society and are socially responsible. Currently there are many taxes that increase a company's costs and reduce wealth creating capabilities, so they need to be reviewed and minimised.

Entrepreneurs can bring tremendous value to society, identifying demand and starting a business to meet that need, going on to provide jobs and livelihoods. Indeed the entrepreneurs take financial risks both with their own and often other people's money. I know, I have started businesses from nothing, just an idea and went on to employ hundreds of people and make a difference to many customers. It is also very gratifying that some of these businesses are still going, even though I have nothing to do with them any more. But entrepreneurs cannot keep all the rewards for themselves, it is a team effort.

India's largest company Tata, which owns Tetley Tea and Jaguar Land Rover, prides itself on its ethics: 66% of the business is owned by charities. Its unique character was shaped by the passion of its founder Jamsetji Tata and his successors. From the outset, and before such things were legally required anywhere in the world, the Tatas showed commitment to labour welfare introducing pensions (1877), the eight-hour working day (1912) and maternity benefits (1921) for their employees. It was Jamsetji's belief that business is sustainable only when it serves a larger purpose in society. *'In a free enterprise the community is not just another stakeholder to business, but is in fact the very purpose of its existence.'*

A tax on corporate wealth seems entirely justified as it returns benefits to the community and it is the basis behind our current system. However we can do more to minimise greed, and maximises success for the benefit of all. I propose a scheme whereby Corporation Tax or corporate Income Tax becomes a Corporate Social Contribution (CSC) where companies make a contribution to government funds based on their corporate wealth (measured by profits and value) but where social responsibility is encouraged through 'social offsetting'.

The taxes due can be reduced or offset according to a clear code of proven social responsibility compliance undertaken by the company. This would improve the lot of the real wealth-creators, it would also encourage companies to fulfil their responsibilities to society. Their stakeholders include not only investors, lenders, employees, suppliers and customers, but also the community, including government, which makes it possible to do business by supplying infrastructure, maintaining law and order, providing education and health services.

The wealth gap is evidence that the current system is flawed, out of date and fails to meet the needs of a multi-stakeholder society. So I am proposing that companies make a corporate contribution to the public services and infrastructure that is vital for them to thrive. This does not mean taking from a company what rightfully belongs to it, nor does it overlook the need to acknowledge and applaud companies that are already socially responsible but, in essence, the aim is to harness enlightened self-interest: doing well by doing good.

The main method of raising government public revenue from business will continue to be based on profits. The road to profitability can be a long one and there is no point in choking off a company that is slowly building a new market, but once it is making a profit, the next decision is how that profit should be used. It could just go to shareholders; it might be used to build savings or go into research and development, or it might fund new equipment or expansion. All and any of these are perfectly legitimate but it should also be used compensate stakeholders. Short-termism is generally bad; it fosters exploitative employment practices and rewards rapacious speculation, and is directly at odds with the concept of '*income for me/wealth for we*'. By cutting payroll tax, introducing a Land Usage Charge, which both acknowledges the social contribution to existing site values and also captures the uplift in site values from new infrastructure improvements, making them self-funding, and using mechanisms such as 'social offsetting', we would aim to create the conditions for profitability and corporate social responsibility.

Wherever possible, covering the social and environment costs of doing business should be achieved through financial incentives rather than greater regulation. Some taxes are levied to improve or compensate for carbon emissions or waste and these are sometime linked to mechanisms such as carbon offsetting. Thus we already link tax and corporate social behaviour but we could go further using 'social offsetting' to help close the wealth gap.

Instead of perpetuating payroll taxes and corporate welfare such as the government topping up poor wages, a charge on company profits could be used to rebalance employment and compensation practices. For example: by linking their contribution to the proportion of employees on low or minimum wage; the greater the number on low wages, the higher the tax charged, and vice versa. Since the money would have to be spent one way or the other most employers would opt to increase wages rather than pay more tax. This would alter the perception that restricting earnings to the statutory minimum is somehow sanctioned by the state and society. It would improve the lot of many poorly paid workers, helping to narrow the pay and wealth gaps. At no extra cost this would bring money into the economy helping to fuel commerce. And, importantly, it would reduce calls on welfare and in-work benefits paid for through the tax system. The provision of training, child care and other facilities at work could also be rewarded by lower tax, to reflect the resulting benefits and savings to the community.

Similar mechanisms could also be used to counter corporate behaviour that exacerbates the wealth gap, such as making huge bonuses part of a general compensation packages or giving institutional shareholders massive dividends while cutting pay. At its crudest, this could be done by mirroring these payments with an impost: matching bonuses or dividends with an equal amount in tax. For every extra million paid to an executive or shareholder a million would go to the community. Shareholder pressure would then be far more likely to curb the excesses of fat cat directors, who are often in control of their own pay and rewards but also remain answerable to general meetings. If these rises and bonuses were paid anyway, the public would benefit from the 'greed tax'. Deferred equity is often used to avoid paying Income Tax on golden handshakes, golden handcuffs and other gold-plated arrangements typical of the 'heads I win, tails you lose' approach to remuneration that helps concentrate wealth. These shares carry no real risk to the holder because they make no real investment. Shares and options used this way have a face value and would be covered by an asset tax. While any rise in their value would be treated as capital gains, any fall would be an opportunity loss, not a real one.

It should be the aim of us all to encourage corporate social responsibility. Companies will be able to reduce their corporate contribution through 'social offsetting' if they implement socially responsible practices. These would include:

- Diversity in pay levels
- Payment of living wage
- Company shareholding schemes
- Active programmes to reward other stakeholders

- Disproportionate political contributions
- Flexible working options
- Positive practices regarding part-time workers
- Use of renewable energy
- Staff welfare, pensions, birth leave, compassionate leave
- Fair dividend levels/shareholder distribution
- Training programmes
- Childcare facilities/funding
- Retaining profits in countries where it was created
- Signing up to an international fair tax agreement

Basically 'good' companies will contribute less in public revenue as they are making a social contribution which otherwise the government would have to undertake. These 'good' companies are saving the government and taxpayers money by taking on responsibilities themselves and giving their stakeholders, mainly in this case the workforce, more freedom. It would not be too difficult to set these socially responsible standards as there are already many rating companies set up to do just this. This could be the basis for a code for a compassionate capitalist system and set the levels of incentive for the various positive actions a company undertakes.

The proposal to abolish current property taxes and replace them with the Land Usage Charge, whereby a firm's contribution to public revenue would reflect the value of benefits bestowed on the site by society, as revealed in its market price. This could give a company that needs to be near labour and resources rather than its market, the incentive to locate in an area of lower land values and so reduce its costs and maximise its profits. This would encourage regional development, helping to narrow wealth gaps between regions. This would ensure that those requiring higher levels of provision from society would pay more for the privilege.

This would still leave the option open for governments to levy windfall taxes or the so-called Robin Hood Tax on financial transactions proposed by NGOs among others. As we know, for many in the financial sector, particularly those trading and consulting, get their fee whether the market goes up or down, whether their client buys, sells or holds on to shares, bonds or whatever, wins a case or looses it. It would seem right that this sector should make an exceptional contribution to the costs of every taxpayer in funding the bailouts and bank acquisitions necessitated by financiers' widespread greed, arrogance and incompetence. As a result of the financial crisis, the International Monetary Fund (IMF) has calculated UK government debt will be 40% higher. That 40% equates to £737 billion pounds, or £28,000 pounds for every taxpayer in the country. *'Having to pay back that debt means cuts in vital services on which millions of people around the country rely,'* says the Robin Hood Tax campaign website.

> A tiny tax on the financial sector can generate £20 billion annually in the UK alone. That's enough to protect schools and hospitals. Enough to stop massive cuts across the public sector. Enough to build new lives around the world – and to deal with the new climate challenges our world is facing.

At first such a tax may seem an anomaly to the principle of shifting the tax base from income to wealth, but it is more of a levy to encourage social responsibility and compensate for potential further irresponsibility.

While a company's primary goal is to make a profit (or not make a loss!) so it can continue in existence, it also has a social responsibility. In addition it is only right that if the contribution to the community is going to come from profits, then other ways of extracting cash from companies that add to the costs (and minimise profits) should be eliminated, in particular the unpopular payroll taxes that employers have to pay.

Taxes on employment distort the market by putting up the cost of labour and ultimately putting up the cost of products and services or reducing profits. Employee payroll taxes like Social Security and Medicare in USA and National Insurance in the UK, started out as an idea of contributing to welfare but have ended up as Income Tax by another name. It would be far better if companies' contribution were to come from the wealth they form 'below the bottom line', not above it. Removing payroll taxes would mean that companies under the threshold for a tax on profits, or indeed making a loss, for instance during a start-up, will have improved margins and a greater chance of survival. In the UK, the current revenue from Corporation Tax is only around £40 billion. If this were raised by a factor of two to bring in £80 billion, then payroll taxes could be significantly reduced or eliminated for many. This would mean that there would be less pressure for wage rises because employees would retain more of their earned income. Eliminating employer payroll taxes in general would enable companies to maximise profit, which would then also be the primary, or potentially only, source of a firm's contribution to public revenue. A company putting profit into investment would be fine but there would also be adjustments for demonstrable social responsibility through 'social offsetting', and that would determine a company's tax liability. The system would therefore be designed to make tax minimisation counterproductive and it would pay to be transparent.

Summary

'social offsetting' provides a catch-all approach to reduce the worst practices in business instead of a plethora of different laws and regulations. It will encourage the best socially responsible practices with financial incentives. It would also enable companies to be seen to be good employers and attract the best staff, as well as develop a strong reputation in their market, so important for a successful sustainable and profitable business. This proposal reduces the accumulation of wealth by the few and enables more of the wealth created to be used by the community as a whole and by those that help create the wealth in an enterprise, in line with the principle of *'income for me/wealth for we'*.

4.3 Working together

Socially responsible capitalism is a fundamental feature of the prosperity agenda, which will only be achieved through cooperation. We are indeed all in this together and we need to get out of it together. This does not mean abandoning the competitive spirit or discouraging creativity. It means that we have a mutually agreed code of practice by which to do business, so the employees are appreciated, the earth's resources are valued and national sovereignty is respected. It means that new freedoms, which come with improved economic security and opportunity, are matched with more responsibility: a responsibility to each other, as well as mutual respect to ensure that power often related to money is not abused.

In January 2016, the OECD announced that rules to stop companies using complex tax arrangements to avoid paying corporate tax have been agreed by 31 OECD members. These rules will make it harder for firms to hide money in tax havens or play one country's tax authority against another. Firms such as Google, Amazon and Facebook must now pay tax in the country where the profits are made. OECD Secretary-General Angel Gurría said the agreement would have *'an immediate impact in boosting international co-operation on tax issues, by enhancing the transparency of multinational enterprises' operations'*. This announcement was combined with incredulity by France and Members of the European Parliament that the UK government had agreed a unilateral deal with Google to pay

£130million in back taxes over the last decade. What UK Chancellor George Osborne naively called a victory has been seen as a very bad deal and grossly under estimated by others.

At a national level, one of the issues is compliance, ensuring companies do the right thing when making the contribution to government revenue from the wealth created. Taxing corporate profits could be liable to abuse as there are many ways that profits can be massaged, either be minimised (to avoid tax) or indeed maximised (to attract sale). However there are certain processes, ratios and indicators that accountants can use to check whether a company is showing a fair profit for its turnover, capitalisation, industry sector, number of employees etc. With 'social offsetting', it will be even more important for companies to show that they are socially responsible while at the same time minimising their tax liability. This desire will lead to greater transparency by business as a way to enhance reputation. So it will be a medal of honour to be making good profits but having the tax liability reduced through exercising social responsibility. So the system becomes self-regulating and encourages compliance.

Transparency is essential so that profits are not squirrelled away or deliberately minimised through various methods or retained in other countries or worse in a deliberately overt offshore tax haven. The US National Bureau of Economic Research has suggested that roughly 15% of the countries in the world (about 30) are tax havens and that these countries tend to be small and affluent. It is the better governed and regulated countries that are more likely to become tax havens, and are more likely to be successful if they do. These include countries like Switzerland, Luxembourg, Bermuda, Cayman Islands and many more.

Social responsibility is much more than money. The right to form a trade union is part of socially responsible capitalism. The value they bring to management and successful development should be embraced. Some will remember the 1960s and 1970s and the power of the trade unions, holding the country to ransom particularly in the UK with the 'Winter of Discontent' in 1978/9. Those days are long gone, so we could now move forward in a spirit of cooperation not conflict. We should not fear trade unions but join them for our own good and respect their role. For it is with a work force that is valued that companies succeed. People are human, they have rights and are not inanimate objects to be shifted around or manipulated at will. Management is a lot flatter in structure than it used to be and new technology has enabled more transparency. So there should be less excuse for the 'us and them' scenario of yesteryear.

Full social responsibility means companies have to pay the full environmental and anti-social costs of their activities. While this may not immediately put more money in the pocket of the lower earner, it would mean that the taxpayer has less of a bill to pick up and it would not be another example of subsidizing company profits. Of course, some of the environmental costs are not so much about who pays, but more about not doing it in the first place to avoid causing irreversible damage. So the sooner environmental charges are realistic, such as carbon tax, the better. We cannot continue to consume more of the world's finite resources as we are robbing future generations. We really do have to move quickly to renewables. There are plenty of options and are great business opportunities. If solar power can be profitable in cloudy Britain then anything is possible!

At an international level, socially responsible capitalism means mutually beneficial trade agreements and cooperation on tax codes between nations. Nations will have to stop setting themselves up as attractive locations for a company on the basis of a favourable tax regime. I believe it is right that companies should make a contribution to government and the nation from their profits, that is, the wealth that has been created by the stakeholders. It all goes wrong when tax due back to one country is not repatriated. The USA may lay claim to taxes on the profits of USA based corporations operating overseas. However, a large part of the profit has been created outside the USA due to the efforts of workers in other countries, so the wealth created (or part of it) should be shared locally. Companies have to pay the taxes due in the jurisdiction in which they operate; this would be easier to enforce if those taxes were considered fair and transparent. An advantage of the Land Usage Charge in this respect is that it cannot be taken offshore.

It needs international cooperation to make this truly effective and there needs to be consequences in their home jurisdiction if this is not adhered to. It is right that a subsidiary makes a contribution to the main holding company and contributes towards its profits, and most multinational companies have a formula for doing this. Often, though, some of these funds are not paid to the headquarters as there is lower tax in the subsidiary country, or the reverse takes place and a company shifts its profit back to the headquarters so that a lucrative satellite operation appears to be making a loss. This gaming of the system stinks. Some US companies in the UK who are paying little or no Corporation Tax to the UK government argue that they make a significant contribution in other ways: they employ people who pay Income Tax, they sell products that attract VAT, and they generally contribute to economic activity. But the other side to this is that their customers create their wealth. These companies just enable them to do so. Under our revised system of corporate contribution, overseas companies would be proud to make a contribution to the economy and wealth-creation of a host country. It is in everyone's interest to ensure that we cooperate and ensure that all companies pay their contribution, wherever they operate.

The problem occurs when a corporation has its regional or indeed international HQ in countries with very low corporate tax rates like Luxembourg. They are just further exacerbating the inequality problem by building shareholder value at the expense of the workers that created that value. There are many organisations campaigning to put a stop to this malpractice, which is currently legal. The only way to move forward is by international cooperation. This can be helped by the 'social offsetting' concept in the corporate tax regime. If a company is not playing fair on international tax and does not sign up to an agreed international code then it will be liable for more tax than a transparently compliant company.

Government must also set an example. The UK prides itself with its low tax on corporate profits. Actually it is a disgrace. Companies should want to do business in the UK because it is an attractive market not just because they can retain more of their wealth so shifting more wealth to the already wealthy.

We already have mechanisms for cooperation through the United Nations and its scope could be broadened. Seventy years ago, in 1945, global change happened when 50 nations came together in San Francisco to draft and sign the United Nations Charter, committing to work together to achieve global peace, prosperity and human rights. We have made good progress, but not nearly enough. It is time to renew our commitment to the United Nations. It is even more important now as nations are ever more interdependent. There are seven billion people on the planet, three times more people than when the UN Charter was signed. No wonder there is renewed call to seek out life on other planets. We could use some help.

Summary

For socially responsible capitalism to provide a basis for sustainable wealth creation and greater social justice, there needs to be more co-operation between workers and management, enterprise and government and between governments. This will help transparency and ensure that, if taxes are considered to be fair and government revenue well managed, there will be less tax avoidance and more chance that taxes are paid in full to the jurisdiction in which they are due. These measures will contribute considerably to ensuring that government revenue comes from those who can afford it without causing hardship. This can be made to happen with the principle of 'social offsetting' so that businesses that comply, reduce their tax payments and retain more of their revenue and have greater say over how it is spent.

Summary of Chapter 4

Fair pay is essential to minimising inequality. This means a living wage at the lower end, with no sex or ethnic discrimination, and a socially responsible level of benefits. It also means that excessive pay is limited at the top end. Basic pay plus performance can be great to encourage individuals and companies to excel, but such performance needs to be based on more than financial considerations. Being profitable and socially responsible are only two signs of a good company, but great customer service and environmental responsibility are also valued attributes. If we can have more companies like this then it will contribute to sustainable business as well as social justice. Internationally, while countries will have different tax regimes, competitive positioning is not a legitimate government practice. So some of the key policy points are:

- The minimum wage must be the living wage related to the living costs of a decent life in a given area.
- Review taxes on company profits, maybe increasing the rates though setting an enterprise friendly threshold.
- Establish a 'social offsetting' scheme and assessment criteria.
- Minimise other payroll and other indirect taxes that increase the cost of doing business and reduce demand.
- Maximise direct taxes on anti-social activity like carbon creation, pollutants.
- Create and sign up for international agreements to ensure tax is paid where due, not at the expense of other nations.
- Encourage employees involvement through trade unions.
- Draft a corporate taxpayers charter which socially responsible companies can sign up to and be seen to be responsible.

CHAPTER 5

Foundations for
the Future

The third major step towards prosperity is to change the way public revenue is spent. A key focus needs to be financing the future to create opportunity for all and a sustainable growing economy, on the principle of 'inco*me* for me/*we*alth for we'.

W E HAVE BEEN neglected. Recent austerity budgets have cut funds for public investment. Even stimulus packages have been pretty tepid when it comes to investing in infrastructure. Yet wise investment brings increased wealth, not immediately but over time. The problem has always been finding a budget to fund infrastructure projects, particularly as there always seems to be more pressing immediate problems, especially those that deliver measurable benefit before the next election which may be a few years ahead. The proposed Land Usage Charge (LUC) captures the increased value of land that results from infrastructure improvements and so provides a return on the investment, making such projects effectively self-financing. These once hard decisions become a no brainer: everyone benefits. While transport is a major component of infrastructure and driver of economic growth, it is not the only element, others include energy, electronic communications, education, health and welfare facilities. All bring benefits to society, in the short term by boosting economic activity and job creation, and in the long term laying the foundations and capacity for a sustainable and prosperous future.

Senator Bernie Sanders proposed a bill in 2015 to spend $1 trillion over the next five years to boost the nation's transportation infrastructure, which he said would cost less than what the US government spent on the Iraq War.

> A $1 trillion investment in infrastructure could support 13 million decent-paying jobs and make our country more efficient, productive and safer. We need a major federal jobs program to put millions of Americans back to work. The fastest way to do that is to rebuild our crumbling infrastructure, our roads, bridges, water systems, wastewater plants, airports, railroads and schools.

The measure has been dubbed the 'Rebuild America Act', but Congress gets bogged down discussing how to find the funds to pay for these infrastructure improvements.

In the UK, there is a constant debate about the benefit of a new high speed rail line from London to Birmingham (HS2). The scheme is approved but too slow and is not extensive enough to have the major beneficial effect needed in the short term. Soon after the election in 2015, amidst calls that it had conveniently left the announcement until after the election, the new Conservative government announced it would have to cancel a promised £38 billion upgrade of the existing rail network. While most people would agree on the importance of good infrastructure, part of the reason why the right level of investment has not happened is because it is seen as a cost that has to come out of current revenue albeit spread over many years. This misconception is because the method of funding for these investments is inadequate and out of date. With a long-term view on return, the case can be made for the investment. High speed rail does more than benefit those who can afford to travel distances for business and pleasure, it increase economic activity. Similarly local mass transit systems enable less well-off workers to get easily and cheaply to their places of work, and indeed secure work.

With the tax reforms proposed and the implementation of the Land Usage Charge, many of these infrastructure projects could now move up the action list. All public expenditure on infrastructure and other socially useful facilities raises the value of the land, not in an arbitrary way, but as measured by the increase in the land component of property prices due to the availability of good public transport, access to high speed digital communications, good schools and facilities. Through the Land Usage Charge a part of this increased value of the land would be returned to public funds to finance more projects. At the same time landowners – I am not just talking about big landowners, but anyone owning their own house – would also benefit from the increase in value of their land, but it will not be quite as much as under the old system where the landowner got it all. So here, we are able to improve facilities, have a fair method to pay for them and everyone is benefitting, not just those who are fortunate enough to own land.

So over the past decades, it is not someone else who has been neglecting us, it is we ourselves: we have not invested in us. Matters are just getting worse the longer we leave it, we will rot and collapse. Investment is needed if there is to be growth. We need to use the funds that are already there, currently in the hands of the already wealthy, in order to finance the future for the benefit of all.

Investment is a very basic human instinct but it can be tainted by the desire for quick results. Any parent knows that the greatest gift you can give a child is time. It is a limited resource and to share it with children to help them grow is an essential need, and indeed joy, of parenthood. So for the farmer, the seeds do not instantly shoot out from the ground bearing fruit, it takes time and it takes investment in watering, cultivating the soil and creating the right environment for growth. It is the same in today's economy: the benefits do not come instantly but they will not come at all unless we invest. With the proposed tax reforms, we will have a way to make funds available to undertake this investment.

Ocean-going sailing ships enabled international trade, the railways in Britain drove the Industrial Revolution, the railroads in the USA opened up the West and later the Interstate highways linked cites. Transportation is a key economic driver but equally important are all the modern developments in communications, which are reliant on the supply of electricity as are schools, hospitals and other consumer services. Whether these infrastructure projects are publicly funded or not, they draw in commercial operations like manufacturing, services, shopping malls, leisure facilities and other businesses, further increasing the value of the land.

A major concern today is the affordability of housing. To make this basic human need affordable for all, we need to appreciate that a 'house' is comprised of two elements, the building and the land on which it stands. The cost of building a house is similar in any part of the country, but the cost of the land can vary enormously depending mainly on its location in relation to the amenities offered by society. It is the high price of the land that makes housing unaffordable for many. One way round this is that a percentage of land in communities is retained or indeed acquired in public ownership, and that the full value of the land not be included in the prices of the housing. Combined with the proposed raising of the Income Tax threshold, more people would have higher disposable income and would therefore be in a better position to pay for housing than before. The Land Usage Charge would also have a dampening effect on land prices, so that smaller mortgages would be required.

Education is a public as well as private good and therefore a key area of investment for the future. It is the best tool for social mobility and a fundamental requirement for anyone to live a full life, but education budgets have been cut, as it is seen as a cost. The cost of a university education is being loaded onto the individual student, which is acting as huge deterrent to many, particularly those in lower income groups. Well-educated people can make a greater contribution to the rest of the world than their own selfish needs. Whether they do so is their choice!

A universal health service is not the first step on the road to communism, as some Americans believe. It is actually the first step on the road to a caring government. It is an example of a civilised society that ensures that the population, its 'customers', are fit, healthy, and able to contribute to the economy and society. This is instead of a healthcare system where the poor cannot afford it or where it is so under resourced, it cannot attend to patients in an acceptable time frame.

Welfare, in its current form, is a huge cost to the economy. Too many people are unable to get work as there are not enough jobs and others, who are long-term welfare recipients, need help back into full society. Yet a large part of the welfare budget is going to support working people because of low wages, effectively subsiding company profits. Pay them a living wage and it puts more disposable income in their hands. We also need to lift low earners out of Income Tax. The result would be a huge drop in the pressure on the welfare budget. I am not advocating reducing the welfare budget as a cost-cutting measure, but reducing the number of people who are dependent on it. So much time and effort goes into debating the best support measures to help the low earners with subsidised childcare, affordable housing and other market-distorting but compassionate initiatives. We will still need this but the real answer is to have a system that means people have sufficient income to live a reasonable life. It is staring us in the face: stop taking money off people who can't afford to pay it and pay people a wage they can live on.

The requirement is for intelligent investment for the future, financed by a public revenue system that draws on funds that would otherwise have remained in the private hands of the few but can be reallocated to care for the public good of the many.

To lay the foundations for the future, there are three areas of policy that will form the building blocks:

1 Integrated Infrastructure
2 Excellence in Education
3 Health and Welfare

5.1 Integrated infrastructure

The first area to lay the foundations for the future is in increased investment in infrastructure. Access to infrastructure such as energy, transport, and telecommunications gives a huge boost to the productivity of private investment and an economy's competitiveness. But for infrastructure to deliver its full value it needs to be an integrated part of an overall plan. By this, I do no not mean an over-regulated, detailed list of dos and don'ts, more of a vision with options that brings quantifiable benefits, as well as a proven return on investment. But however great the ideas and schemes, the stumbling block is always: how can this be financed? There is no money! The reality is we cannot afford *not* to finance the right projects. With the proposed Land Usage Charge there is a way of making ideas a reality and laying the foundations for the future.

Globalisation, population growth, and urbanisation are placing considerable strains on infrastructure around the world. Advanced industrial economies are focusing on repair and replacement of their ageing infrastructures. But the developing world faces the more daunting task of creating new transportation, communication, water, and energy networks to foster economic growth, improve public health, and reduce poverty.

Infrastructure development has always been a vital component in encouraging a country's economic growth. Good infrastructure enhances a country's productivity, helping firms to be more competitive, and boosting a nation or region's economy. Not only does infrastructure in itself enhance the efficiency of production, transportation, and communication, but it also provides economic incentives to public and private sector participants. The accessibility and quality of infrastructure in a region help shape domestic firms' investment decisions and determine the region's attractiveness to foreign investors.

According to the World Economic Forum (2014), global spending on basic infrastructure – transport, power, water and communications – currently amounts to $2.7 trillion a year when it ought to be $3.7 trillion. The gap is almost as big as South Korea's GDP. And it is likely to grow fast.

Research by the World Bank in 2014 shows that every 10% increase in infrastructure provision increases GDP by approximately one% in the long term. Improved infrastructure quality accounted for 30% of growth attributed to infrastructure in developing countries.

The BBC reported in 2012 that economists estimate that every £1 spent on construction generates almost £3 in economic activity. According to the National Infrastructure Plan, £400 billion needs to be invested in the UK's infrastructure between 2012 and 2020 if the country wants to remain competitive in a global market.

The need is urgent, but we are kept waiting. An example of this is the outrageous decision on airport capacity in the United Kingdom. In 2012, Prime Minister David Cameron said he would postpone a decision on a third London airport until after the general election in 2015. That's a further three years later, yet all the time international flights are using other European airports with capacity at the expense of the UK. Part of this particular problem is that the wrong question is being asked. The focus seems to be on airport capacity for London whereas from a UK perspective it would be sensible to enhance the regional airports to encourage more intercontinental links. So instead of seriously considering a regional airport enhancement or even a large extendable international airport built on a man-made island in the estuary of the River Thames, the discussion is just focussed on trying to land more aircraft on a small strip of concrete in west London or in the Sussex countryside at Gatwick.

The government displays a complete lack of urgency and yet these decisions are vital for international trade and prosperity. I sometimes feel that this lack of priority for fast and efficient business communications is that most politicians are part of the elite who have never worked in commercial enterprise or if they have, never been responsible for bringing in the sales to provide jobs for the team. George Osborne, the 44-year-old Chancellor of the Exchequer has never had a job outside politics so has never had commercial financial responsibilities, and yet is in charge of a budget of £750 billion! Similarly 49 year old Prime Minister David Cameron has always worked in politics apart from a seven year stint in corporate affairs for a TV company, so basically has no previous experience of managing a team, let alone an entire country!

This lack of urgency is also reflected in the slow progress on high-speed rail construction. In the UK there are only 75 miles so far, the USA has none (as defined by international standards), yet Japan has had high-speed rail for 50 years. The discussion about a third airport in London has been going on since the original proposal for an airport in the estuary of the River Thames at Foulness in the 1960s is still not resolved. The UK should be focussing on expanding its regional airports as major hubs and ensuring fast interconnecting rail links between them, rather than making the country even more London focussed. Having done business in many countries, I know how vital great airport facilities are and how it does affect your travel plans; it needs to be made easy for people to do business anywhere in the world, and indeed for leisure travellers too.

Transport makes trade possible, from the first paths across the mountains and plains, the horse, the sailing ship, the steamship, the railways, roads, airways, it all enabled trade further a field and faster as the years progressed. Based on comparative advantage, trade is the basis of our capitalist society. It makes wealth creation possible. I can make shoes cheaper (better, in less time) than you because I am good at it and you can make bread cheaper and better than me, so let's trade. That's fine in your own community but in order to grow, we need new markets. Transport is the key, that needs to be powered by generated energy and also electronic communications (internet, email, video) are now the highways of instant communication and need full attention so that we get superfast speeds everywhere in the country.

However the present tax system means that infrastructure development is perceived to be a burden to the taxpayer, especially those who do not live or work near the project. But with carefully coordinated planning, large and small-scale infrastructure projects can provide economic stimulus, create jobs and give a lasting competitive legacy to any nation. Certainly it seems China realises this, whereas some other advanced economies do not. However, infrastructure development is not acceptable at any cost, for example where it has negative effects on climate change or is compromising safety.

So a nation whatever its size, needs a comprehensive transport infrastructure plan which combines all current mass transit methods, that is, rail, air, roads, water, for both passengers and freight. For the UK, this means upgrading regional airports to attract more intercontinental and regional travellers (so spreading the hub traffic away from London), but these need to be connected by high speed rail with other UK metropolitan areas, which in turn need to have a good regional and metro rail systems. Similarly with freight: airports and seaports need good rail connections, not just road, so that more freight between main urban areas can be shifted off the overcrowded roads. In the USA, metropolitan areas within five hundred miles of each other could benefit from high speed rail rather than relying on airports, and to move away from motorised inter-urban travel when research suggests that 30% of car travel in cities is actually looking for parking!

The Crossrail scheme for fast metro trains across London from east to west, costing £15 billion, is an example of how an infrastructure development can not only be made to pay for itself, but at the same time help reduce inequality. Due to open in 2018, it is already causing an increase in property prices along the route. In October 2012, the BBC reported that house prices along the Crossrail route could rise by up to 25% over the next 10 years, adding £5.5 billion to residential property values within 1km of the new stations on the route by 2021 (three years after the opening). This is just residential property and does not include commercial. The *Daily Telegraph* reported in May 2013 that property prices within a 10-minute walk of central London Crossrail stations have risen by more than 30% since the project was announced in 2008. The growth in values was 8% greater than wider improvements for central London, according to a study by estate agent Knight Frank. It now forecasts prices will increase by 40% over the next five years, rising at an additional 1.2% a year above wider rises in prime areas of the capital.

At present the government has no mechanism for recovering the expense of building Crossrail except through general and business taxation, which falls on everyone regardless of whether they use the service or not. Apart from the benefits the users of the service receive, for which they pay, the major beneficiaries are those whose properties will have increased without any effort or cost, save as a taxpayer, on their part. The proposed Land Usage Charge (LUC) would not only provide the government with a means of benefiting financially from the subsequent property price increases as a method of funding the project, but also ensure that those who received financial benefit also contributed. The LUC would only apply to the public value of these increases (i.e. the land) and not to any private value (e.g. buildings), which the Council Tax currently does. Thus with a change in the way the government raises its funds, a percentage of the increase in value from Crossrail would be returned to the Treasury, enabling it to recover the cost over 30 years, a reasonable time frame in investment terms.

Quite apart from the increase in property values, Crossrail will generate huge economic benefits to users through the reduction in travel time and ease of access. The extra footfall will stimulate new business and wealth. So, with a better way of collecting revenue and funding, the decision to embark on such infrastructure projects is not difficult: they pay for themselves. Also there is the very important point related to reducing inequality by ensuring that the poorest do not pay through their taxes for the enrichment of wealthier citizens through the increase in the value of their property. Instead those who benefit pay in proportion to their gain, but they too will have benefited from the raising of the Income Tax threshold.

Sometimes there can be other forces at play. In the 1960s, big cuts, known as Beeching's Axe, were made to Britain's railways. They were implemented by transport minister Ernest Marples, who at the same time was closely associated with Marples Ridgway, the firm that was given the contract to build the M1 motorway. In the USA, the building of the interstate highways in preference to the continuation of rail was probably even more dubious!

Despite the fact that infrastructure development provides a strong economic stimulus, recent efforts have been fairly piecemeal. For instance, the UK has one of the lowest mileages of high speed rail in Europe with only 67 miles opened in 2007. It will not have the next phase, known as HS2, completed until 2025, 18 years later. There have been periods when the importance of transport has been realised more than others, and some countries seem to get it more than others. The Japanese have had bullet trains since the 1960s, France and Germany developed electric railways after the Second World War whereas the UK was building coal fired steam locomotives up to mid 60s on the premise that it had a plentiful supply of coal.

In the UK, 1.3 billion passenger journeys are made per year over 9789 miles of track compared to USA with only 27 million over 139, 679 miles. That means 683 times more journeys over one mile of track in the UK than in the USA. That is a lot of under-utilised passenger track in the USA, which could be leveraged for improved public transit, resulting in higher land values, increased government revenues and the potential to reduce other more regressive taxes. This is happening in Marin County, Northern California, where a new passenger service is taking over a 70 mile stretch of the old Northwestern Pacific railroad.

For years, while the United States has focused on its highway and air-transport systems, passenger rail has been an afterthought. In 2010 the President announced a plan to spend $8 billion from the American Recovery and Reinvestment Act to build 13 high-speed rail corridors in 31 states. The investment was expected to produce about 320,000 jobs and roughly $13 billion in economic benefit. Overall a nationwide high-speed rail network could mean 29 million fewer car trips and 500,000 fewer plane flights annually, according to a 2006 study referred to by the Environment Law and Policy Center. That would save six billion pounds of carbon dioxide emissions, the equivalent of removing a million cars from the road annually. And yet, amazingly, several states rejected this funding.

The USA was yet to build any true high-speed rail even though it owed so much to railroads in the past such as enabling the settlers to spread west. Despite this, today there is real hesitation about building high-speed rail in many states. Even in California, there are regular attempts to 'derail' and delay the project. I went to listen to Dan Richards, the chairman of the California High Speed Rail authority talk at the Commonwealth Club in San Francisco in 2014. He outlined how this was a long-term project and it is designed to cope with the increasing population and the excessive travel requirements between the two main conurbations of the San Francisco Bay Area and the Los Angeles/San Diego area. Florida was one of the states that rejected the high speed rail funding. Yet in July 2014, a more enlightened private freight railroad operator announced plans to construct a $2.3 billion 240-mile passenger line between Miami and Orlando by 2016. The company sees much of the return and profits to come from the real estate development in the proximity of the stations which it owns!

The increased land values from new transport systems can generate more property tax revenue (if the property tax system is reformed to capture the increased value of land for the benefit of all) to fund public services and balance local budgets. Research clearly shows that family residences located near commuter rail stations in St Louis command a 32% premium over homes located elsewhere. In 2002, commercial land located within 1,300 feet of the VTA Light Rail in Santa Clara County (San

Jose, California) commanded a 120% premium, according to a Recon-
necting America report. A $17 million renovation of the Milwaukee
Intermodal Station is projected to increase land values around the
station by $227 million and create 3,000 new jobs in the Milwaukee area,
according to multi-state economic impact study. Building out the entire
3,000 mile Midwest HSR corridor is expected to produce an overall
economic benefit of $23.1 billion, creating 57,450 permanent new jobs at
an average of 15,200 new jobs annually. Unfortunately, today much of the
financial benefit goes to the landowners, instead of some being returned
to the public purse to fund the development, ultimately at 'zero cost'.
Currently all taxpayers, many of whom will never use the trains, and
irrespective of their financial status, contribute to the cost of building and
maintaining the system which clearly benefits the users and brings
significant wealth to the landowners without any effort on their part,
further redistributing wealth the wrong way!

As transport is key to economic activity it makes sense to proactively
create residential areas close to good transport links. This has always
been how our towns developed, often close to rivers and later on beside
man-made constructions of railways and industry. A concept that has
popped up recently is in fact an old concept: transit-oriented development
(TOD). TOD is designed to maximise access to public transport in a
mixed-use residential and commercial area and often incorporates
features to encourage transit ridership. A TOD neighbourhood typically
has a centre with a transit station or stop (train station, metro station, tram
stop, or bus stop), surrounded by relatively high-density development
with progressively lower-density development spreading outward from
the centre. TODs generally are located within a radius of a quarter to half
a mile (400 to 800 m) from a transit stop, as this is considered to be an
appropriate scale for pedestrians. Such developments can provide
affordable housing and good low cost (of use) transport links which bring
considerable benefit to those on lower incomes.

An example of the TOD concept in London was 'Metroland'. This
was the name given to the suburban areas built to the north west of
London in the early part of the 20th century that were served by the
Metropolitan Railway (the Met). The Met was financed largely by buying
up large stretches of farmland in advance and then selling it off in higher
priced lots for housing around the new stations. Dulles Airport close to
Washington DC opened way back in 1962 was developed in exactly the
same way – the surrounding land was bought many years in advance,

and later sold off for development, and this paid for the construction of new terminal buildings, runways, etc. So it is a well-tried method.

Then there were the garden cities, such as Welwyn Garden City in Hertfordshire UK, just 19 miles by rail to Kings Cross rail terminus in London. Founded in 1920 it was designated one of the first 'New Towns' in 1948. Sir Ebenezer Howard initiated the garden city concept for urban planning in 1898. Garden cities were intended to be planned, self-contained communities surrounded by 'greenbelts', containing proportionate areas of residences, industry and agriculture. He claimed to be inspired by Edward Bellamy's utopian novel *Looking Backward* and Henry George's work *Progress and Poverty*. The garden city would be self-sufficient and when it reached full population, another garden city would be developed nearby. Howard envisaged a cluster of several garden cities of 50,000 people as satellites of a central city, linked by road and rail.

Transport infrastructure is just as much about moving freight as well as people, and it is the freight that keeps the economic blood circulating. Similarly freight transportation needs to be more integrated so that seaports have good rail connections and regional and metro areas have good distribution centres and capacity for swift and clean local delivery. This type of infrastructure development can be managed by the private sector but it needs a visionary local or regional or national government to create the environment to make it happen.

Robert Reich promotes the importance of investing in infrastructure in his article on actions that would shrink inequality.

Many working Americans – especially those on the lower rungs of the income ladder – are hobbled by an obsolete infrastructure that generates long commutes to work, excessively high home and rental prices, inadequate Internet access, insufficient power and water sources, and unnecessary environmental degradation. Every American should have access to an infrastructure suitable to the richest nation in the world.

The fact that so many infrastructure proposals get dismissed through lack of funding is surprising. One of my early lessons in economics and politics was cost/benefit analysis: analysing what the strengths and weakness of a policy proposal are in relation to the costs. An infrastructure project could still win acceptance on the basis of a cost benefit analysis i.e. it would bring benefit greater than the cost, but still not get implemented because there were no capital funds or indeed other priorities or allocations were already approved. However, with a property tax system that captures the increase in the value of land resulting from new infrastructure and returns part of it to the government, such projects can be funded for the benefit of all. This timidity has been especially true in the recent years of enforced and unnecessary austerity where public funds have not been made available, resulting in further crumbling infrastructure.

Summary

So by returning some of the wealth of the very wealthy for public use through the proposed Personal Asset Contribution (PAC) as well as through the Land Usage Charge (LUC) that captures the value of land, it enables us all to share in more of the wealth we create. With more wealth returned to the nation, significant investment in infrastructure is possible and will further increase public revenue. It is a way of putting the private wealth accumulated by the few, to work for all. This is good for everyone, good for business and good for the country. Significant investment in integrated infrastructure can be a major contributor to reducing inequality and creating a better life for all.

5.2 Excellence in education

A good education is a public good not just a private benefit. It is in a nation's interest to ensure that its population receives the best possible education at every level. Education is generally acknowledged as the greatest social mobility tool and a key driver for any emerging and indeed advanced economy. It is not just about how it is funded but also about the quality of the education which ultimately rests with the training and support for the teachers.

Our children are being neglected. Every parent wants to do the best for their children and will try hard to make that possible. To prepare our children for today's world and give them the right skills and ambition to lead a full and purposeful life, we need good education, good teachers and a commitment to learn and excel. But sadly many, many parents do not have the choice for their children: it is often a lottery to get in to the best schools, those that get all round results, not just academic achievement.

Education needs more funds: funds to train and support good teaching, building facilities and education resources from early stage through to university. At one time loans for students seemed like a good idea to assist higher education funding instead of the formerly free system, but this has proved a real millstone and a major driver in increasing inequality of opportunity. Those from less well off backgrounds are less likely to take on debt and go to university despite having the ability, even though there are many funding programs. As a full-time student leader, I campaigned against education cuts and also for improvement in student finance. Ironically a fellow campaigning friend of mine from those days went on to become Secretary of Education in the Tony Blair government but did not succeed in switching the system! We know now that the level of student debt is causing significant personal anxiety as well as reducing spending power and further reducing demand and slowing economic progress, once again, exactly the opposite of the intention

I have been fortunate to benefit from university education having obtained an honours degree in Public Administration and previously studied at both independent and state run schools in the UK. And now many years later I have had the opportunity to attend lectures at University of California, Berkeley. I like to know what is going on and be part of the decisions. I was on the academic board and governing body of my university and also member of the National Union of Students (NUS) Education committee, representing students in national negotiations. Later as a parent, I was a governor of the two local primary schools my three children attended; they all went on to gain university degrees higher than mine!

To provide a better education and more opportunity for all, more funds are required. In the UK the current budget is around £98 billion, 13% of government expenditure and is about the same percentage in USA. According to figures from the World Bank, this is the same as Sweden, higher that Germany or France, Finland, Denmark, India but less than Finland. Many underdeveloped countries are also spending a high percentage of budgets on education. Whichever way, more needs to be spent and spent wisely.

The answer to additional funds for education once again can be found in the principle 'income for me/wealth for we'. More of the wealth locked away for private use could be put to better use for the nation, to truly bring opportunity for all, the millions of people who could really benefit from the life changing effects of a good education.

The Personal Asset Contribution (PAC) I propose could more than cover the proposed reduction in income taxes for the majority of people and provide additional funds. The change in property taxes to a Land

Usage Charge will increase revenue from those with higher value land and reduce it for those with lower value land, while increasing government revenue from this source overall.

Good schools increase the attractiveness of a residential area and have an impact on land values. Estate agents are always highlighting the schools in a particular area in which a property is located and there are many stories of families moving to be in the catchment area of a good school. So if good schools increase the value of property, let's invest more in good schools. Then with the Land Usage Charge some of that increased value will come back to fund the schools. However this does not mean poorer areas will automatically have worse schools, far from it, they would be the priority for funding.

Education has to be priority, as the Universal Declaration of Human Rights makes very clear in Article 26:

(1) Everyone has the right to education. Education shall be free, at least in the elementary and fundamental stages. Elementary education shall be compulsory. Technical and professional education shall be made generally available and higher education shall be equally accessible to all based on merit.

(2) Education shall be directed to the full development of the human personality and to the strengthening of respect for human rights and fundamental freedoms. It shall promote understanding, tolerance and friendship among all nations, racial or religious groups, and shall further the activities of the United Nations for the maintenance of peace.

(3) Parents have a prior right to choose the kind of education that shall be given to their children.

Many nations are falling far short of keeping to this declaration even though they signed up for it. While many nations have free education at fundamental and elementary stages, tertiary education, while accessible on merit, now depends on the ability to pay. There is a lot that could be done to improve education and bring more opportunity to more people, enabling them to move out of poverty and low incomes and lead a fulfilled and prosperous life.

Summary

Education is the key driver for social mobility and a route out of poverty. So it needs to be accessible and free to those who will benefit. The experiment of student-funded higher education has failed and we are paying the price with a debt burden and exclusion for many. Education can be funded from a fairer tax system whether it comes from the Personal Asset Contribution or Land Usage Charge or both. The funds are there; they are just tied up in the banks of the wealthy. If they could be released then everyone will benefit from a first class education at all levels and no one will get hurt, another win-win situation!

5.3 Health and welfare of the nation

For any government, the health and welfare of its citizens should be a major priority as it is a major component of prosperity. How it is funded and how much needs to be spent is a matter for continued discussion, one thing is certain more funds are always needed. Good health and welfare provision is a major factor in limiting inequality and reducing poverty, helping to build a sustainable economy with greater social justice.

1 Healthcare

Most European countries consider universal healthcare provided though taxes as a key role of government but in the US, a public health service is seen by many as 'socialised medicine' and the first step to a communist state. Yet, access to universal healthcare is absolutely critical to a fair and just society where everyone has the opportunity for a prosperous life. Without good health, we cannot reach our full potential which means we all need to take responsibility for our own care, but it would be against the principles of social justice to be excluded from healthcare access because of cost and inability to pay.

In the UK, the expenditure on universal healthcare represents 20% of the government budget and welfare (presented as social protection and personal social services) represents a further 35%, a total of 55% of government spending. In the USA healthcare represents 21% of total government spending of $6.4 trillion (Federal, state and local) and welfare including pensions 26%, a total of 47% of government spending (source: usagovernmentspending.com).

However, the healthcare provision funded by federal government in the form of Medicare (for seniors) and Medicaid (for those in need) covers about 100 million Americans, that is, only a third of the population, whereas in the UK 100% of the population are covered for the similar proportion of government budget. For reference total government revenue in the USA is about $5,900 billion for a 316 million population, that is $18,670 per head, in the UK government expenditure is £648 billion for 64 million population, that's £10,125 per head or about $15,300 at current exchange rates without adjustment for parity.

Having had personal experience of healthcare services in both the UK and the USA in recent years, I know what great work doctors, nurses, technicians and support staff do, and the level of service is similar. Early in my career I worked for eight months on the management team commissioning a new general hospital, it was a lesson in the commitment and dedication of healthcare providers.

Recently I had need to visit a doctor in the UK, who happened to be American and had been in the UK for twenty years. He said that, if he ever returned to the USA, it would not be to practice medicine, but he did comment that hospital doctors in the USA had 'more toys to play with'! He added if I had gone to a doctor in the USA, I would already have had a full CT scan. As it happened he could not find any problem, but at my request he did refer me for an ultrasound scan at the local hospital and I got an appointment within a few days on the National Health Service. They gave me a clean bill of health – but no bill! In fact the nurse who did the scan told me his wife had had to have a caesarean section. When his brother who lived in California heard, he had been concerned about the huge financial burden as it may not be covered by health insurance but, of course, in the UK it is was all taken care of medically and financially. What a relief! (And no paperwork). Obamacare may be a step in the right direction but there is a long way to go before the health provision is truly universal.

In the USA, I visited the Emergency Room regarding a problem with my knee and secondly when I fell off my bike and subsequently had a small fracture in my arm. I can honestly say that there was no discernible difference in provision, doctors, nurses and other medical staff are dedicated and hard working and always do the best for you wherever you are.

My view seems to be supported by others. Writing in *Business Insider*, Jim Edwards, an American who spends half his life in the US and half in the UK and so is used to both countries' healthcare systems, concluded that he preferred the UK's NHS to the American private system. He noted that: '*The NHS is a little more inconvenient in terms of appointment times, but due to the fact that its free, has no paperwork, and the treatment on the day is super-fast, the NHS wins.*' As he notes the NHS covers everyone equally, whereas Americans get care based on their ability to pay, leaving tens of millions with only minimal access to care.

However, many people are in bad health due to economic circumstance or lack of knowledge or access to preventative care. This even happens in a country with a national health service like the UK with full access to healthcare. Though in countries with commercial healthcare like the USA, this means that those in poverty and even the economically squeezed middle classes miss out on healthcare with severe implications for a healthy life and indeed life expectancy (Obamacare may have improved this but there are still those without access to healthcare). Universal healthcare with a good level of resources is essential to a good life as well as the life of a nation.

The amount of money spent on health care does not correlate with better results based on key indicators like longevity, child mortality and days off work. To many European who have been used to a comprehensive national health service for 50 years or more, it is very difficult to understand the USA's resistance to implementing a so called 'socialised medicine'. Instead they have fudged half-cocked plans which have had to be devised just to get it though the political process and, even then, there are constant attempts to derail it. The federal government now covers half the cost of healthcare with its Medicaid and Medicare programs

According to the OECD, the US spends two and half times as much on healthcare per capita ($8508) as the UK ($3405), yet Americans do not appear to be healthier or live longer? Americans have a life expectancy of 79.8 years and the Brits of 81 years (Source: World Health Organisation). Another indicator could be the under-fives child mortality rate which is seven deaths per 1000 live births in USA; the UK's is five per 1000 (still too high – Japan is three per 1000).

The total amount spent on healthcare in the US in 2012 was $2.8 trillion, the share of the economy devoted to health spending was 17.2%. For 2014, Forbes.com estimated total healthcare spending was actually $3.8 trillion, that's over $12,000 each, which is actually 3.5 times the per capita expenditure in the UK with its full universal healthcare provided by the state (this compares with the OECD estimate of 2.5 times above). In the US about half the total cost of healthcare comes out of personal insurance. The federal government budget for healthcare in 2015 was $1.4 trillion. That amounts to $4430 for each of the 316 million people (source: usagovernmentspending.com), while in the UK, where everyone gets 'free' access to a health service that is funded out of taxes, £133 billion is budgeted for 2015 so that is £2078 or approximately $3166 per head.

The federal government is already spending 40% more per head on healthcare than the UK. According to the United States Census Bureau, in 2012 there were 48 million people in the US (15.4% of the population) who were without health insurance. People in the UK would all agree that the NHS could benefit from more resources. If it were to spend the same per head as the US federal government, then it would have a 40% uplift, that is, another £53 billion. The real issue is that anyone in the UK can walk into a doctor's surgery or a hospital and get seen or referred to a specialist at no direct cost. Rich or poor, you are covered. It seems to me that a key role for government is to provide for the health of its people, all its people.

The US's patchwork system of private providers and insurance companies is dramatically different from the British National Health Service which is, as all Americans know and fear, a completely public 'socialised medical' system. Dr Ben Carson, Republican presidential candidate, one time director of Paediatric Neurosurgery at Johns Hopkins University and Hospital, author of bestseller *One Nation* and darling of the right wing Tea Party, drew a parallel between the Affordable Care Act, or Obamacare as is commonly called, and 'socialised medicine'. He cited communist leader Vladimir Lenin's support for government-run health care as the '*keystone to the establishment of a socialist state*'. Dr Carson said that Obamacare '*was never about healthcare. It was about control*' and making all Americans '*subservient to the government*'. The fear is reminiscent of the McCarthy era politics where people where frightened of communism creeping in and having 'Reds under the bed'. A universal national health service with no cost at the point of access is more about a civilised society caring for its people than it is about socialism. Why are so many Americans scared of such great and more simplified service? The Canadians, north of the border are not.

Comparing three nations' satisfaction with their healthcare systems a 2003 Gallup poll found 25% of Americans are either '*very*' or '*somewhat*' satisfied with '*the availability of affordable healthcare in the nation*', versus 50% of those in the UK and 57% of Canadians. 44% of Americans were '*very dissatisfied*', but only 25% of Britons and 17% of Canadians. Regarding quality, 48% of Americans, 52% of Canadians, and 42% of Britons say they are satisfied.

Canadians strongly support the health system's public rather than for-profit private basis, and a 2009 poll by Nanos Research found 86.2% of Canadians surveyed supported or strongly supported '*public solutions to make our public healthcare stronger'*. A Strategic Counsel survey found 91% of Canadians prefer their healthcare system to a US style system. Plus 70% of Canadians rated their system as working either *'well'* or *'very well'*.

About half of Americans have their healthcare costs covered by employers, in the form of insurance plans, this puts a big extra burden on the employers. A universal healthcare system would eliminate these costs and increase profit margins and possibly increase public revenue from corporate Income Tax. Looking to the future and laying the foundations for the benefit of all, the US needs to give up its hostility to a public health service and embrace its benefits. Of course, one of the challenges is the huge financial vested interests involved including the pharmaceutical and health insurance companies whose huge profits depend on the status quo. At the same time as providing healthcare, the US system is taking money off the squeezed middle and indeed employers for health insurance and creating corporate profits which contribute to distributing funds from the poor to the rich. This needs to be reversed. Callers for a single payer service, such as Democrat presidential candidate Senator Bernie Sanders, need to be reassured that such a universal free to access healthcare system is entirely practical and will deliver excellent results, with no increase in federal budget. It would save the country a trillion dollars in the unproductive activity of the layers of for-profit insurance companies!

For countries like the UK with a national health service, the focus needs to be on better resources and better management to ensure better outcomes and better personal service. This means more funds, which, in my view are available. Currently they are in the hands of the wealthy who can by definition already afford to pay for their own private healthcare.

2 Welfare

Despite welfare programmes being in place in many advanced economies, there still remains a high and undesirable level of inequality and poverty. Our priority must always be reducing and eliminating poverty as it is a disgrace that such hardship exists in our advanced world today. Governments, despite good intentions, have failed to deliver the results. The pressure to reduce welfare budgets, making life more difficult for the most vulnerable people and perpetuating slow economic growth, now compounds this.

The practical policies outlined in this book will not only raise the income of the lower paid without harming the economy, which in turn will actually reduce pressure on the welfare budget significantly, making more funds available for the most needy.

I can remember being unemployed, claiming benefit and 'signing on'. I was lucky, at the time I only had myself to support, but for millions there is frustration and despair everyday. I also saw it from the other side when I worked in an unemployment office when I was a student.

Once again most of the problems that necessitate welfare are man-made and so are the answers. The low earners continue to pay income or payroll taxes, as well as regressive consumption taxes. It is a bureaucratic nonsense then to receive benefit back in welfare and tax credits. If, as I propose, Income Tax and ultimately payroll taxes were abolished for the lower paid, many would not need welfare and pressure would be taken off the welfare budget. The UK spends £30 billion on child tax credits and working tax credits, effectively topping up low wages paid to those who are employed. This is where the policies in this book are interlinked: as the abolition of Income Tax would reduce government revenue but also reduce the welfare budget, there is no need to cut it, it will reduce itself as we shift the tax contribution from income to wealth on the principle of *'income for me/wealth for we'*.

When discussing welfare, the issue always arises about 'scroungers' or benefits cheats. There are those who live on extended or perpetual welfare, expecting the state to provide, though they are in many cases capable of working but the financial incentive is not sufficient. Similarly there is a perception that there are a large number of people defrauding the welfare system. The UK Department for Work and Pensions (DWP) defines benefit fraud as when someone obtains state benefit they are not entitled to or deliberately fails to report a change in their personal circumstances. The most common form of benefit fraud is when a person receives benefits, but continues or begins employment. Another common form of fraud is when the recipients are financially supported by a partner or spouse yet claim that they live alone. The DWP claim that fraudulent benefit claims amounted to around £900 million in 2008-09. So that is about 0.4% of total welfare budget or approximately 0.7% of the welfare budget excluding pensions. It is still a sizeable amount of money which could be put to much better use, but is a minor amount when compared to corporate and personal tax avoidance schemes and the use of tax havens. All of these socially irresponsible actions need rectifying: tax-payers want to see a clear plan to eliminate such practices if true social justice is to be achieved.

Maintaining the welfare budget is important, though it will reduce as more people enjoy higher incomes from the reduction in taxes at the lower end and more are able to get work. However we still want to improve support for those in genuine need. The priority is to minimise the hardship of poverty and this is all tied in with affordable, decent housing, personal support services for the needy, strengthening of social services, raising working-family incomes, providing more work for single parents, and engaging better with high-risk racial and ethnic minority groups. Work and Pensions Secretary Iain Duncan Smith, in an interview with *The Guardian*, said many people on benefits see those who take up job offers as '*morons*' and, the paper reported, claimed it wasn't worth coming off 'the dole' for less than £15,000 a year. As a comparison, in October 2014, the Equality Trust reported that a minimum wage earner would have to work for 342 years to earn just one year's average pay of Britain's top bosses. People are unwilling to pay taxes and particularly more taxes if they feel that some of it is going to freeloaders. So this means tackling fraud more effectively, being transparent as well as reforming the tax system so that it is considered fair by all.

Poverty plan

By removing the squeeze on the financially insecure, a stronger middle class can emerge that in turn provides more opportunity to move up out of poverty. Such interconnected actions to minimise poverty would include:

1 Create jobs through infrastructure development, including affordable housing, transport, energy generation, schools.
2 Care for workers, partner with employers:
   a Raise minimum wage to a living wage;
   b Ensure pay equity;
   c Establish work schedules that work for families;
   d Ensure benefits reach those who need them.
3 Invest in education, early as well as adult, especially basics for the young, training to meet skills required plus wider opportunities for higher education.
4 Make basics affordable by eliminating income and social security taxes for lower incomes, provide affordable housing and high-quality child care.
5 Improve support services such as training, rehabilitation for ex-offenders and credit rating recovery.

Health and welfare summary

Whether countries have a private or public healthcare systems, it seems that the quality of care and the health outcomes are not significantly different. Doctors, nurses, paramedics and support staff are dedicated and committed the world over. For those countries like the UK that provide healthcare as part of the tax package, there certainly needs to be further resources for improved services as well as reinstating a full service for essential services like dental and optical care. For those few countries, such as the United States, that consider healthcare provision as a private matter, it is time for change in mindset. The financial argument is strong enough on its own, the country is wasting over half of the money spent and could have a full universal free (paid for by current levels of taxation) health service on a pro rata basis with no extra funding required. The current system, even with Obamacare, still leaves 15% of the population without healthcare and burdens others with a significant personal expense in addition to paying taxes, not to mention the paper work involved.

The welfare budget provides support for over half the population in the UK. The fact that so many rely on welfare shows that the capitalist system is not working as it should do. Instead of spreading the income and the wealth, the system is channelling it to the wealthy by keeping wages low so that profits are higher. The base cost of employment should be a wage that a worker can live off, not one that needs a top-up from the government. Recent proposals in the UK to make the national minimum wage a national living wage are a step in the right direction, but is not nearly enough and too slow. Many will still look to tax credits and welfare, but the government is cutting the benefit budget. This should not happen until a real living wage is in place. As some have pointed out the proposed living wage will not have a big impact in reducing poverty as, while wages go up, tax credits are going down. A higher wage, lower tax and, ultimately, a lower welfare economy is the right thing, though it won't happen all at once.

Foundations for the future summary

A nation cannot live just for today and ignore the children of tomorrow. It has to lay the foundations for the future, which means strategic planning and allocating funds today that will provide a better life for the next generations. Nowhere is this more obvious than climate change and renewable energy, if we don't act, there will be no planet or at the very least an inhospitable place not capable of providing a comfortable existence. I have not addressed climate change in detail here as in my view it is absolutely obvious that we have to act responsibly as a matter of urgency. Meaningful longer term investments in infrastructure can be funded with reformed property taxes, which capture the value of land, the investment can be recouped through the Land Usage Charge and so develop a virtuous circle of further self-funded development. Together with contributions from personal assets the budget for education could be increased to provide access for all and a better quality of provision. Similarly with health and welfare provision, by unlocking funds accumulated for private use we can improve provision for all.

The principle of *'income for me/wealth for we'* enables more resources for funding the future, empowering the poorer members of society, giving the majority access to the prosperity pot, and a chance to build a better life. The policy points to ensure solid foundations for the future include:

- Integrated infrastructure strategy at a national and regional level to include transport, utilities, education and recreation.
- Change property taxes to Land Usage Charge so that benefits of infrastructure increase public revenue and fund projects.
- Significantly increase infrastructure spending, funded by new revenue.
- Restore free access to higher education based on merit.
- Write off student debt in a phased and equitable fashion.
- Raise the profile and standing of the teaching profession with improved pay structures, career opportunity and resources.
- Improve secondary/high school facilities to include more education for life such as social skills, domestic skills, democracy, human rights, retain and support sports, music, arts for all-round education.
- Introduce universal free access healthcare in the USA, it is already paid for, no extra taxes and the end of personal health insurance costs.
- Increase health budget in UK by 10-20%, funded from PAC and LUC revenue streams.
- More resources for preventative care and health education so reducing pressure on other resources and leading to healthier lifestyle.
- Maintain welfare budget and only reduce in line with decrease in demand as a result of rising wages.

PART III

Moving Forward

'The future depends on what you do today.'

Mahatma Gandhi

'SHARE the wealth' ran the headline to the CNN story on Pope Francis's address to Congress in September 2015. It was particularly poignant to me as I was in Washington DC at the same time and watched the whole speech live. The Pope told Congress: *'It goes without saying that part of this great effort* [to deal with the problem of poverty] *is the creation and distribution of wealth.'* His clear message: we need cooperation and inclusivity. Politics, he noted, *'cannot be a slave to the economy and finance'.* Politics must instead be, *'an expression of our compelling need to live as one, in order to build as one the greatest common good. I do not underestimate the difficulty that this involves,'* the Pope added, *'but I encourage you in this effort.'* We sure do need encouragement in this effort. The political rhetoric around how we can reduce extreme inequality has typically little to say about practical proposals to help us become more equal.

Whichever sector, group or position you are in, the simple principle of *'income for me/wealth for we'* provides a sound basis for social justice, where economic growth benefits all, where our precious democracy is restored and where the miseries of the majority can disappear.

Over the last 300 years, there have been several promising starts to create a more socially just and responsible society but then greed and vested interests have overpowered commitment and hope. The challenge is to lay the foundations for a new era in human history that is inclusive, compassionate and sustainable, a model for the 21st century. If we want freedom, we have to take on responsibility.

When I have talked about this book, many say they understand and really like the concept of 'income for me/wealth for we'. It makes so much sense and is very fair, but they say it will never happen because those in power will not let it. We shall see, let this not be an excuse to give up but for greater determination to push forward. The problems are so extreme; they are bad for everyone, rich or poor, and those in the middle. I believe we are very close to a tipping point now. If we do not act there will be chaos, collapse and revolution. It is not when, it is now!

The movie, Selma, about Martin Luther King Jr and the events in Selma, Alabama in 1965 brought home not only the importance of not giving up on what is right and just, but also the power of non-violence and of hope. These are values that underpin the Agenda for Progressive Prosperity. Martin Luther King memorial in Washington where some of his most momentous and inspiring words are engraved on the wall is very impressive

The campaign focus today needs to be not only on influencing the decision-makers but also on the deniers, the cynics, escapists, the apathetic, so that there is a huge unstoppable groundswell of opinion and change becomes inevitable. The majority and the minorities, the rich, the poor, the squeezed middle and the politicians must be convinced that an agenda for change will benefit all and we can make it happen, if we are smart and focused, as well as non-partisan, in our approach. But if I was to pick one key group we need to influence to bring change, it is the wealthy, the 1% and above. If we can convince those close to the levers of power that this is in their interests too, then change will happen: if we attack and vilify them, they will roll up the drawbridge and they will not participate.

I was talking to a New Yorker who described himself as being 'in finance'. I outlined the theme of the book and his immediate response was, 'So you're a socialist then!' This is just a small indication of the high level of misunderstanding and prejudice. There is a huge task to educate everyone with the truth and facts. But we must not insult those with opposing views. If we do they will switch off immediately. We need to listen, observe and respond. However in the year since I had that conversation the word socialist in America has become almost acceptable and some policies once considered socialist are now becoming mainstream such as single payer healthcare.

A key element of the 2008 Obama campaign was the hope that real change would come. As I write this book it would be a pretty fair assessment to say that many of those living in hope of 2008 are still hoping. This is despite some determined effort, but real change has been blocked by a stalled political system and the key to political collaboration seems to have been lost.

At the 2010 general election in Britain, the Conservative slogan was '*Vote for change*', but that double meaning of change was clearly more about vote for change of party from the previous Labour government rather than any radical change to move society forward. Austerity policies (for the many, though it has been business as usual for the wealthy few) were applied which meant the economy only slowly crawled out of recession. It would have happened a lot quicker with bolder, more decisive policies. Then as a result of apathy and lack of a credible alternative, the UK voted for more of the same by re-electing a Conservative government in 2015, even though only 25% of the electorate voted Conservative.

There will always be some inequality, that's human nature, but we all want to strive to do better. I do not accept that greed is good or that breeding the conditions of generational under-privilege is necessary, desirable or wise. This Agenda is not about restoring the American Dream or just making Britain great again. It is about building a fair and just society that is sustainable. As we have seen where greed exists, it creates more greed. If these levels of extreme inequality continue, we are likely to turn into savages. It is time to listen to the majority. There is a once in a lifetime opportunity for the USA and Britain to lead the way.

We do not need more government, we maybe could do with less government but, above all, we just need better government. I understand the frustrations of libertarians who want to cut taxes and think there is too much government, which is taking away our freedoms, but will a reduction in government activity bring the outcomes they seek? I would say Government exists to serve the people, all the people, not just the few. The government creates the environment for prosperity to flourish. It provides services collectively for the people who cannot provide them for themselves individually, and the resources to take care of those who may be on hard times and need support to get back on track. The government enables freedoms to grow.

This Agenda will bring benefits in the long and short term. When pushing for reform, it must be done with the certainty that these proposals will actually deliver the change we want. Then a campaign needs to be developed to make it happen. The choice is yours. It is up to you whether you want to make it happen or be a bystander. There are many things you can do. But above all, we have to come together to make the change happen. It is not just about voting, it is not just about talking to others: it is about collective action. Then we can move forward.

The most urgent goal in my view is to enable the poor and the lower income groups to have more disposable income. There will need to be some increased redistribution efforts in the near term in order to make the changes take effect quickly. An environment needs to exist in which it is feasible to move out of the welfare culture but still provide a safety net. The poor are used to being lied to or overlooked. They need to see signs that what is proposed could and will become a reality.

As mentioned, it is key to persuade the rich and the powerful that these proposals are in their favour too. Nick Hanauer and Eric Beinhocker summed up the need to engage private and public interests in a 2014 article for the journal, *Democracy*, headlined *'Capitalism Redefined'*:

> Understanding prosperity as solutions, and capitalism as an evolutionary problem-solving system, clarifies why it is the most effective social techno-logy ever devised for creating rising standards of living. Realistically, the public sector is going to play a big role in many parts of the economy as well as in many aspects of society. So governments need to be problem solvers, too. It is imperative that we bring the evolutionary processes of problem solving inside the walls of government and build public institu-tions that have incentives to innovate and space to experiment.

In this last section of the book, I look at how we can make the Agenda for Progressive Prosperity a reality. The foundations for a sustainable economy and greater social justice need to be laid in order to remove unnecessary hardship and bring greater opportunity for all to lead fulfilled, purposeful and happy lives.

CHAPTER 6

Hope into Reality

THE MOST successful advertising campaigns have a simple, clearly understood message, so too with a campaign for political reform. The message needs to resonate with the audience, influence them, change their attitude and spur them into action. The principle of '*income for me/wealth for we*', can provide us with a central message of fairness, freedom and opportunity.

When I started my first career job in marketing, I thought selling was about getting people to buy what they did not really want, the hard sell! Of course, you can't get people to buy what they don't want by the very nature of the decision (unless there is some threat involved!). I also thought that it must be very difficult to sell because you have to know everything about a product. But I was wrong. Selling is about communicating a message to bring action; it is about listening, listening to what people want and then meeting their needs. This may mean tailoring your product to meet the customer's requirements. It does mean overcoming all their objections and once you have done that they will buy from you. So too in politics, it is about listening to what people really want and meeting those needs, not just peddling what you have to offer. After just two years in two different advertising agencies, it was time to go it alone and I founded my first advertising/PR agency and have had my own businesses ever since. We felt we could offer a more strategic approach based on agreed outcomes and measurable tactics. So too in politics today, a clear vision is essential but if it is just supported by sound bites and rhetoric it will go nowhere. Only when a campaign is measured in stages can it be sure to arrive at the desired result. Just as the most successful companies have a bold vision and determined leader, so too in politics but that has been lacking in recent years, hence reform is slow.

171

The Agenda for Progressive Prosperity needs advocates that under-stand the inclusive message. A political agenda is about emotion and branding but above all, about substance. A brand has to live up to its promise. Having spent a career communicating on behalf of clients, it is very gratifying to see so many that have been tremendously successful not only financially but also in terms of bringing real, not just perceived, benefits to a large number of people. Establishing and maintaining a good reputation contributed significantly to their success.

Blogger Alex Myers summed up the political approach in his blog post in February 2015:

> It seems that generations of scandal, expense-dodging and PR gaffes have stuck the heads of political parties so far into the sand that they've become blind to the fact that winning an election is NOT about telling people what you will do if you win. It's not even about how that is slightly different to what the other political parties will do. It is WHY you intend to do what you intend to do that wins genuine support. Just as with a brand, a political party should not focus on sales but on advocacy. People BUY a product but they JOIN a cause. Like Simon Sinek says, there's a reason it was the 'I have a dream' speech and not the 'I have a plan' speech.

In politics that does not mean blindly agreeing with what any voter says to please them. You have to start with principles and outline policy, but, of course, to be completely acceptable, you have to listen to people's needs and tailor your offering accordingly, if you are to achieve political success. So the content of the Agenda may change and also the method by which it is delivered, there will always be room for improvement. However, I hope the overall inclusive message and vision will not be lost. In any political campaign, it is very important to manage the message, but not to the point where it loses authenticity. The message must be positive, simple and true. It is about how good the 'offer' is: it is not about how bad the other guys are. There is no place for negativity and insults in any campaign. The views of others must be respected. As soon as opponents are insulted, they switch off and stay opposed. We cannot rely just on great ideas, as they will not be fully understood initially. Our policy-makers and, indeed voters, think in the traditional way, old answers to old problems. We want new answers to all public policy prob-lems. So we need a constructive, comprehensive and consistent campaign for change. Alter the way we think about the problem. It takes time to change attitudes.

There have been many warnings and volumes of words about what is wrong with our society but much less in terms of fresh ideas about what we can actually do to fix the problems. It seems to be the same old ideas that are put forward in a piecemeal and often non-specific way: build more affordable housing, create more jobs, pay better wages. Let's get specific. Let's get practical. Some of the actions can be immediate like cutting Income Tax for lower earners. Others will take longer. It might take a year or more to have all land valued so that a contribution to public revenue from land values can be implemented, for example. Campaigns need goals, messages, strategies, tactics, outcomes and budgets, all planned, and a means of measuring success.

The Agenda for Progressive Prosperity may be bold but it is also practical and financially feasible. By the time all the policies have been implemented in the first four years, a budget surplus can be achieved and a public revenue stream will grow in line with the increase in the wealth of the nation, wealth that can be spread more equitably. Many people will have their lives changed for the better and a few will find their wealth and even income slightly reduced but with no threat to their quality of life.

In this chapter I will look at how the policy proposals in the Agenda will achieve the goals outlined at the beginning of the book. Then look at our audience in more detail, how it is segmented and how the message can be effectively tailored to each group. Finally consider the strategy and tactics for achieving these goals and how we can come together as a non-partisan movement to make change happen. Then we will truly move From Here to Prosperity.

6.1 Towards progressive prosperity

Prosperity is being stifled by extreme inequality and a corrupted capitalist system in conflict with the interests of the majority. These have collectively undermined democracy so that changes in the interests of the majority simply do not happen. By reforming the tax system and using it as a toolbox to create a fair method of collecting government revenue for the services we need, inequality can be minimised and we will make progress to prosperity.

We are all fed up with austerity, and so we should be: it was unnecessary. However we should still be prudent and not extravagant. While we can blame the greed of the banks for the financial collapse and subsequent recession, we would have expected government to take a bold lead to ensure catastrophes like this do not happen, as they are in fact completely avoidable and down to human failings.

Having said that, the Great Recession did happen, but why did it take so long for nations to recover and why, eight years later, is the global economy still described as fragile? The global economy is becoming increasingly interdependent and technology is having a huge impact on the nature of work and the conduct of our lives. Still the basic human problems remain, too many people are going hungry, are not healthy and are under constant financial pressure. We cannot blame globalisation and technology.

The reason the austerity policies lasted so long was due to lack of vision and a preponderance of traditional thinking. More could have been done to improve economic growth and further steps could have been taken to minimise inequality and reduce poverty. But it was not, because plutocrats believe that it is irrelevant that the rich get richer (and even believe that in doing so, they help others, the old trickle down notion) and that is just unfortunate that the poor stay poor. By tightening everyone's belts, wages stagnated, jobs were lost, demand dropped and those who were already wealthy, gained even more.

What should have happened is that some fire should have been injected into the economy. Extracting taxes from the poorer members of society should have been stopped. Instead public revenue could have been generated from those who can afford it, as they hold the wealth that others have helped create. By shifting the emphasis of taxation from income to wealth especially land values, a stream of revenue that increases with the growing wealth of the nation could be tapped for public revenue. This process will produce additional funds without depriving anyone, and by investing in the future of the country it would create more opportunity for all. Such activity would reduce welfare budgets, not interfere with the market, and simplify government.

If we are to constantly monitor the progress of our campaign, the goals must be quantified, so that it is clear what the definition of success is. Major advances can be achieved in a four or five-year time frame, a typical lifetime of a government. That means we have to be specific as to the data:

- By how much do we expect to reduce extreme economic inequality, and in what time frame?

- By how much we expect to reduce poverty, and in what time frame?
- What growth rates should be achieved?
- How will we define when the government is working in the interests of the majority?

Not having access to full government economic data makes it difficult to put numbers on the goals right now. But such quantifiable goals should form part of the commitment of a government, which has access to all the data and can predict what is realistically achievable.

At the beginning of this book we outlined the three main problems that need to be solved. These can be summed up in three goals:

1 Reduce extreme inequality and persistent poverty.
2 Improve economic progress.
3 Restore democracy so the government is working for us.

So let's put Austerity behind us and summarise how the policies proposed in the Agenda for Progressive Prosperity actually give us the outcomes we desire.

1 Reduced Inequality and poverty

The urgent priority is to end the hardship of the poor and lower paid by increasing incomes. Next is to strengthen the middle class, increasing consumer demand, encouraging economic growth and expanding wealth creation to be shared more equitably. So for those at the lower end and in the middle of the income and wealth spectrum there would be the following benefits:

- **More money to spend or save**
  - The introduction of a living wage will give a welcome pay rise to about 20% of the workforce.
  - Abolishing Income Tax for most employees will give a pay rise of up to 15%, though the full effect may not immediately be felt as current income also includes welfare and tax credits.
  - Abolishing payroll taxes for most employees could give up to 10-15% more income for many.

- **Less money to pay out**
  - Changing property taxes to the Land Usage Charge will encourage the development of more affordable housing and result in reductions in housing costs for many homeowners and renters.

- ○ Reducing sales taxes on necessities and basic items means less to pay out.
- **Increased opportunity**
  - ○ More domestic income will increase consumer demand.
  - ○ This will create more jobs.
  - ○ More people will have more choices, enhancing the sense of freedom.
  - ○ Revised property taxes will provide more funds for education, health and infrastructure which in turn will facilitate upward social mobility.

At the same time poverty can actually be reduced by strengthening the middle class, particularly the lower paid, putting more money in their pockets, leading to increase in consumer demand. More jobs would give greater opportunity for the unemployed and lowest paid and those in the poverty trap to move up. With less demand on the welfare budget from the working poor, there will be more funds for the unemployed poor to provide a better quality of life and more opportunity. This will be combined with better education opportunities giving more access to those who were previously denied through social circumstances. Together with a greater supply of affordable housing, society can better meet the basic needs of its entire people.

2 Greater economic progress

The measures taken directly to tackle inequality and poverty will boost economic growth, as it will significantly increase consumer demand. Higher growth rates will lead to the creation of more wealth to be shared by the many, not just the few.

- **Higher growth rate**
  - ○ The living wage together with reduced income and payroll taxes, plus potentially reduced property taxes and sales taxes will maximise disposable income.
  - ○ This in turn will boost consumer demand, increase jobs and create more opportunities personally and for business.
  - ○ Higher growth rates should increase company profits and, with 'social offsetting', will encourage social responsibility and greater shared wealth.

- **Shared prosperity**
  - Company profits will be increased from reduced payroll taxes with more opportunity to share in the wealth created. Though profits may be temporarily decreased from paying a living wage and fair wages this will be offset by savings in absenteeism, recruitment and quality of work as well as potential increase in property taxes.
  - 'Social offsetting' of company profits will allow the wealth we all create to be shared by the many stakeholders, not just the few shareholders.
  - The introduction of a tax on personal assets will return more of the wealth created to the community, to be invested in education, health and welfare.
  - A contribution from personal assets (PAC) provides funds to make up shortfall based on ability to pay.

- **Investing in the future**
  - Fairer property taxes will enable more investment in infrastructure which will pay for itself.
  - This will unlock private funds for public investment in education.
  - Enable more investment in health and welfare.

3 Democracy restored

When the Agenda for Progressive Prosperity is fully implemented, it will mean at least that the government is acting in the best interests of the democratic majority. Democracy needs to live up to its definition as a system of government in which power is vested in the people, who rule through freely elected representatives. Once the government is acting for the majority, it will mean that the money of the minority of plutocrats will be ineffective and eventually unwanted by a new breed of bold, visionary and trustworthy politicians.

- **Social justice:**
  - Implementation of a true living wage.
  - Tax system reform so that it is fairer and easier to collect.
  - Tax avoidance minimised especially overseas funds, increasing tax revenues.

- **The will of the people**
  - Political funding reform to end plutocracy and corruption, and encourage responsibility.

- ○ Corporate 'social offsetting' will encourage social responsibility to benefit all.
- ○ Investment in the future will benefit all from infrastructure, education, health and welfare.

- **Economic Justice**
  - ○ Measures will encourage shared wealth creation.
  - ○ 'Social offsetting' of corporate tax will encourage this.
  - ○ Encourage hard work, minimise need for welfare (but will still be available).

Summary

In moving towards prosperity, I am recommending a serious reduction in taxes for the poor and the lower paid. This may not bring immediate significant increase in income, as a large proportion relies on welfare benefit and credits to top up income. However in the longer term, it will give more people more control over their lives and the respectability of earning enough to live on instead of relying on welfare. It will at the same time reduce the welfare budget. In addition there are other measures such as the living wage that will significantly increase disposable income and sales tax adjustments that will reduce family costs. Some of these measures will reduce government income, by how much depends on how far the approach is taken. Either way it will have to be gradual, but with some immediate measures like the living wage and a reduction in Income Tax. The alternative measures to fund government will not only replace the revenue but the Land Usage Charge in particular will act in a way to increase public revenue. These measures will be progressive, fair and cause no hardship.

Prosperity is possible for the many, not just the few. It is not out of our reach, though it may seem so now when income and wealth is concentrated in the hands of a minority of people, despite the fact that we have all helped to create it. To make progress towards a fairer and more sustainable system, we need to think differently, think boldly and think decisively. We want to minimise the interference in the free market, but we have a responsibility to create a system where enterprise thrives, jobs pay well and basic goods are affordable. We want freedom but it comes with responsibilities. This is also the meaning of '*income for me/wealth for we*'.

6.2 Convincing the confused

Not everyone has the same needs or indeed the same viewpoint. So while for many of us the Agenda for Progressive Prosperity may make a lot of sense, there will also be many who don't understand it, don't believe it or just disagree with it. Worse still, there will be those who ignore the fact change needs to happen if we are to end hardship for so many. So the confused need to be convinced.

This has been particularly apparent when I have met with politicians and academics. Some politicians have found the ideas too bold and radical and suggest problems of implementation. The academics, who are used to precise data, take my proposals at face value but are sceptical. To them I say it is about the principle and the moral reasoning. If that makes sense, we will find a way of making it happen. Those who have been more excited are the political campaigners and think tanks who realise the need for new ideas. I hope they can build on these ideas and we can add further data. If it is the right thing to do then any problems can be overcome.

One of the first tasks when developing a marketing campaign is to be clear about the audience. The message must be tailored to that audience so that they actually do something, whether it is to buy a product or change an attitude. The main challenge for a campaign for change is to convince the audiences that these proposals affect them and to persuade them of the benefits and ultimately of action. While most people understand the problems (because they feel them), they don't know what can be done, or think nothing can be fixed, or indeed don't know what they could do. The audience could be segmented into many groups but I have chosen to keep it simple with three main target groups:

1 **The Majority**: those in poverty, the working poor, the new insecure with low incomes, the squeezed middle.
2 **The Rich** who have accumulated most of the world's wealth and who also control the political agenda.
3 **The Political Establishment** who influence and take the decisions on our behalf, but have actually been making matters worse.

1 The message to the majority

As the first of the measures proposed would make a significant difference to the majority of people, namely the abolition of income related taxes for over half the population, you would think that voting for it would be obvious. Apparently not, a pledge of £7 billion in tax cuts by the Conservative Party in December 2014 met with potential rejection. This proposal included raising the Income Tax threshold from £10,000 to £12,500 and the higher 40% rate from £32,000 to £50,000. The London *Evening Standard* did a survey published on 22 December 2014, which gave rise to the headline: *'We can't afford Cameron tax cuts says 53 per cent of voters'*. Staggeringly only 22% of Labour voters actually supported this idea, which, given the usual demographics, is a bit like turkeys voting for Thanksgiving in the USA or for Christmas in the UK. Further to this, 80% of Labour supporters believe Britain is not in a position to pay for tax cuts. The problem is that so many people associate tax cuts with reduction in government spending on key services and are conditioned to thinking in terms of Income Tax. Instead we should be thinking that there are many people who could pay more and it would cause no hardship to them.

Educating the electorate is critical to bring change. This includes presenting like-for-like, comparable data. It means being non-partisan in the approach so that we do not alienate others by a strong party political extreme line. It is important to listen to what the key concerns are. For most people it is financial security. The manifestation of prosperity is also high on the list. Above all it has to be proved that the initiatives in the Agenda are practical and possible not just blue-sky thinking.

The fact is the UK, the USA and most western democracies can afford tax cuts for the squeezed middle which could be more than made or from other sources with a greater ability to pay. The shift in contributions to public revenue from income to wealth will balance the budget and increase public revenue, so providing much-needed funds to finance the future. It will take funds that are idle or making a low returns and put them to productive use on behalf of all the people. The Agenda will create the possibility of progressing to prosperity not just in the financial terms with more money in people's pockets, but also provide great opportunity for upward social mobility through better and more accessible education and training. Better infrastructure would provide the environment for a healthy and growing economy. Backing for many of these initiatives has some support within the major parties on either side of the Atlantic. In order for this support to coalesce, our Agenda will need to gain visibility.

The issue is that the necessary funds are in the wrong hands and some adjustment needs to be done for the benefit of all. That's why I came up with the strategy of *'income for me/wealth for we'*. It is easy to understand;

it is simple and it brings together the key principles that make for a sustainable economy and greater social justice. The benefits of the Agenda of Progressive Prosperity for the majority of the population can be summarised here:

a More money in your pocket and more choices as to how you spend it.
b Lower household costs enabling a higher standard of living.
c Better and more accessible services leading to more opportunity.

2 Reasoning with the Rich

The benefits of the Agenda for the rich may not be so obvious – certainly for the rich who may have the fear of being 'soaked'. If the poorer have more money and yet pay fewer taxes then surely someone is going to have to pay more and that someone will be the rich. Those who already have enough to live on, have a greater ability to pay. This wealthy group is likely to be those in the top 5%, with a greater contribution coming from the top 1%. In the UK, the 1% would be those with over £1.5 million in assets, in the USA this could mean those with over $2.5 million. So we are not talking about impacting the slightly-above-average Joe who owns his own house, has some shares and has a good pension plan. We are talking about those with serious wealth and a very comfortable lifestyle.

Extreme inequality is very troubling, not just for those at the bottom of the income and wealth pyramid but also those at the top. Here are three good reasons why the wealthy should support proposals to reduce inequality even if it means they pay more:

a It makes good business sense and would be an excellent return on investment.
b Their wealth will still increase.
c It is socially responsible.

a Good business sense and an excellent return on investment: Paying more back for the benefit all of the community will not only give an excellent return on investment, it will also create greater economic stability and an environment for greater business opportunity. No one likes paying taxes whether rich or poor. Many people go to great lengths to avoid it, mainly the already wealthy as they can afford the advice. With the money raised from taxes going into a great big pot to be allocated according to political will, many feel there is mismanagement and funds are wasted. However if the public revenue raised was visibly well managed and its allocation transparent, then like all good investors, those funding the operation may be more willing to do so. Investing in transport, energy (renewable), communications, education and health and welfare can bring huge returns by providing the environment for economic growth and prosperity for us all, the wealthy included.

Those with a portfolio of expensive properties will find there is more to contribute, once property taxes have been re-valued to an up to date location value. That just seems fair: the more you benefit, the more you pay. You get what you pay for and with a flourishing economy that value can only increase. The funds raised from the land value charge will pay for infrastructure, not just transport, but health, education and recreational facilities to make an area even better. One of the proposals made earlier was that a tax on assets could be used to fund education, an admirable and good use of the assets from the wealthy which no one can shy away from. Such revenue could be enough to improve all levels of education and make university education free to those with the ability to achieve it. The concept of ring-fencing or hypothecation, allocating the money raised for specific budgets has been frowned upon in the past, but maybe its time has come. It could be a way of raising more money and also meeting the general approval and compliance of the wealthy with less effort on avoidance, which will result in benefit to all.

Economic stability depends on a strong middle class who can afford to buy products and services on a regular basis. When times are tough, aspirational people on lower incomes have massive incentives to take on too much debt to support and maintain their living standards, even for basics like keeping the car on the road to get to work. This exacerbates the propensity of the economy to swing from boom to financial-crisis bust. So ensuring the less well off have fair wages and the opportunity to earn and achieve more, maintains economic stability for the good of all. This also has repercussions on a global scale when decisions are made on allocation of funds, as Robert Peston, the former economics correspondent for BBC noted:

> The operation of markets in the circumstances of modern globalisation both leads to extreme concentrations of wealth and increasingly irrational outcomes when it comes to the dispersion of funds to combat threats such as diseases or promote public goods.

Such investments tend to favour the richer nations and the needs of the rich in particular.

Successful business relies on demand; demand increases sales revenues, profits and business opportunity. This Agenda will create more demand, more jobs and more opportunity to sell products and services, enabling the creation of more wealth. If the majority of the population continue to be tightly squeezed, no progress will be made. The poorer members of society as a whole can spend more than the rich. There are only so many shoes, jeans, motorcars and yachts a billionaire even a millionaire can own, so much of the super-rich's wealth sits idle, not generating income or creating jobs. Therefore growth tends to be faster when income is more evenly distributed so that those at the poorer end can spend more. Put simply, there is a bigger market.

b Wealth will still increase: With the proposals outlined in the agenda, the rich are not about to be soaked. Even with the payment of a small percentage on all personal assets, those with wealth will still make more money on their assets but not quite as much. The rate of the proposed Personal Asset Contribution is still well below the expected return from a broad asset portfolio.

c It is socially responsible and the right thing to do: Being socially responsible may not initially seem to be a high priority for the rich, though many people with wealth do actually want to give back and do want to be seen to be doing the right thing, but are not sure of the best way to do it. Unfortunately the current system means those who are philanthropically inclined are actually setting the social agenda, deciding how 'spare' funds should be spent. This is not in any way to denigrate the philanthropic intentions of the rich, as many have contributed to great socially valuable work. It is just that our current system allows for the accumulation of great wealth by the few who may lavish it on their personal enjoyment rather than the wider community. As others and I have attempted to demonstrate, wealth is in fact created by the many not the few, and it therefore seems fair to share it more equitably than it is now. I still want to encourage both the creation and accumulation of wealth but in a socially responsible way.

There are signs of increasing awareness amongst the plutocrats that wealth should be spread. The millions of people that own their own home, have a share portfolio, pension plan and feel they are 'doing OK' are unlikely to be contributing any more to the public revenue under my proposals. But those with plenty will need to contribute more. It is not about taking away, it is about giving back, being grateful not greedy. Paying taxes because you are wealthy is a way of giving back because the wealth accumulated was created by the many. It is economic patriotism to invest in the nation. There is an initiative from a group known as the Patriotic Millionaires, over 200 millionaires, who are actually asking the US government to increase taxes on the wealthy. Once the wealthy see these changes as fair, the idea will catch on, the switch to public revenue from wealth instead of income will seem like the new normal, instead of some threatening removal of rights!

According to researchers from Harvard and Yale universities, making others better off is not our main motivation for giving: we cooperate because it makes us look good. So it could be with paying taxes, if paying more taxes (that are fair) makes the rich look good then people will think more highly of them – that is a strong motivator. It could be that conspicuous consumption will be come unfashionable. For many it is not money that is the prime motivator it is status. Contributing more could indeed enhance status.

The rich and the super-rich have controlled the political agenda to ensure that the status quo is maintained and that policies that favour them win through. This is the 1% controlling the 99% and it cannot go on forever. The pitchforks will come out unless changes are made and, besides, this Agenda creates more opportunity to create additional wealth. The future of the wealthy is tied up with the well-being of those who create the wealth, so unless action is taken now to benefit the majority of people, revolution will come and it could all fall apart.

3 Winning policies for politicians

There are three reasons why politicians should now act boldly for social justice:

   a It is a vote winner
   b It is a non-partisan issue (or rather it is an issue for all parties!)
   c It is the right thing to do

a It is a vote winner: A platform of inequality reduction is clearly a vote winner. Over 80% of people in the UK agree the gap between rich and poor is too great, with nearly 70% believing that it is the Government's job to reduce this gap. However this did not seem to have much prominence in the General Election of 2015, where inequality seemed low on the agenda. According to Sir John Hills of the London School of Economics, of 25 policies that affected inequality offered by the winning Conservative Party, only one was shown to have a positive impact, the rest were all set to make matters worse. Incredible really!

Two out of three Americans are dissatisfied with the way income and wealth is currently distributed (Gallup, January 2014) and have few doubts that inequality has grown. About two-thirds of respondents (65%) said the gap between the rich and everyone else had increased over the past decade, versus just 8% who said it had decreased (Pew Research Center, January 2014). But when asked why the gap had grown, the answers were all over the place. In another survey, 72% agreed that '*right now, 99 per cent of Americans only see the rich getting richer and everyone else getting crushed*'. Though Americans are more concerned with equality of opportunity (97% of Americans think everyone in America should have equal opportunities to get ahead) than with equality of results, high levels of inequality reduce the opportunity for people to get ahead.

Similarly, a *New York Times*/CBS News poll conducted in late May 2015 revealed that 66% of Americans favoured the redistribution of '*the money and wealth in this country*' along more egalitarian lines. A key reason for Americans' desire to share the wealth more equally is that many of them think that riches are amassed unfairly. 74% of respondents said that large corporations had '*too much influence*' in '*American life and politics today*'. When it came to unions, however, only 37% said they had '*too much influence*', while 54% said they had '*too little influence*' or '*about the right amount of influence*'.

There is widespread demand for government action to counter economic inequality. The Pew Research Center's January 2014 opinion poll found that 82% of American respondents favoured government action to reduce poverty and 69% supported government action '*to reduce the gap between the rich and everyone else*'. *The New York Times*/CBS News survey reported that, by 57 to 39%, Americans favoured using government to '*reduce the gap between the rich and the poor in this country*', and most Americans back specific government programs along these lines. The survey found broad public support for the following programs: raising the minimum wage (71%); increasing taxes on the rich (68%); and requiring employers to provide paid family leave (80%). Even the more unusual approach of limiting the pay of top corporate executives received the backing of 50%. Other recent polls reveal similar priorities: between

71% (CNN/ORC) and 73% (Pew) of Americans favour raising the federal minimum wage; 52% favour *'heavy taxes on the rich'* (Gallup); 54% (Pew) support raising taxes on the wealthy and the corporations; and 70% (Gallup) support federal funding of pre-school education, according to an article published by the news site Common Dreams.

This data suggests that it is the will of the people that action is taken. Yet surprisingly, these issues have only been picked up by a handful of politicians such as Bernie Sanders and Elisabeth Warren in the USA. They have virtually been ignored by most politicians in the UK and have certainly not been a priority for the new Conservative government apart from few platitudes. We know that money and vested interests play a huge part but it clearly shows that any politician that speaks up on these urgent hardship issues will have support.

As the simple changes to Income Tax proposed bring benefit to the majority, it is a vote-winning tactic and a practical promise that can be fulfilled. At the same time it works for business, the engine room of the economy, creating more demand and more growth. Politicians hold the key to turning our agenda into action. Letting the majority of the people keep more of the money they have earned, has to be a vote winner and a means of salvaging respect.

b Non-partisan issue: All political parties say they consider inequality a key issue, yet none have come up with a strategy for correcting this – just a few piecemeal suggestions. This Agenda for Progressive Prosperity is not more party political rhetoric: it is non-partisan. As most of the recommended initiatives have some level of support within all major parties on either side of the Atlantic, this agenda or indeed part of it could quite conceivably become theirs. Just think of the way that environmental polices once characterised as hippy nonsense have made their way into the mainstream, buoyed by research, but also by developing public awareness. This Agenda is based on the belief that a government's role is to serve the people and that the capitalist system is a great way to create wealth, for the many, not just the few.

c It is the right thing to do: Tackling inequality and relieving unnecessary hardship is the right thing to do and will make it easier to resolve other economic and social issues. There will be opposition to the Agenda from entrenched interests as our cherished democracy is now a plutocracy in which the super-rich wields power through a self-perpetuating political elite. Money talks. In the USA the amount spent per elected seat in Congress is 1,200 times as much as per elected seat in the House of Commons. This has been caused in part by the Supreme Court's 2010 *Citizens United* decision that allowed corporations and unions to spend unlimited amounts to influence elections as long as they operate independently of candidates. A separate High Court ruling in 2014 abandoned the limits on the total amount of money an individual could give to candidates, political action committees and political parties in an election, making matters even worse. Large political contributions need to be capped and attract significant tax liabilities, which will reduce the power of super-rich individuals and corporations and create the conditions for other voices to be heard.

Even in the UK, with regulated political financing, money still buys influence and increasing amounts are spent on lobbying by special interest groups, who win out over the underfunded but nevertheless valid interests. Having wealth makes it easier both to stand for political office and influence political decisions.

It would be naive to regard well regulated political financing is a panacea on its own. It will not cut through social networks or throw open club doors, but it comes as part of a package aimed at improving civil society. Measures to incentivise companies to be socially responsible through the tax system will also help, as they will be implementing the new social agenda, paying a living wage and helping to close the pay and wealth gaps. With greater prosperity and more enriched lives, more people will engage in the political life of the country, vote and get involved in community activities, all of which contribute to a more effective democracy.

Summary

So if we are to have any hope of achieving a reform agenda to minimise hardship and bring prosperity, the benefits of the Agenda for Progressive Prosperity have to be tailored and addressed clearly to the three main audiences. The Agenda has to be inclusive: it is not about them and us, it is about us. The rich and politicians should not be demonised but their help should be enlisted in bringing change and prosperity for the majority, not just for the few. If we can achieve this then democracy will be restored. The government will be working for us to minimise inequality and poverty, and to boost economic growth, bringing more wealth to be shared more equitably.

6.3 Campaign for change

Many political campaigns are divisive, doomed to failure by pitching one side against another, us against them. Disrespect, name-calling and ridicule causes conflict and deteriorates into anger, distrust and opposition, reducing the likelihood of bringing change by consensus. If there are no good ideas then attack the opposition!

To succeed, a campaign for Progressive Prosperity needs to be inclusive. The majority of the population, suffering from unnecessary man-made hardship, will clearly benefit from the proposals. However in the past, the electorate have voted against their best interests, such as voting against tax cuts for the needy because they believe it will mean cuts in services. It does not have to be like that. The message of this campaign is that change can happen.

The real challenge comes not from convincing the majority who will clearly benefit, not from voting in the politicians but from the need to persuade the very small number of wealthy people that it is good for them too. It is because the wealthy control the agenda. They can afford to lobby, they can afford to contribute to political campaigns and candidates, and they have the circle of contacts to network with others who are influential, so reinforcing and maintaining the status quo.

If this campaign is to succeed, there has to be a different strategy, otherwise insanity: making the mistake of doing the same thing again and expecting a different outcome! It was this insane approach that lost the UK Labour Party the election in 2015, when it focussed more on what it had to offer rather than what people wanted. According to polls in mid 2015 when the extended marathon campaign got underway, presidential nomination candidate Bernie Sanders, the self-declared democratic socialist is reflecting the wishes of the people. He is clearly having an effect on Hillary Clinton who has been exceptionally cautious in putting forward proposed policies. She has been slightly more progressive than she might otherwise have been if there had been no Bernie. On the Republican side we see a wide range or differing proposals, but it seems at this stage all candidates are talking to the converted. The challenge is to talk to the unconverted. While Bernie Sanders appears to be representing a majority of ordinary Americans, his rhetoric is a fight against the billionaires, Wall Street and the big banks. This is the very target group that needs to be convinced, instead of forcing them into opposition and entrenchment. However, this does not mean cosying up to the wealthy and abandoning reform because of the high financial stakes and funding. A clear case for reform needs to be made and at the same time to reassure the majority that what we want to accomplish can be achieved.

It is not that the wealthy are evil, far from it: many have done and are doing great work for the benefit of mankind. However with wealth, there often becomes greed and the lust to create more wealth. The justification is that it is creating jobs and providing opportunity, but the fallacy of 'trickle-down' economics has been well documented.

Once the wealthy realise that an Agenda for Progressive Prosperity is good for them too, then change will happen. The strategy is to play the game and then change the rules rather than try to change the rules without playing the game! As the wealthy will be contributing more to the nation, the concept of tax needs to be more attractive and acceptable, for everyone, not just the rich. There are three areas to consider in making tax more palatable and fairer:

1 A tax need not be a tax.
2 Tax needs to be fair.
3 Tax and spending needs to be transparent and well managed.

1 A tax or a charge?

If we define a tax as a *'compulsory contribution to a public authority irrespective of the exact amount of service rendered to the taxpayer in return,'* then a voluntary payment to a public authority where the amount is directly related to the service rendered is not a tax. To illustrate, London's Congestion Charge, designed to keep traffic flowing and cut pollution, is levied on vehicles driving through the central zone during peak hours. The motorist has a *choice*: to drive through the zone during peak hours and pay the charge, or to avoid the central zone in peak hours. Those choosing to drive then are paying for the benefit of having less congested and polluted roads, so it is a usage charge rather than a tax. Moreover, by law all surplus income has to be reinvested in infrastructure. In its first 10 years of operation, it provided London with an additional £1.2 billion to spend on roads and public transport. Similarly the UK Road Fund Licence, paid by vehicle owners wishing to drive on the roads, was meant to cover the cost of highways, but that cost is nowhere near covered today. However, were the Land Usage Charge in operation, the higher land values of properties benefitting from the roads, would become available to help with infrastructure costs. Another option would be to increase the road licence fee. National Insurance Contributions, although a compulsory levy, were initially a contributory system of insurance against illness and unemployment, and later also provided retirement pensions and other benefits, but the revenue from this source no longer covers the outgoings. Time for a readjustment?

Income tax is clearly a tax as it is compulsorily removed from most of us before we even see the cash, and there is no correlation between what we pay and the benefits we receive. That's one of the reasons I would abolish Income Tax for all but the highest earners. Similarly other payroll taxes are a tax and are extracted from us whether we like it or not and are generally regressive, hitting the lower incomes harder in percentage terms.

The proposed Personal Asset Contribution, while it will be compulsory is a contribution back to the community. It will be levied on assets over a certain threshold. On the principle of 'income for me/wealth for we', a sizeable part of the wealth held by a few rightfully belongs to the rest and should therefore be returned through a contribution to public revenue. Such a system will not adversely affect lifestyles of the wealthy to the point whereby they fall below a good standard of living.

Today's property taxes are undoubtedly taxes and regressive ones at that. The proposed Land Usage Charge (LUC), however, is not a tax because the charge is directly related to the services received at the site concerned, and the occupant has a choice whether to live or work there. Public infrastructure projects and local services make some areas more desirable than others, increasing land values accordingly. The LUC reflects these varying land values and captures a proportion for public revenue. This creates a virtuous circle: the greater the benefits conferred on a site, the more valuable it becomes and the higher the LUC payable to the government, making more revenue available to fund further improvements. This principle could and should be extended to more areas of local and national revenue collection, eventually arriving at a public revenue system without taxation.

For companies, current taxes on profits and payroll are undoubtedly taxes. However I would say that the proposed Corporate Social Contribution is not a tax in the traditional way as it is directly related to the wealth created by business, which belongs to the stakeholders not just the shareholders and part of this can be returned to the stakeholders through a contribution to public revenue. This is a contribution towards supporting all society, which can be reduced or offset in direct relation to the social responsibility of the company. So, while this is a compulsory contribution, it is in relation to the wealth created by the business that is due to the stakeholders.

2 Tax needs to be fair

There was a lot of comment on the proposal in the UK to charge a mansion tax on houses worth over £2 million. This was a lazy proposal, as what is really needed is a complete reform of the out-of-date property taxes – residents of some of London's more up-market boroughs would regard this as the last straw. The real issue here is that the property taxes are woefully out of date with the highest tax band being on properties over £320,000, when the average house price nationally is over £250,000 and the average in London over £500,000, clearly favouring those with more valuable homes. The valuations are based on 20-year-old data. If these were updated to reflect today's values, there would be a considerable increase in revenue from this source with the rich paying a higher proportion than now, which would be fairer. However, a revaluation on the same basis would not be entirely fair because current valuations include the building, so it penalises those with the best kept properties. As we have outlined the whole system needs to be revised so that it distinguishes the publicly created value of the land from the privately created value of buildings.

3 Tax and spending needs to be transparent and well managed

As all taxes are paid into one big pot, irrespective of the source. How it is allocated and prioritised is a political decision, but some don't like to think it is going to fund scroungers who strain the welfare benefit system and do little to find work. The British government made an effort on this front by sending a note to the 30 million Income Tax payers, setting out how the money raised from their tax was spent, but it was just Income Tax. This is not the whole picture: it did not take into account a nearly equal amount of revenue raised by sales and property taxes. The taxpayer needs to have the confidence that the money that is contributed is well spent and well managed, not wasted. Then there may be less avoidance.

However, there is a case for hypothecation, which is the technical term for ring-fencing revenue raised for specific purposes. It could then be argued that it is not really a tax, as it is a payment for services rendered. This could encourage transparency and the acceptance of the tax. President Obama suggested corporate profits held overseas, if repatriated, would be used to fund infrastructure, in an attempt to appeal to companies to come clean. Many taxes, such as the UK Airport Tax or the Road Fund Licence were supposedly designed to fund specific expenses but now they are just paid into the pot.

The idea of the large pot for all government revenue could be abandoned altogether. Revenue from different sources could be allocated to budgets for particular government services so that taxpayers knew what they were paying for. This could make tax more palatable.

Writing in the Fabian magazine in January 2015, Charles Clarke, a former senior cabinet minister in the last Tony Blair Labour government suggested that we need hypothecation to strengthen transparency, notably for the National Health Service.

> In addition, 'copayment', where beneficiaries of public spending make an appropriate and socially just contribution to costs, as with university tuition fees and congestion charging, will strengthen the public sense of contribution. However, the Treasury's traditional opposition to such change plays into the hands of the anti-taxation campaigners. The public needs to support how their tax is spent. It should be acknowledged that public spending, which might easily have gained public support decades ago, now needs serious re-evaluation in modern conditions.

Making increasing demands on the taxpayers and extracting large amounts are damaging to the economy, but the revenue raising initiatives I propose are not additional taxes. They are a first step towards replacing harmful taxes with more efficient and less damaging ones. Coming more from accumulated wealth they are not taking money out of the economy, they are in fact injecting it back in. So this process is going to boost economic growth, which increases more wealth and more public revenue over time. Obviously the realisation of the full benefits will take time. For example, it takes time to recruit good teachers, train them, organise on-going training, build new facilities etc, but as investing more in education is agreed by virtually everyone as top priority and the key to social mobility, we must find a way to fund it.

Being pragmatic, it may not be possible to allocate revenue precisely to each budget, though it would at least make up the majority. As an example revenue received by UK government could be allocated as follows:

1 The infrastructure budget could be funded out of the revenue raised from property taxes based on location value, the Land Use Charge. Infrastructure projects have the effect of raising the value of surrounding land, and so increasing public revenue to help recover the investment costs as well as contributing to the bigger pot.

2 Education could be covered by revenue from the Personal Asset Contribution (PAC). So the individuals with significant accumulated wealth generally, though not always, have a good education and this has helped them become wealthy. Everybody believes that education is the key to social mobility so it is a very worthwhile use of accumulated wealth, it would be good to be seen to be contributing. Of course, I am not suggesting that those who pay tax on their wealth decide the agenda for education!

   For example in the UK, the education budget is £98 billion: a 20% increase would make a considerable difference. That would require £120 billion to be raised. The proposed PAC could deliver £100 million or more. No one over the eligible threshold of £1.5 million in assets could argue effectively that such gesture is unfair: they would be using their accumulated wealth to create a great education system for the next generation. Some super-wealthy do this anyway, in a philanthropic manner but to their personal agenda.

3 Universal health care is vital to reducing inequality and moving towards prosperity. As businesses want a healthy workforce for social as well as commercial reasons, they want to minimise days off sick! Of course in the UK and most advanced countries, healthcare is provided by the state as part of the tax system. However instead of retaining payroll taxes, which is in effect, a tax on personal income and on employment, the contribution to healthcare costs could come from the tax on company profits, the proposed Corporate Social Contribution.

   Once again using the UK example, the healthcare budget is £140 billion (about 19% of the government budget). Currently the revenue received from tax on company profits is just £41 billion, so that would mean a three and half times jump to cover it, so currently this may not be possible or practical. However the proposed reforms would reduce direct and indirect taxes on companies and therefore increase profits and the resultant government revenue. However added together with VAT revenues of £111 billion, it could cover the entire national health service.

It is already accepted in the USA that companies pay health insurance for their staff as the norm, and at great expense, separately from the tax system, so significantly adding to employment costs. However in addition there are Federal Insurance contributions paid by the employers and employees. Overcoming the ideological and cultural opposition to 'free' national health services would be an uphill battle, but I am sure most corporations would prefer to have the opportunity to make high profits without the cost of healthcare as a direct employment expense.

4 Welfare: It would make sense that this was covered by income related taxes as this is the contribution to a rainy day when you can't work or can't get work and indeed for pensions. So Income Tax could be abolished altogether and be replaced by insurance contributions?

Summary

There is a clear case that the principle of '*income for me/wealth for we*' will bring benefit to the majority of the population. In order to build a more equitable society, the biggest challenge is convincing the wealthy that this is a good idea. There is no hiding the fact that those with substantial wealth will be contributing more, but still making money. In order to bring change, the idea has to be 'sold' to the rich. Fortunately, there is a very strong practical argument in addition to a moral case for the wealthy to support this agenda. Hopefully their attitude towards tax and avoidance can change.

Summary of Chapter 6

Prosperity is possible for the many, not just the few. It is not out of our reach, though it must seem so for so many people when a minority are concentrating income and wealth in their hands despite the fact that we have all helped to create that wealth. To make progress towards a fairer and more sustainable system we need to think differently, think boldly and think decisively. We want to minimise interference in the free market, but we have a responsibility to create a system where enterprise thrives, jobs pay well and basic goods are affordable. We want freedom but it comes with responsibilities.

The Agenda for Progressive Prosperity recommends a serious reduction in taxes on the poor and the lower paid. This may not bring immediate significant increase in income as a large proportion relies on welfare benefits and credits to top up income. However, in the longer term it will give more people more control over their lives, and the respectability of earning enough to live on instead of relying on welfare. At the same time it will reduce the welfare budget. In addition there are other measures such as the living wage and reduced payroll taxes that will significantly increase disposable income and sales tax adjustments that will reduce family costs. Some of these measures will reduce government income, but this could be replaced by the proposed reform of the property tax in a revenue neutral way. The shift will need to be gradual but with some immediate measures, like living wage and reduction in Income Tax. The replacement measures will stimulate economic activity and increase revenue. They will be progressive, fair and cause no hardship.

So if we are to have any hope of achieving a reform agenda to minimise hardship and bring prosperity the benefits of the Agenda for Progressive Prosperity have to be tailored and addressed clearly to the three main groups I have outlined. It has to be inclusive, it is not about them and us, it is about us. The rich and politicians should not be demonised but their help should be enlisted in bring in change and prosperity for the majority, not just the few. If we can achieve this, then democracy will be restored, the government will be working for us to minimise inequality and poverty, and to boost economic growth to bring more wealth to be shared more equitably.

CHAPTER 7

And Now, It Is up to Us

*Ask not what your country can do for you;
ask what you can do for your country*

John F. Kennedy, inaugural address,
20th January 1961

THIS ALTRUISTIC duty is key to our Agenda for Progressive Prosperity. We cannot sit around waiting for other people to do things for us. If our elected government does not deliver, then we have to take action. If we want change, it is up to us, every one of us. The odds are currently stacked against us but we can still win. One of the biggest obstacles is our lack of belief: we have to believe that change can happen. Do not dismiss the possibility and despair. There is hope, despite the fact that large numbers of people have been known to vote against their best interests, believing that is how it has to be. No, it does not. Poverty, financial insecurity and lack of opportunity are not inevitable.

The political plutocratic elite still has a stranglehold on government and it is going to take determination to break this established mould. This can only be achieved in an inclusive, not divisive way. Unfortunately, we only have ourselves to blame for the present situation. It is not that the elite are inherently bad; it is just our traditional thinking. It only needs a change of mindset about how public revenue can and should be raised, then the trend of taking from the poor and giving to the rich can be reversed. But there are rays of hope.

The British people found themselves with a Conservative government after the general election of 2015, bringing to an end a coalition of the Conservative and Liberal Democrat parties. Things had been tough for most people during the previous five years of austerity politics but, surprisingly, the voters voted for more of it! This was partly due to the opposition Labour Party losing the election because of a lack of a clear message and strong leadership. So evidence would indicate that the UK electoral system needs reform, as 75% did not actually vote for the party that formed the government. Though 37% of voters of those who voted, voted Conservative, there was only a 66% turnout, which suggests there was no clear mandate for austerity. It was a very disappointing campaign with no bold ideas, no clear vision and no real answers to the underlying problem of extreme inequality. In the end, fear, uncertainty and doubt decided the result. More than half the country was left disappointed, disenfranchised and in need of answers.

A lot of hope was placed on the shoulders of Barack Obama when he was inaugurated as President in 2008. At first he only had the House of Representatives with a Republican majority but in 2014 the Senate went Republican, making a progressive legislative program very difficult. The Democrats have a lot of work ahead to swing both houses of Congress back to the Democrats. The last thing any Democrat President would want to inherit is an Obama stalemate with a polarised legislature at odds with the Executive and a Judiciary that has not really eased the stalemate either. The populist agenda of Bernie Sanders and his courage to stand up to the establishment of big money seems to be resonating with the country, tired of being squeezed with ongoing financial insecurity while the rich get richer. Unfortunately, Bernie consistently talks of bashing the billionaires and busting up the banks, hence alienating the very people that will in fact be the instruments of change. A successful candidate needs to be inclusive and bring in all factions and groups for a common cause, both rich and poor; it needs to be us together, not us and them. So the challenge is sincerely to reconnect with the American people and not be in the pocket of the wealthy. Bernie may do a great job at representing the will of the people, forcing the agenda, but he, like so many candidates, is in need of more policy substance and not just rhetoric. The United States cannot go on as it is, but there is still hope to make the will of the people prevail.

Meanwhile in the United Kingdom, it will not be an easy run for the Conservatives as they only have a slim majority. By-elections and dissent can make it difficult to keep that majority together after the honeymoon period. The Labour Party seems to have a new direction but it is still confused. The only hope for the UK is that the Labour Party, and for that matter the decimated Liberal Democrat Party, to get their act together and reflect the views of the people. Or there may be a new movement, hopefully for Progressive Prosperity, which will help move the political agenda to represent all the people, not just the few. That is why it is up to us to act, now.

It is time for a new, non-partisan direction, a new Agenda for Progressive Prosperity. This is an inclusive agenda that can bring immediate and sustained relief to millions of people by abolishing Income Tax for the majority of taxpayers, giving them a significant pay rise at a not very great cost to government revenue. It could be made revenue neutral through a small tax on assets over and agreed threshold from those who already have enough to live on. They are already enjoying a comfortable income from their investments so that a small percentage tax would not have a big impact on their living standards. We can stop squeezing the middle and keeping so many trapped in poverty. Together with a living wage, this would inject billions into the economy and create growth, more jobs and a chance of a better life for all. There is a clear case for change and there is a body of evidence to support that case.

7.1 Body of evidence

Despite the level of awareness of economic inequality being at an all time high, with the majority of the population in poverty or in the squeezed middle, feeling the hardship every day, there are still no bold, radical, coherent measures to tackle it. But the talk is increasing.

President Obama focussed on inequality in his 2015 State of the Union address, the World Economic Forum meeting of plutocrats in Davos in January 2015 highlighted it, Janet Yelland, US Federal Reserve chairman said it was a grave danger, Christine Lagarde, managing director of the International Monetary Fund said inequality hampers growth. Then in February 2015 inequality was mentioned for the first time in a communiqué from the G20 group of finance minister. Even Republican potential presidential candidates have made reference to it. During the first two months of 2015, BBC TV screened Jacques Peretti's 'The Super Rich and Us', the BBC World Service 'A Richer World but for Whom?' and BBC Radio 4 from Robert Peston, the harbinger of doom for the 2008 economic crisis, presented a thoughtful two-parter called 'The Price of Inequality'. In the USA inequality is a regular feature on media like moyers.com and

Mother Jones. Denying inequality is like denying climate change, arguments can be made as how bad it is, or what we can do about it but its existence is obvious and we are still slow to act

The evidence of the problem is clear, there is the data from Thomas Piketty, Emmanuel Saez and Gabriel Zucman, together with detailed reports from Oxfam, the Equality Trust, institute of Policy Studies and others and combined with the learned works of Joseph Stiglitz, Anthony Atkinson, John Hills and many more.

Joseph Stiglitz, Nobel laureate and professor at Columbia University New York and Anthony Atkinson, Senior Research Fellow of Nuffield College, Oxford and Centennial Professor at the London School of Economics have been cooperating since 1976 when they proposed the Atkinson-Stiglitz theorem of public economics. In March 2015 Sir Anthony Atkinson published his latest 300-page work: *Inequality and what to do about it* which outlines 15 key proposals mainly from a UK perspective. Then in April, Joseph Stiglitz published his latest: *The Great Divide, Unequal Societies and what we can do about them*, which is mainly a collection of recent articles with an American focus.

While Thomas Piketty seems to be the poster boy on the inequality problem, it is interesting to note that he has known Anthony Atkinson for 25 years since he (Piketty) was a student at the London School of Economics and cites Professor Atkinson as one of his two main influencers. Thomas Piketty now Professor at the Paris School of Economics is one of the trio of well respected French economists who have all worked together and are now on the international stage, this group include Emmanuel Saez at UC Berkeley and Gabriel Zucman at London School of Economics and now back at UC Berkeley.

All these recent works are well researched and thought through but like many scientists they love the theory and proving how a set of inputs produce a given set of outputs. This was brought home to me when I attended a seminar given by Emmanuel Saez at the Institute of Fiscal Studies in London on 'Generalised Social Marginal Welfare Weights for Optimal Tax Theory'. It was full of formulas and hypothesis (unsurprisingly with a title like that), well above my advanced level mathematics and my basic university economics (my degree was in Public Administration), indeed many from the floor where chipping in with even more hypotheses. Now, this work is valuable and helps us get a better understanding, but I can't help thinking: This is all very well but can't we get on with fixing the problem, the real life problem with some bold decisive action.

At an event at the LSE in May 2015, just after the general election in the UK, Sir John Hills, the director of the new International Inequality Institute presented a clear set of graphics of polices. There were four areas: Capital taxes, Direct taxes, Benefits, and Pay They were taken from the manifestos of the main parties, showing their expected contribution to increasing or decreasing inequality. It was dismal showing for all parties. Out of the many policies, all but one (pension growth above earnings) proposed by the new Conservative government could be shown to be contributing to even more inequality. It is frightening, especially when only a quarter of the electorate actually voted for a Conservative candidate.

But we must not give up! I am convinced that we will reach a tipping point when the will of the people will become so strong that change will happen in the UK, USA and other countries with extreme inequality.

So I think we have more than enough data on the problems of inequality. We could argue that some of it is not accurate, but the sheer volume of evidence indicates we have a problem. As mentioned, it is not the inequality so much as the fact that so many people suffer unnecessary hardship and miss the chance to lead a fulfilled and purposeful life. It seems many think that extreme inequality, not just economic inequality, is a natural by-product of a growing industrial society. Well, it is not, we have a choice; extreme inequality it is not inevitable. As Joseph Stiglitz believes, our choice is not between growth and fairness: with the right policies, we can have both.

Despite the enormous amount of data on the problem, there is only a limited amount as to what can be done to fix it. Much of it is very sound advice but, to me, it does not present a clear theme nor is it part of a bold strategy for sustainable reform. The recommendations amount to a collection of piecemeal solutions to lightly related problems. For example, Anthony Atkinson made 15 proposals for the UK in his latest book. In the Roosevelt Institute's latest paper: *Rewriting the rules of the American economy: an agenda for shared prosperity*, authored by Joseph Stiglitz, 37 action points were proposed under eight headings.

I have tried to offer you a simple theme from a common sense point of view under the principle of '*income for me/wealth for we*'. I hope this will make the strategy easier to understand.

When I put my proposal to abolish Income Tax for the lower paid majority to one of the learned academics above, the response was: '*Hmmm, but if you raised the tax threshold you would be giving tax breaks to everyone.*' No, I said, it could be managed through adjusting marginal tax rates with steeply progressive Income Tax above the threshold, or even a reformed tax credit system. His final word to me was, '*Aahh, I will have to think about that.*' I concluded that he saw merit in the idea but had concerns as to how it could be implemented. Good. Because to make progress we need to think differently, figure out what is the right thing to do and then how to implement it. I talked later that week to another economist who studied at the Paris School of Economics who was now working in the 'real world' of finance not as an academic. He immediately understood my proposals and liked the simplicity of the '*income for me/wealth for we*' approach. He agreed that practical issues could be overcome if the will was there and the outcome was extremely beneficial and desirable.

The case for raising government revenue from wealth is overwhelming given the fact that wealth continues to increase and continues to concentrate. Any 'tax' based on wealth is still going to leave the wealthy getting wealthier but by not quite so much. It just takes the funds out of storage and puts them to use. It is not about punishing individuals but doing what is best for the country.

In the UK, families hold a combined wealth of more than £9.1 trillion – the equivalent of £326,414 for every household in the land (enough to buy a house outright at the average house price with £50,000 left for pension!), according to analysis from Lloyds Bank Private Banking in 2015. Average household wealth has grown by more than £126,000 in just 10 years, but it reveals a deep divide: the richest 20% hold 105 times more wealth than the poorest fifth. People already on the property ladder or with good pensions are accumulating personal wealth fast. The value of property and other personal assets grew by £1.5 trillion in 2014, a staggering but unsustainable 16%, the largest annual increase in household wealth since records began in 2001. Average house prices rose by 9% in 2014, adding £452 billion to the total. However, housing now accounts for just 39% of total UK wealth, compared to 45% in 2004. Other financial assets, such as the pension pots and life assurance funds, have doubled in value over the same period to £5.5 trillion, and now make up 61% of total wealth. So at the levels of the asset tax proposed, there would be no hardship for those payers and yet considerable relief for those that would no longer be paying Income Tax

The Equality Trust, citing the Office for National Statistics, reminded us that the majority of the UK population (66%) hold no positive financial assets at all – with the combined £9 trillion held privately in the UK spread between the remaining 34%. So on that basis 34% (nine million house-holds) would have an average of million pounds each!

So it could be said that the problem of extreme inequality is now on the political agenda, there is much discussion on the problems, but lack of initiatives to solve it. Apparently one European Union official cynically commented that most politicians know what needs to be done but they just don't know how to get re-elected afterwards.

A platform of inequality reduction is clearly a vote winner. Over 80% of people in the UK agree the gap between rich and poor is too great with nearly 70% of people believe that it is the Government's job to reduce this gap. And yet this was not tackled head on in the UK general election. It is clearly the root of most of the other problems in society: solve this and we move forward. Surprisingly the Conservative Party chants that it is the party of working people and that it will reduce taxes for 30 million people, yet it still continues with punitive taxation on those who can't afford it and not on those who can.

In a poll taken just after the May 2015 election, voters were asked whether the government *'should give priority to working for faster economic growth or reducing the gap between rich and poor,'* 50% of voters said inequality was more important. Meanwhile only 43% said that economic growth should take priority. People who voted Tory at the last election were at odds with the public view. A huge 78% said that economic growth should take priority, compared to only 17% who were concerned with inequality. Of course, the issue here is that it is a loaded question because by careful well-conceived policies we can have both economic growth and reduction in inequality as a priority. They are not mutually exclusive. So the will of the people is to reduce inequality but among Tories this is a low priority, oh dear!

During the election campaign, Prime Minister David Cameron vowed to introduce a law guaranteeing no rise in Income Tax rates, VAT or National Insurance before 2020 if the Tories won the election, which they did. While this was considered a comforting pledge to the regular voter it was also undoubtedly a great ruse for the rich who can now have no fear of tax increases on their ever-expanding wealth pot. So, even though social justice stresses that the better off have the ability to pay more, that clearly is not going to happen in the near future.

The Tories are, however, proposing to raise Income Tax threshold from £10,500 to £12,500, a step in the right direction but very timid. This move will take 1 million more of the lowest paid workers out of Income Tax

(I should hope so!) and will give a tax cut to 30 million more, equivalent to about an extra £1 per day. As they say every little bit helps or 'better than a kick in the teeth', but this is derisory and still leaves 30 million people struggling to make ends meet. At the same time it is proposed to raise the 40% threshold from £40,000 to £50,000, meaning those on £50,000 (in the top 10%) would take home £1,620 more a year or £135 per month, £4.50 per day, a 3% rise – useful but not significant.

Inequality is also a high-profile topic in the US, where President Obama called for higher taxes on the rich in his State of the Union address. Americans across the ideological spectrum see inequality as a big problem, including majorities of Democrats (89%), independents (77%) and Republicans (60%) in a Pew Research Center 2014 poll. However, the view that inequality is a very big problem is much more common among Democrats (59%) and independents (49%) than among Republicans (19%), and there is a big partisan divide over how the issue should be addressed.

If we are to bring real change and sustainable improvement, then bold policies are required. The academics are saying it, the people are saying it, but the politicians are not doing it. So our challenge is to convince the politicians to follow the will of the people.

7.2 The time is now

This impasse on government action on inequality or more importantly ending hardship for millions means that the people have to show their strength of feeling. Clearly voting is not enough.

Government is visibly not working for the majority, as it continues to allow such unnecessary adversity to persist for the majority of the population. To fix it, vast sums do not need to be raised from punishing taxation, wide-ranging welfare programmes do not need to be expanded, ineffective austerity packages which have made matters worse do not need to be continued. Public revenue can be sought from sources where there is plenty and ensure that companies pay fair wages instead of forcing taxpayer top-ups. The government is serving the interests of the few and the few would like to keep it that way.

As a result of extreme economic inequality, democracy has been eroded and we find ourselves in a plutocracy, effectively ruled by a wealthy few. It is this group that have the money to influence political decisions and the network to move in the circles of the political elite. Government needs to reengage with the people who elected it as well as those that did not, all the people.

You can decide to do nothing or do something, or better still act with purpose, not alone but together. Work together to change attitudes, embrace new thinking and say *'Yes, it can be done and we are going to do it.'* If you do nothing, you risk your country falling into turmoil as civilised society falls apart. The poor and the oppressed, the 75% in the middle will not keep quiet forever. Indeed the top 5% and even the top 1% (in income and wealth terms) are starting to realise that they cannot go on like this forever. It is fair to say that most of us don't want a French or Russian revolution but a considered and acceptable plan of action, which brings results as swiftly as possible over just a few years. We should not be afraid to use the system to change the system. We should join forces with like-minded organisations and individuals to create a movement that understands the system and how to change it from within. It requires commitment and determination.

So, if a movement is to be built that seeks prosperity for all, and organisations and individuals are going to support it, there needs to be a clear agenda, definite policy proposals that will bring change that the government will be mandated to action. I have suggested just five policy areas. In order to get consensus they will need to be broad but also effective and deliverable. The success of the movement will be in the detail and the immediate and strong action that brings rapid results. There needs to be a renewal of the social contract between the government and the people a new 'promise to the people'.

The rich say it does not matter that the rich get richer as they help the poor get richer too. After years of trickle-down economic theories, most people now realise this no longer works or, rather, that it never did.

Maybe we are being naïve in believing that we will ever persuade the super rich to act, even though the likes of billionaire Nick Hanauer and groups like the Patriotic Millionaires are pushing the case for the wealthy to pay more (and the less well off to pay less). And maybe we are naïve to think that the politicians (not all) who, as a group, have more wealth than the average Joe, may be willing to make changes, especially as their plutocratic paymasters are calling the shots. If the politicians will not act and the plutocrats control the agenda with big money, then this could reduce our choices to just one option: revolution?

The best way to bring change is through the democratic process, but even then there is the possibility of voting for appealing personalities with little substance, or for political parties to which people feel some aspirational attachment or where there is just stubborn resistance or even irrational prejudice. Voter ignorance is a real block in our route to democratic effectiveness. We need to be better informed of the facts, be aware of the possibility of change and to believe in its possibility of achievement, if we are to win through.

As America knows only too well, candidates rely on donations from corporations and wealthy individuals to fund their campaigns. They are, therefore, beholden to their donors to ensure that funding continues. This was highlighted by a report in the *Washington Post* on 26 January 2015 that a network of conservative advocacy groups, backed by Charles and David Koch, aims to spend a staggering $889 million in advance of the 2016 elections. This massive financial goal was revealed to donors during an annual winter meeting hosted by Freedom Partners, the tax-exempt business lobby that serves as the hub of the Koch-backed political operation.

However, money can't buy everything. The majority of the nation does not have access to such funds so the way to bring change is through a new movement of interested groups and individuals coming together to create a strong clear message to politicians and plutocrats, as well as the whole nation, that this is the will of the people and it must prevail.

It is different in the UK where there are precise regulations to protect the democratic process, but there is nevertheless a significant and increasing amount spent on lobbying and influencing political opinion. There is nothing wrong with lobbying, but it can be bought and that needs money. Sometimes lobbying is essential to achieve your objectives, but as President Chirac of France declared (before the selection of London instead of Paris as the host of the 2012 Olympics was announced): lobbying is an English word!

There are three options to turn the wishes of the majority into a strong political force that will make change happen:

a Progressive groups within the existing party system.
b A new party.
c A new movement outside the party system.

a Within the party system: There is the opportunity to bring reform through the democratic process using the ballot box, but this may not be enough to make change happen. In many western democracies the current party political system is failing us. The rigid two party system in the USA makes it exceedingly difficult for a third party to break through, yet the two main parties appear to be at each other's throats in constant conflict. With a Republican congress and a Democratic President, where has consensus politics gone?

The UK recently had a coalition government, unheard of since wartime. There have been other parties besides the two main ones, the Conservative and Labour. The most persistent has been the Liberal Party, now morphed into the Liberal Democrats, but with the rise of the UK Independence Party (UKIP) which, as its name suggests, is a single issue party, though it is developing policy on a whole range of issues. Perhaps the nearest to a radical third party in the UK is the Green Party with only one Member of Parliament. Then there is the Scottish Nationalist Party which won almost every seat in Scotland.

b A new party: I was a founder member of the Social Democratic Party (SDP) in 1981 and stood for election under that banner in both Manchester and later in Windsor and Maidenhead. At the time the Labour Party was tired and left wing and the Conservatives where too far to the right. I remember well the enthusiasm and excitement of a potential breakthrough as well as the warm and positive reception from the electorate, boosting our hopes of winning. However when it came to Election Day, voters reverted to form and voted for their traditional party, and the SDP made some but not a lot of progress. Sadly, it was merged with the Liberal Party to become the Liberal Democrats in 1988.

As has been seen in recent years, the traditional parties, wherever they are on the political spectrum, have failed to come up with bold visionary measures that actually improve the lives of the majority – though recently we have seen a new party win a majority in Greece and a new party in Spain leading in the opinion polls. Their clear message is enough is enough, there is a better way (even though there are challenges along the way!). Such a call is clearly very popular but it is also practical. As I have tried to show in this book, some of the answers to our recurring ills are actually very simple, but they will only be changed with bold leadership which has the firm belief that justice can prevail. We do not have to be stuck in some medieval time warp of neo-feudalism.

c A new movement outside the party system: However clear and organised an independent movement may be, it may still not break through. Its success requires media attention which is often subdued, though as there is now a lot of user-generated media that reaches vast numbers, this is less of an issue than it was. A movement for Progressive Prosperity will need to make strong representation through the democratic process but also bring people out in shows, not of force, but strength of feeling. The ideals we hold true like human rights and also property rights must be upheld, with no destruction of property or vilifying, just plain logic and compassion backed by very strong determination. A new movement needs to be more than a public demonstration. Time and again, in demonstrations that steal the spotlight and shine light on injustices, end up being ignored. History tells us results do not happen unless there is disruption and sacrifice, combining in forceful ways. A new movement needs clear goals, a determined strategy and a plan of what we will do when we get there. Movements fail if they are not fully thought through, but above all the movement needs people, people to lead, people to organise and people to do. It must be peaceful and constructive at all times, it must be compassionate and understanding, it must be inclusive and not in conflict. It must be a movement for the majority.

To get started, there are many like-minded organisations that would need to come together under the umbrella of the movement and sign up for the key planks in the platform for Progressive Prosperity. Putting this in a US perspective, these views are shared by Robert Reich who noted in an article that appeared in *The Nation* in May 2014:

> Having served in Washington, I know how difficult it is to get anything done unless the broad public understands what's at stake and actively pushes for reform. That's why we need a movement for shared prosperity – a movement on a scale similar to the Progressive movement at the turn of the last century, which fuelled the first progressive income tax and antitrust laws; the suffrage movement, which won women the vote; the labor movement, which helped animate the New Deal and fuelled the great prosperity of the first three decades after World War II; the civil rights movement, which achieved the landmark Civil Rights and Voting Rights acts; and the environmental movement, which spawned the National Environmental Policy Act and other critical legislation.

Most success stories are a team effort, a coming together of the right group of people committed to making it happen, whether it is a tech start-up, a sports team, a neighbourhood group or a political movement or even a band. A movement needs to build a platform of support and endorsements from other organisations, political figures, academics, business leaders, community leaders influential writers ... and you. If traction is to be built for a new agenda, not only those who agree need to be educated but also those who don't, particularly those who may reject what is being proposed because they do not fully understand it, its simplicity, its moral justification but also its true and immediate impact.

One thing that was made abundantly clear to me all those years ago when I was canvassing for the Social Democrats in Manchester, was how very few people had any idea how local or national government worked and what its purpose and responsibilities were. As a result they tended to revert to the status quo and vote for their traditional party, the gut feel. So we have a challenge in articulating the message of the movement and actually getting people to act on it. That's why it will be important that we have respected and notable people supporting the movement, such as academics, writers, journalists, broadcasters, professionals, people from show business, politicians, millionaires, billionaires, entrepreneurs, in fact a good cross-section of the influential who in turn will influence others to take action. We all agree, no one really likes paying taxes on their hard-earned income, including members of the media. The media are interested in what will interest their audience but not in one-sided messages. This is where you come in!

The media love real people and real experiences that chime with those of their readers, viewers or listeners. You know, you like reading personal stories rather than just a description. Several years ago I had a client who developed a price comparison service for utility bills. The best way for us to get media coverage in the personal finance sections of the national newspapers was to find examples of real people who had benefited from switching gas, electric or whatever, and the savings they had made. Surprisingly, this was quite difficult but a few sentences and a photograph would make the phones ring for 24 hours. So too with a new movement, real people, real stories of hardship and determination, not just data. This is about communication, a two-way process. At the same time potential objections to the proposals in the new agenda need to be addressed head on. It is no good just being right: we also have to get it right!

It is blatantly obvious that most of our current economic policies only benefit a minority. So if the political will can't be shifted by conventional process, then to get the government to act for the majority requires mass mobilisation to show strength of feeling and pressure to be kept up until our goals are achieved. This is not a protest movement; it is a call to for action. This is not a fight against an oppressor, though it might feel like that sometimes! It is about freedom, freedom to choose, and the possibility of leading a purposeful life. We are not out to bash the politicians or plutocrats but to persuade them that what we propose is not just good, but good for all of us, that it is morally right. Apologists for plutocracy claim that the super-rich create wealth and that it will magically trickle down to the poor. They don't and it doesn't. We create the wealth, they hold on to it. The policies proposed in this book are aimed to bring real benefit to the vast majority of people. Yes, it will be at the expense of the better off, but not to the point that it significantly impacts on their wealth and lifestyle. We currently have a system that has developed structural flaws, which are not compatible with a compassionate, dynamic and enterprising society. It is time for not only comprehensive capitalism, but also compassionate capitalism that acts in the interest of all stakeholders.

Many people were surprised at the strength of feeling and the involvement of people from all walks of life in the Occupy movement. The civil rights movement needed a major Washington rally in 1963 to get legislation passed the following year. The poll tax demonstrations, indeed riots, overturned a very unpopular tax in the UK in the 1980s, and contributed to the downfall of Margaret Thatcher. The peaceful and annual 'ban the bomb' marches in the UK also reinforced the will of the people. This time we have an agenda for action.

But we are not out to win victory over an enemy. We are out to overcome our own failings. We are all in this together, rich and poor, and those in between. We need to achieve change that is good for all of us and provide the basis for a stable and sustainable society with greater social justice. This cause is a common cause and it is about peace, reconciliation, human rights and a desire to do better for all.

There is a lot we can all do ourselves that could to make a difference:

1 Read informed media, research online, watch relevant videos to learn the facts and develop a considered and concerned view.
2 Discuss with your friends, not just the problems but also what the answers could be, ask your friends what they think we can do, listen to those that disagree with you as you will learn something. Bring people together in your area.

3 Engage online by identifying stories in the news, tweet/blog about them or make comments, re-tweet on interesting informative pieces that further the cause.

4 Join and/or be active in a political party or organisation that truly represents you and is going to take up the message of the Movement for Progressive Prosperity.

5 Contact your elected representatives, express your concerns, suggest actions and ask for their support.

6 Participate in collective actions that show strength of feeling.

7 Listen, plan and act in peace, understanding and non-violence.

It may be no wonder our elected representatives can get out of touch with reality and caught up in their own bubble. The average wealth of a member of Congress is $3.9m and the pay is nearly $200,000. In the UK, the salaries of Members of Parliament put them in the top 10% of earners and membership is skewed to come from a privileged background, but then members of the non elected House of Lords receive only £300 per day for attendance. However, the fact that someone is well off does not mean they can't understand the circumstances of the poor and the squeezed middle, but they do not have the sense of urgency and desperation that is felt every day by those in need.

Government seems to have lost its way as to what its purpose is, why it is there at all, and what is it doing. We all know that, once we are immersed in a culture, we cannot see the key issues objectively. It happens in organisations and businesses as well as politics. With so many career politicians who have had little experience of outside work or being responsible for the bottom line or building a business, it is no wonder they get out of touch. I certainly noticed this when I stood for local council elections, and on the occasions when I have made regular visits to the Houses of Parliament. It is a different world, removed from everyday reality.

Since the Great Recession there has been poor growth, a rise in exploitative employment practices, poverty wages and excessive and unnecessary hardship. Out of respect for our fellow human beings, this must stop.

The good news is that it can stop. It is not difficult, it just takes the political will to make it happen. Quite frankly, unless there is change there will a revolution in certain major economies. There have already been warnings. Voters have lost faith and trust in politicians. There has not been the change that was hoped for, the promises from politicians have not been fulfilled. It is time to make some new promises, some promises to the people and for the people. The investing of power by the people in the government has long been defined as a social contract. It is the basis of the American and other written constitutions, but governments are not working for the people, at least not all the people and not even the majority of people.

The role of government within a democracy is to provide a service to its people, to deliver on its promises, and to be accountable. The government is not just a legislator, making laws, it is not just a judiciary upholding those laws and it is not just executing the will of the people. The government should be a partner with the people and has three main roles to play for the benefit of all:

- Provider (services: health, welfare, education, infrastructure),
- Enabler (investment, enterprise, wealth/profit),
- Protector (democracy, rights, law, freedom, defence).

The Universal Declaration of Human Rights, enshrines natural law with social justice. The UDHR, which was adopted by the UN General Assembly on 10 December 1948, was the result of the experience of the Second World War. Much of this was due to the leadership and determination of Eleanor Roosevelt, the widow of former President Franklin D. Roosevelt. With the end of that war, and the creation of the United Nations, the international community vowed never again to allow such atrocities to happen again. But sadly, they are still happening, though not on a world scale as in the two world wars, but they are still happening and that is not acceptable.

Let us remind ourselves of a key paragraph in the preamble:

Now, Therefore THE GENERAL ASSEMBLY proclaims THIS UNIVERSAL DECLARATION OF HUMAN RIGHTS as a common standard of achievement for all peoples and all nations, to the end that every individual and every organ of society, keeping this Declaration constantly in mind, shall strive by teaching and education to promote respect for these rights and freedoms and by progressive measures, national and international, to secure their universal and effective recognition and observance, both among the peoples of Member States themselves and among the peoples of territories under their jurisdiction.

7.3 Next steps

Let's not make it difficult for ourselves. There has been a lot of rhetoric that something must be done about extreme economic inequality, slow growth and restoring democracy, but there has been less about what could and should be done to make this hope a reality. That is why I have looked for a simple theme: *'income for me/wealth for we'*. I have shown you some commonsense answers to our everyday problems that would make a difference to millions of lives; bringing significant financial relief and in the process causing no hardship to anyone.

I think the ultimate goal of a sustainable and just society, where public revenue was raised without taxation, is entirely feasible and desirable as clearly demonstrated in my father's book. My view is that we first have to do some preliminary work before we can bring this about. Politically our mindset has to be changed to a recognition that there is a better way. The priority is to reduce unnecessary suffering for the majority of people so that they can lead fulfilled lives. The five key initiatives proposed here would have a significant positive impact. Once this mindset is changed and inequality reduced, then tax as we know it, could be abolished altogether. Yes, we would still be paying money to the government, but it would be for the services provided, just as we would pay a builder or accountant, hence it is not a tax. *How much we pay* would be determined by the market estimation of the value of all the benefits conferred on the site we occupy to live or work by government and society. This would relieve us of the punitive extractions from our hard earned income.

The proposals in the Agenda for Progressive Prosperity may be challenging to implement, but only because they are bold and therefore require strong leadership to carry them through. This means no more pussy-footing politicians focused on re-election but authentic, committed people who believe in doing the right thing. I have the strong belief that 'where there is a will there is a way'; we just need to have the will. I recollect winning pitches for public relations campaigns and thinking, *'How are we going to implement this?'* However, I would never give promises I knew we could not deliver. The fact was, I always knew what was possible and focussed on winning the contract and then working out how to deliver. This particularly happened when we were asked to undertake multi-country marketing campaigns in up to 50 countries, which the bigger agencies could not do, but we found a way, found partners and we delivered. It is the same with these policies, if they are fair, if they improve the lives of millions of people, then we will find a way of making it happen.

Most people seem to have little idea how government works, the different levels and their different roles. No wonder they are disengaged. When canvassing on the streets as I have done on many occasions at local elections, it is clear how many people are confused as to what the election is for and why they are voting; or if they had a complaint about something, did not realise that it was actually a matter for national government. Voters need educating on the value and benefit of government, so that more people can make better informed decisions rather than voting traditionally or just emotionally. This should start in schools with citizenship classes. To live a fulfilled life you need to be participating or at least be aware of how things affect you, don't just let things happen to you. That is why, when my children started school, I agreed to become a governor of the school, though it was an unpaid advisory and limited policy making role, but at least I got to know what was going on!

As part of the need for an increased transparency and engagement, government has a role to demonstrate that it is carefully managing our tax money. The first recent step in the UK was a breakdown sent to each Income Tax payer as to where their money went. However this only applied to Income Tax, but it was stated that an average household in addition pays nearly the same amount in indirect taxes for which no breakdown was provided. The government needs to do more of this if it is to regain and retain the confidence of the people.

If taxpayers had a better understanding of how their tax money was spent and they could be confident that it was well managed, then they would be less reluctant to pay taxes. This could be helped by ring-fencing or dehypothecation where specific revenue sources are allocated to specific budget. Such openness could help convince the rich that they need to pay more – no one likes to hand over money and not be sure of what they are getting in return, which is the case with the current tax system. If there were such shoddy service from a business supplier, you would find another. The government is a monopoly supplier, however, and we can't choose to whom we pay tax, unless we relocate – which is only the privilege of the already rich! Similarly, we all need to know that our taxes are not going to prop up lazy people who are not prepared to make their fair contribution to society

There is a lot of convincing to do for us all to realise that the tax source can actually be shifted from income to wealth, for we have been brainwashed to believe that taxes on incomes has to be the main source. However younger people are seeing more of their income taken away as a result of tax and repayment of student loans, they are feeling the near impossibility of ever being able save and to buy a house. So many are horrified when they realise the rate of Income Tax they have to pay and ask why. Exactly! Why is it necessary?

I have also wanted to provide a short simple approach to reducing inequality and improving millions of lives, a common sense approach that could be understood by all and not need an economics degree to comprehend. Many of the learned proposals put forward are about regulation or additional laws to force companies, organisations or individuals to do something. It is better to incentivise to make things happen rather than beat with a stick.

The Agenda for Progressive Prosperity must move into the main stream. With recent polling in the USA, it seems the views of the onetime outsider, progressive Democrat presidential nominee Bernie Sanders, are now considered mainstream, that is, it means that this was what most people want. It was similar in the UK, having lost the 2016 election, the Labour Party saw a surge in membership, to become the UK's largest party by membership, and then elected the outsider candidate, Jeremy Corbyn, as its new leader in September 2015. So many have kept quiet for so long, no one being bold enough to upset the wealthy governing elite. The principle of 'income for me/wealth for we' is for every man and every woman. By applying this sound strategy, funds can be taken out of storage and the wealth we all helped create can be made to work for all.

One reasons there has been no bold, decisive action to tackle inequality has been that we do not know what is the best thing to do. There is so much information and discussion on the problems and very little on answers. Certainly our politicians while making piecemeal efforts show no clear vision that would benefit all.

I am hoping both the USA and the UK could lead the way in showing what makes a country great and a true nation of the world. By creating more opportunity, reducing inequality and poverty, restoring a true democracy and having a multi-stakeholder economic system, social attitudes will change, there will be a more compassionate society, more mutual respect, and hopefully there will be no turning back.

This is not a partisan fight against oppressors; it is a radical rethink as to how we organise our society and how we treat our fellow human beings. It is about consensus not conflict; it is about making our people prosperous.

One day we will wonder why we ever taxed income so insensitively that it caused hardship for so many people; why we let the wealthy amass such large unearned sums and assets, while there was homelessness, hunger and poverty. I hope too that we will look back in amazement that we ever allowed such hardship to exist and indeed get worse everyday. We now look back in disbelief that we ever allowed slavery, gender discrimination, racial segregation and oppression (though clearly not eliminated completely). Similarly we will look back on how we let polluting vehicles be around for so long or filthy factories belching climate threatening fumes. The Agenda for Progressive Prosperity will help close the wealth gap and lay the ground work for a sustainable future and greater social justice.

As Martin Luther King said in 1963: '*No, no we are not satisfied, and we will not be satisfied until justice rolls down like waters and righteousness like a mighty stream.*'

We have no time to lose; the unnecessary suffering has to end and it can end. It is in our power, all of us together. We will realise and be glad we made that change, the world and its people will be better for it; if we believe we can, we will, we can move From Here to Prosperity.

This is not

THE END

It's just the beginning...

Index